Nostradam...
The Final Prophecies

Nostradamus:
The Final Prophecies

A revolutionary new interpretation
for today's world

Luciano Sampietro

Souvenir Press

First Published by Edizioni Piemme, Spa 1999
Translated from the Italian by Lowell Fitzgerald

This edition published 2002 by
Souvenir Press Ltd,
43 Great Russell Street, London WC1B 3PA

Reprinted 2002 (twice), 2004

ISBN 0 285 63639 1

Typeset by Rowland Phototypesetting Ltd,
Bury St Edmunds, Suffolk

Printed and bound in Great Britain by
Cox & Wyman Ltd, Reading

Dedicated to
Michel Nostradamus

Contents

Preface to the English edition

Two years have passed since the publication in Italy of the first edition of this book and the events that have occurred in the interim have made possible to compare predictions with reality; the result has been surprising. The crisis of the financial market which began in 2000 is still happening now, a new Intifada has exploded with hundreds of dead and, just as Nostradamus predicted, it has coincided with the conjunction of Jupiter and Saturn. The United States have been victim of a dramatic attack by Islamic terrorism, awakened after a long period of sleep, Bush has become president of the USA, the Islamic world is in turmoil, and it is possible to foresee future scenarios, in which religion, or more accurately religious fanaticism, will have a major role in determining the destiny of nations.

However, events have also enabled me to clarify meanings of some of the quatrains, and in conjunction with what has already been unravelled from my analysis of the obscure verses and cryptic sentences, these have transformed figures shrouded in mist into characters of our time.

What I predicted two years ago and has now happened, exactly as was said, convinces me that my proposed chronology is correct.

Hence, I can confirm that the prophecies of Nostradamus will end on 2 June 2025, and still I say with certainty that Nostradamus wrote his *Centuries* for us, children of our time and witnesses of the most crucial moments in the history of humanity.

Trieste, 1 October 2001
Luciano Sampietro

Preface to the Italian edition

Nostradamus: the mere sound of his name has always aroused obscure fears and anxieties – fears of the unknown.

Most of people prefer to take each day as it comes, without thinking of, or indeed without fearing, the future, like an ostrich burying its head in the sand. Then, out of the blue, surprising things happen, bringing upheaval and suffering. However, the dawn of the new millennium has revived an interest in the work of Nostradamus, and in 1999 alone, numerous books on the Seer of Salon have been published or printed.

After studying the hundreds of works that, over the course of centuries, have commented on the *Centuries*, it is possible to see a common, characteristic denominator: an enormous disparity in interpretation.

Once this is realised, it is easy to understand why Nostradamus has been viewed as an ambiguous and obscure Seer, in whose work everything and its opposite can be read. The main reason why this has happened lies in the fact that, until now, no one has been able to put forward an acceptable dating for the *Centuries*. So certain data would be attributed to a past event which bore similarities to them, or to another, or even to some vague time in the future, hence confusion and ambiguity, and the frequent accusation against Nostradamus of being a Seer of events that had already occurred.

And yet, the Seer, in the part of his work written in prose – the letters to his son César and Henry of France – as well as in some of his verse, did reveal the existence of certain keys, which would have made it possible to determine the chronology of his predictions, and, most significantly, to establish a time-span for his prophecies. The only problem was that these keys were masked in such a way as to make them difficult to understand, or at times, even recognise. So, to avoid well-trodden paths, I've chosen a completely different course: which springs from a need to define, first and foremost, the chronology of Nostradamus's work, so then we can identify the moment in time to which the prophecies extend. Only in such a way as this, is it possible to place the verses in a precise temporal context, and so give future events in a well-defined setting. I have been able to do this through identifying and subsequently resolving the numerous puzzles hidden throughout Nostradamus's work, the astonishing concealed double meanings, the anagrams, the subtraction and addition of letters, not to mention problems connected with astrology.

It thus became possible for me to establish, down to the very year, month and day, the exact date to which the prophecies extend, and that is 2 June 2025, a date by which everything that has been prophesied and has not yet been fulfilled will come to pass.

It is quite possible for a mistake to be made in the timing of a single event. However, the general chronology is precisely defined and not readily open to dispute. Any error that arises in the detail does not challenge the validity of the overall picture, which appears, after much analysis, to be borne out by numerous verifications.

So for the first time readers may have the opportunity to judge for themselves the extraordinary skill of this, the greatest Seer of modern times.

L.S. 1999

Acknowledgements

I should like to express my thanks to the following:

Professor Mauro Messerotti of the Astronomical Observatory of Trieste for his cogent and precise information on astronomical matters; Mrs Luciana de Leoni of Aiello del Friuli (UD) for her penetrating observations on astrology; and my office colleagues who through their personal sacrifice allowed me the necessary time to write this book.

My old friend Marino for his help in making possible an English edition.

Finally, and most importantly, my wife Lori and my sons Giulio and Carlo, for having understood how little time I could give to them in the last two years, and from their support during this time.

L.S.

Michel Nostradamus at the age of 59

Introduction

Nostradamus's entire work revolves around his mysterious chronology, in which he subdivides the past, present and the future into eight millennia, during the course of which the drama of mankind unfolds. In the vast sweep of time, events, wars, deeds, personalities are drawn into a gigantic fresco, where certain scenes are in detail, while others are lightly sketched, almost as if the artist wished to leave the background to the events shown to the viewer's imagination.

Everything is closely surrounded in mist, in which we glimpse warriors and saints, peoples and individuals in a state of agitation, the flashing of swords, the blaze of explosions, duels in the air, sinking ships, and hear screaming, praying and tragedies of every sort. The history of mankind is for the most part underscored with sorrowful, apocalyptic events – glance through any history book: what is remembered are wars, battles, slaughter and revolution, while peace treaties are readily forgotten, viewed at best as parentheses between two wars.

And you only have to read any daily newspaper to understand immediately that what appeals most to readers are tragic events, not happy ones: while readers may glance at a piece on a marriage, their attention will be riveted by a death, a murder, a massacre.

The work of Nostradamus is not at odds with this common sentiment: he seems almost like a reporter from the past, come to eavesdrop on future happenings, someone who lingers at a newspaper stand to read the headlines and events, steadfastly taking notes on those of major importance, the ones in bold letters, which are for the most part sad and distressing.

This is why, but for a few rare exceptions, the quatrains

and sestets are concerned with dramatic, grim episodes, almost like painful stages on a human highway, marked by the toll of a death-knell. It is for this reason that his work is often viewed with a sense of fear and repulsion: man has always based his hopes on a better future, and to read that the future will be no different from the past, and perhaps even worse, creates an overwhelming sense of disquiet. Many have approached the Seer's work seeking to attribute a meaning to his abstruse prophecies that depends on occurrences and their timing, but no one has yet written a work that is systematically and organically coherent, by, first of all, establishing the chronology of events before attributing them to their protagonists. Many events have been identified once they have taken place, but the future has remained shrouded in mystery. What is to happen has not yet been assigned a particular time.

This has happened mainly because either interpreters have not taken into account the mystical aspect of the Seer's work or they have not considered the historical context in which he lived, or the content of works that were available to Nostradamus when he wrote his prophecies.

At first glance, it must be said that the Seer did not make use of any mechanical scientific system to predict the future.

Astrology on its own was certainly not an adequate means of gaining admittance to future occurrences. It is well known, in fact, that astrology, whether it be a scientific discipline or a pseudo one, was conceived to assist individuals: through their date and place of birth, astrology makes it possible (for those who believe) to define their personality, inclinations, fate and future, but it cannot determine or reveal general events involving thousands if not millions of individuals.

Astrology, on the other hand, was useful to Nostradamus in determining the timing of certain events through various astral combinations. But, in fact, he made greater use of astronomy than of astrology. It is as though the Seer had witnessed a precise future occurrence and having witnessed it, had observed the sky, and scrupulously annotated the position of the stars, and was thus able to define the exact time. It is no coincidence either that in many places of his work events are visualised through the stars' positions in the Heavens, which correspond with the date of the occasion described. That his method is not purely mechanical or scientific but principally mystical is borne out in his letter to his son César, which serves as a preface to the first seven of his *Centuries*. In it he writes:

> *And seeing that it has pleased the Immortal God that you were born to the light of day in this region of earth and I do not wish to speak of your years which are not yet threaded with gold, but rather (of your) Martial months, incapable in your fragile intellect of admitting what is to come when my days are over: I perceive that it is not possible to leave you in writing what will be forgotten by the outrages of time: for the hereditary gift of occult prediction will remain sealed within me . . .*

In this passage the Seer is clearly saying that his son will not be able to inherit his powers: a confirmation that such powers are not the fruit of study or learnable technique, but rather a divine gift that is not transmissible. Nostradamus, therefore, can be defined in modern-day language as a natural talent, refined by a historical, linguistic and scientific culture, both polyhedral and profound, which did not exclude astrology, during his lifetime considered the science par excellence.

It was therefore his mystical nature which enabled him to detach himself from the contemporary material world in order to wander with the spirit of time and space, where past, present and future are a unique unity, as if the earth represents the present, the shining stars we see light years away, the past, and the spirit, which is without form and infinite, is the vehicle through which to perceive what has not yet happened.

The historical period in which Nostradamus lived, and that is the first half of the sixteenth century, is known for the oppression by the Catholic church, manifested in the constitution of the Tribunal of the Holy Inquisition and in the connected trials for heresy or witchcraft, which in most cases ended by condemning the unfortunate to the stake. Nostradamus, apart from being an astrologer, was also an alchemist, but he carefully kept these studies secret, being well aware of the impending dangers, were these leanings to be revealed.

For these reasons his entire work is laced with professions of faith and a scrupulous observance of the religious canons. He was descended from a Jewish family, who in order to remain living in France was obliged to embrace Roman Catholicism. His origins alone were reason enough to arouse mistrust for in these times Jews were seen as 'God killers', people who had crucified Christ. So, the historical, socio-political and religious milieux of his time would not have allowed the Seer to express himself freely, not to reveal his true feelings, or his religious or philosophical convictions.

Here, then, is why his work should be stripped of all its religious tinsel and of its numerous and redundant appeals to the Catholic faith. In his heart, Nostradamus was not a religious person; just as his great friend Rabelais was not. His true faith was the freedom to exist, without restrictions or dogma, to be able to delve into the secrets of the universe without compromising, to express in knowing the true essence of man, the mystery of his birth and death.

His membership of the Order of Rosicrucians, like Rabelais', an uncontested historical fact, throws some light on his true essence, on his way of thinking and of conceiving the cosmos, and makes it possible to understand how his work should be read in a quite opposite key from the religious canon by which it appears to be inspired. The Rosicrucians are respectful of everyone's religion and faith and do not claim supremacy in any of their mystic truths. They force no one to believe certain dogmas. The Rosicrucians seek to understand man's spirituality and his division into three: body, spirit and soul. They study the relationship between these three different entities and they seek to explain themselves and to unravel the mystery of existence. They are the heirs to the ancient mysteries of Egypt and of their initiatory schools, the continuators of Pythagoras and Plato. When the Renaissance was at its peak, Nostradamus assimilated its culture to the point where he became one of its most luminous symbols of scientific knowledge, methodology of research and intellectual curiosity. It drove him to investigate every field of knowledge till he ventured into such unexplored territory, as the study of Ancient Egyptian hieroglyphics.

The Rosicrucians recognise Christ as the greatest of the cosmic masters, who came to earth to reawaken man's spirituality, in the way others before him, such as Buddha, had done. But they do not identify the Catholic church as the instrument decreed by Christ to achieve this goal, especially as the church does not recognise the Laws of Karma, the linchpin of Rosicrucian teachings.

Nostradamus's work is, therefore, governed by caution and prudence, in fear of the times in which it is written. This is clear in his letter to César, in which he writes:

> *Consider the teachings of the True Saviour – nolite sanctum dare canibus nec mittatis margaritas ante porcos, ne conclucent pedibus et conversi dirumpant vos ['Give not that which is holy unto the dogs, neither cast ye your pearls before swine, lest they trample them under their feet, and turn again and rend you']. This was the reason for which I held my tongue in check, and did not speak publicly, and kept pen from paper. For these reasons I preferred to use abstruse and perplexing sentences to explain future causes, as well as more imminent ones, of future events of general interest, and occurrences for which I perceived some human change happening that would have upset delicate ears, it is all written in a veiled manner rather than in more prophetic way, following the principle 'abscondisti haec a sapientibus et prudentibus, id est potentibus et regibus et enucleasti ea exiguis et tenuibus' ['You have concealed from the learned and from the prudent, that is, from those with power and those who rule, and you have explained it to the weak and the frail'].*

A reading and interpretation of this work cannot be separated from such a fundamental fact, nor can they be done without studying the texts that preceded it, texts which Nostradamus would have had at hand.

Foremost among these are the Old and New Testaments, of which most significant is St John's Apocalypse. Then there are the works of the Fathers of the Church, of the classical philosophers, of the medieval mystics, as well as classical texts on Egypt and its history, texts on astrology and on alchemy and whatever else may have been part of a scholar's baggage at that time. Only with the help of such elements it is possible to approach the Seer's work seriously and give an objective, rather than a fantastic or arbitrary, interpretation of his prophecies.

Many scholars have done their utmost to search for a secret key to reading the *Centuries*, but such a key does not exist, as is demonstrated by the total incoherence of what has been written so far: the Seer limited himself to setting down the quatrains in chronological order, only to reshuffle them later without any logical criteria. In consequence, each quatrain has to be interpreted on its own and then compared to others in which a reference to the same period of time can be verified. Reading Nostradamus's work makes for a fascinating journey into a time that has yet to come, in the hope of finding there the certainty of a better tomorrow for our children and for mankind.

A short biography of Nostradamus

Before embarking on details on Nostradamus's fantastic work, it seems appropriate to give a brief biography, so that readers approaching his *Centuries* for the first time can have an idea of who the author was and how he lived.

Michel de Nostradame was born at Saint Rémy, a small town in Provence, on 14 December 1503 in the Julian calendar, son of Jacques and Renée de Nostradame. The family was quite well off, thanks to the two maternal and paternal grandfathers. Renée's father, Jean De Rémy, was doctor to Renato, King of Jerusalem and Sicily and Count of Provence. Jacques' father, Pierre de Nostradame, was doctor to Giovanni, Duke of Calabria and of King Renato's son. Nostradamus's father was a notary, a profession that was as well paid as it is today, especially in view of the fact that in this times there were very few literate people.

His maternal grandfather Jean, a profoundly cultured humanist, took little Michel into his care, giving him an education which was unique of its kind. Under his guidance, his grandson learnt Latin, Greek and Hebrew and was introduced to a study of the stars. Jean therefore played a positive role in the boy's development and from a very tender age Michel showed surprisingly sharp intelligence.

After Jean's death, Michel, by now an adolescent, was sent to Avignon to further his studies. There he enrolled in the faculty of philosophy. In this environment Michel soon revealed his surprising gifts of observation and memory and an acute mind, very quickly earning the esteem and respect of his teachers. So much so that when he had brilliantly completed his studies, which included philosophy, rhetoric, Latin, mathematics and astronomy, he was entrusted to give lessons in astronomy.

On his return to Saint Rémy, the young Michel found himself having to make decisions about his future: he would have preferred to dedicate himself exclusively to astronomy, but the need to take up a profession, which would offer a pleasant lifestyle, led him to choose medicine as both his grandfathers had done. Nostradamus enrolled in the faculty of medicine at Montpellier, one of the most prestigious of these times. Here he pursued his studies with excellent results, just as he had done at Avignon. And here he came to know François Rabelais, a shining example of renaissance culture and author of *Gargantua and Pantagruel*. Rabelais was the second person in Nostradamus's life, after his grandfather, who was to influence him notably. This was an era full of contradictions: there was opposition against the urge for knowledge and scientific research in all fields from the rigorous doctrine of the Catholic church, which suspected heresy in every field of study held not to be in keeping with the Bible. This was an epoch in which alchemists prospered, alchemists, who, in their quest of the philosopher's stone, studied metals and their composition, thereby establishing the foundations for modern chemistry and physics.

In 1524, when Nostradamus hadn't yet completed his studies, the scourge of the plague devastated France and the university was closed in order to prevent the spread of infection. So the young Michel set to work helping the stricken townspeople. He had conceived a therapy to cure the plague, shrouded in mystery to this day but probably obtained from medicinal herbs, which he applied as part of preventive hygiene measures, which at the time were practically unknown: draining away sewage, burning mattresses belonging to victims of the plague along with their personal belongings, lime-washing their dwellings, boiling drinking water, a ban on eating raw vegetables, or eating them only after they had been thoroughly washed. Wherever he went the disease regressed until it disappeared, and his fame as a healer of the terrible plague rapidly spread, bringing him renown and not inconsiderable economic rewards, as various communities compensated him for his services.

When the plague had died down, Nostradamus returned after
a lapse of four years to the University of Montpellier to complete his studies, in an aura of fame and honour. After a short
while he received his laureate in medicine with honours, and
an offer to remain at the university as a teacher, but didn't
think this was the right course for himself.

As soon as he became a doctor, he latinised his surname,
as was the custom of the day, thus becoming Doctor Nostradamus. Around 1530 Nostradamus took a wife and went to live
in Agen. Two children were born of this marriage, but within
a few years the entire family perished, probably from diph-
theria, a disease which was unknown in those days and which
had been imported to Europe from the colonies. Once again,
he was alone, Nostradamus began to wander around France.
His fame was such that his intervention was requested all over
the country. Although the plague had lost its virulence of
former years, it occasionally broke out, nonetheless, here and
there. His wealth increased along with his fame, and not
yet thirty, he could consider himself a well-to-do physician.
Thanks to his affluence, Nostradamus was able to travel a lot,
especially to Italy, a country that he particularly loved and in
which he had numerous friends. His wanderings lasted about
ten years, until he decided to settle in Salon, where on 11
November 1547, at the age of forty-eight, he married the young
and well-to-do widow of a merchant, Anne Ponsard, with
whom he had six children, three boys and three girls.

From time to time the plague made its return, sometimes
virulently, and Nostradamus, by now the most famous physician in France, was unfailingly called upon to assist those
stricken and to organise appropriate sanitation measures. So,
first he went to Aix en Provence and then to Avignon, to battle
against the black death. He managed to defeat the disease by
using strange pills made from herbs and petals, and earning
gratitude, wealth and honours. It was time now for him to turn
his attention to his favourite subject of study: astronomy and
astrology (then considered a science).

For some time now, at Rabelais' encouragement, Nostradamus had belonged to the initiatory movement of the

LES
PROPHETIES
DE M. MICHEL
NOSTRADAMVS.

*c'est à françois ~~xxxx~~ Courtol~
nous voyal~*

Centuries V-II. IX. X.

*Qui n'ont encore jamais esté
imprimées.*

A LYON,
PAR BENOIST RIG

Frontispiece of the first (undated) edition of the second part
of the Centuries

Rosicrucians, which in great secret, for fear of the Inquisition, pursued their doctrine of the tripartite: spirit, soul and body, and studied the arcane ties which bound man to the cosmos as well as to Earth. Fortified by his immense humanistic culture and that of astronomy, Nostradamus's studies progressed rapidly, and he came to the recognise that he possessed an incredible, innate faculty of divination. So he would spend night after night in the attic of his house in Salon, scanning the stars and, scrupulously annotating the information he gained from them and from his arcane faculty concerning the future of humanity. Everything came to him in the first place in a clear and unequivocal fashion, but the times and his own instinct led him into rewriting these prophecies in an obscure, ambiguous way.

In 1555 the first 353 quatrains were published. Then in 1557 they were republished along with the additional 286 in the hand of Antoine du Rosne, among these the *Centuries I, quatrain 35*:

Le Lyon jeune, le vieux surmontera,
En champ bellique par singulier duelle,
Dans cage d'or les yeux lui creuera,
Deux classes, une puis mourir de mort cruelle.

The young lion will surmount the old
On the battlefield in a duel, one against one
In a golden cage his eyes will pierce,
Two wounds in one, a very cruel death.

On 30 June 1559, King Henry II of France, in the course of a knightly tournament, dressed in his gilt armour, fought his last encounter against the twenty-nine-year-old Duke Gabriel of Montgomery, who wore a lion on his insignia. The lances were equipped with a ball of leather at their tip. In the encounter, however, the duke's lance broke and the remnant of its shaft penetrated the sallet of the King's helmet, going straight through one eye and emerging from an ear. After ten days of atrocious suffering, the king died.

Nostradamus's fame as Seer grew immediately and out of all proportion: Caterina de Medici, Henry's widow, wanted him at court and held him among her most trusted counsellors. The Seer, however, apart from his visits to Paris, preferred living in his house at Salon (a house which is still standing and which has been transformed into a museum).

In the meantime, in 1558, Nostradamus had completed his work by writing the last three *Centuries*, which were preceded by a long letter, apparently dedicated to Henry II of France, that is, the king who had been his contemporary. In reality, the seer's intention was to dedicate the last part of his work to a future king named Henry, who has still to make his appearance on history's stage, and whom Nostradamus knew would have a decisive role in the victory over the Antichrist.

Strangely, enough, this second part of the *Centuries* was published in Avignon only in 1568, that is, some two years after the death of the Seer, as demonstrated in in-depth bibliographical study by Michel Chomarat, who deserves merit for having rid the *Centuries* of distortions that have arisen in various editions and for having restored the work to its original form.

This second part brought Nostradamus immense success as well. In the meantime, however, his health worsened. Gout and dropsy gave him little peace. The few days remaining to him before his death were just long enough for him to set down his will and write his last prophecy:

> Du retour d'Ambassade, don de Roy, mis au lieu,
> Plus n'en sera, sera allé à Dieu,
> Parens plus proches, amis, freres du sang,
> Trouué tout mort pres du lict et du banc.

> *On returning from embassy, the King's don lay down,*
> *No more shall he be, he will have gone to God,*
> *Close relatives and friends, blood brothers,*
> *Will find him quite dead, twixt bed and board.*
>
> (Prophecy 142)

And this it was that friends and relatives found him on the morning of 2 July 1566.

PART ONE

THE SEVENTH MILLENNIUM

1. Nostradamus's letter to his son César

Au reuolu du grand nombre septiesme,
Apparoistra au temps ieux d'Hecatombe,
Non esloigné du grand eage milliesme,
Que les entres sortiront de leur tombe.

At the end of the great septennial
It shall appear at the time of the Hecatomb Games,
Not far from the age of the great millennium
That the buried shall issue from their tombs.
                    (*Centuries X, quatrain 74*)

Vingt ans du regne de la Lune passés,
Sept mil ans autre tiendra sa monarchie,
Quand le Soleil prendra ses iours lassés,
Lors accomplit & mine ma prophetie.

When twenty years of Moon's reign shall pass
Seven thousand more its monarchy shall hold.
When the Sun has reclaimed its days left
Then shall my prophecy come true.
                    (*Centuries I, quatrain 48*)

With these two enigmatic quatrains Nostradamus makes a specific reference to the seventh millennium, at the end of which one can hope for a better future.

One can easily sense the importance of identifying this long period, since it signifies a clear distinction between the world as we know it and a future world, where relationships among men will be governed by radically different rules and criteria, and life itself will have a greater spirituality, in a great aware-ness of the mystery of life and death.

To be able to identify the dates of the beginning and end of the seventh millennium is of crucial importance to under-stand the work of Nostradamus, and especially to find the first date to use as a background for the quatrains.

To do this, we can use the starting points in Nostradamus's letter to his son César, employed as a preface to the first seven *Centuries*, as also the letter to King Henry of France, which prefaced the final three. In this chapter, however, we shall just look at the letter to his son César of 1557 (see Appendix II for the original French version). The letter to Henry will be analysed fully in Part Two.

As already noted, Nostradamus used this letter to his son César as a preface to the first seven *Centuries*. The first edition of this first part of his work was printed in Lyon in 1557. We have to thank the initiative of Michel Chomarat, who founded the Association of Friends of Nostradamus in 1983, among other things, for a truly valuable anastatic reprint of this first part. The letter appears to be complete, save for the last few lines, which are missing in this particular edition, but are given in successive ones.

In his epistolary preface, Nostradamus not only talks of the prophetic spirit, and of astrology, defined by him as 'judicious' *(Judicelle),* he also tackles the timing of events, though in a language which is intentionally obscure, so much so that even today these references to time have still not been deciphered by anyone.

To my son César Nostradamus, long life and happiness.

Your tardy arrival, my son César Nostradamus, has led me to wile away my long hours of continuous night watches by writing to you, leaving you a memory after the body of your progenitor has died – for the general good of mankind – of what I have learned from the divine essence through the revolutions of Astronomy. And, seeing that it has pleased Immortal God that you were born to the light of day in this region of earth – and I do not wish to speak of your years

*which are not yet threaded with gold, but rather of your
Martial months, incapable in your fragile intellect of admit-
ting what is to come when my days are over, I perceive that
it is not possible to leave you in writing what will be forgotten by the outrages of time: for the hereditary gift of occult
prediction will remain sealed within me; considering also
that the adventures of mankind are uncertain, and that
everything is regulated and governed by the inestimable
power of God, who inspires us, not through bacchanalian
fun, nor through apathetic inertia, but through the truths of
astronomy. 'Only those filled with the divine breath can
foretell particular things, thanks to the prophetic spirit'.
For however long and repeatedly I have predicted the far
future and what has happened in the meantime and in particular regions, I have attributed these prophecies to courage and divine inspiration; this also applies to other happy
or sinister happenings, speedily foretold, that have since
come true in the world's climes: I would have preferred to
remain silent and refrain from putting all this in writing,
and this, not only because of abuse, not only in current times
but also in the greater part of future time, for kingdoms, sects
and religions will undergo changes, even ones diametrically
opposite to the present, that if I were to report what the
future holds, those belonging to a kingdom, a sect, a religion
or faith would find themselves so gravely at odds with their
perceived fantasy that they would come to condemn so much
of what through future centuries will be recognised as seen
and understood. Considering also the words of the true
saviour 'Give not that which is holy into the dogs, neither
cast ye your pearls before swine, lest they trample them
under their feet, and turn again and rend you'. This was
the reason I held my tongue in check, and did not speak
publicly and kept pen from paper. For these reasons I preferred to use abstruse and perplexing sentences to explain
future causes, as well as more imminent one, of future events
of general interest, and occurrences for which I perceived
some human change happening that would have upset delicate ears, it is all in a veiled manner rather than in a more*

prophetic way, following the principle: 'You have concealed from the learned and from the prudent, that is, from those with power and those who rule, and you have explained it to the weak and the frail' and to the Prophets: they have received the spirit of prophecy through Immortal God and his good angels and through him they see the remote causes and come to foresee future events: for nothing can be obtained without him, so great are his powers and his goodness towards his subjects, who, while they are in themselves subjected to other aims, imposed by an inspiration towards goodness, that warmth and prophetic power come close to us, just as do the Sun's rays that come to cast their influence on elementary bodies. As for we humans, we cannot know anything through our natural knowledge and intuition of God, the Creator's inaccessible secrets. 'Since it is not for us to know either the time or the moment etc. . . .' Even though, in these times, people can exist, to whom God the Creator has wished to reveal some secrets of the future through visionary impressions, by means of Judiciary astrology, as has happened in the past, when a certain power and volitional faculty came through them, like the appearance of a tongue of flame inspiring them, they were judged as divine and human inspirations. For divine works which are totally absolute can only be achieved by God; those in between belong to the Angels and the third sort to the malevolent. But, my son, I am speaking too abstrusely to you. However, as to the occult prophecies which come to be received through the subtle spirit of fire, which can, when we are contemplating the highest of the stars, as though it is keeping watch, sometimes be disturbing in their content, so much so that we are surprised by the written word, uttered without fear and with very little boastful loquacity: but why? Everything progresses from the divine power of the great eternal God from whom all goodness flows. Furthermore, my son, although I have been called a prophet, I do not want to attribute such a sublime title to myself, for the present: 'since who nowadays is called prophet, once was called Seer': for my son, properly speaking, a prophet is someone who sees things that are beyond the natural know-ledge of all creatures. And it comes about that through the perfect light of prophecy, things divine as well as human manifestly appear to the prophet, something that cannot be attained, and he sees the effects of the prediction reaching far into the future. For the secrets of God cannot be under-stood and actual power, dependent on a long extension of natural knowledge, having its closest origins in free will, makes causes appear, about which information cannot be had for it would reveal what they are, and this cannot be done neither by human Seers, nor through other means of knowledge, nor through any occult power that exists under the dome of the sky, as well as in the presence of total eternity, which encloses all time within itself. But by way of that indivisible eternity, through agitated assembly of Heracletian proportions, the causes come to be known from the movement of the Heavens. I do not say, my son, so that you may understand well, that knowledge of this material cannot as yet be impressed upon your fragile intellect that very distant future causes are not within the remit of know-ledge of a reasonable creature: in truth, if there are present distant causes, this not withstanding, for a creature with an intellectual soul, these are neither occult nor evident: but full knowledge of the causes cannot be acquired without that divine inspiration: seeing that every prophetic inspiration receives its principal impulse, first of all, from God the creator, then from time and from nature. Since it is true that causes are indifferent and are indifferently produced or not produced, the prediction happens when it has been predicted. Since intellectual understanding cannot see into the occult, except through the voice that comes from limbo through of the tongue of flame in which part future causes are determined. Furthermore, my son, I beg you never to want to commit your intellect to those illusions and follies that render the body arid and damn the soul, disturbing the fragile senses: above all the folly of utterly despicable magic, already rejected in the sacred scriptures and in the divine canons, from which is excluded knowledge that comes through judiciary astrology: through which and by way of inspiration and divine Revelations, and by way of continuous calculation, we have written down our prophecies. And, true though it is that occult philosophy is not rejected, I have not wanted to represent its wild suggestions, notwithstanding numerous books I have come upon that have been hidden for long centuries. But fearing what was capable of happening after reading them, I made a gift of them to Vulcan, and while he was devouring them, the flame that was licking the air had an unusual brightness, brighter than a natural flame, like the light from a flash of lightning which suddenly lights up a house, as if it were suddenly on fire. So, in order that in future they not be misused, observing the principles of perfect transformation – solar as well as lunar – and that of the incorruptible subterranean metals subjected to occult waves, I reduced them to ashes. But, as concerns the knowledge that is obtained through investigation of the Heavens, this I would like to explain to you: for having knowledge of future causes, putting at a distance the fantastic imaginings that can come about, limiting the description of places, through divine supernatural inspiration, attributing to the images in the Heavens, places and a part of time that has occult properties, with the power and divine faculty, in the presence of which the three times are compressed into eternity, awaiting the revolution of the stars to past, present and future events: 'since all things are naked and open, etc.' because, my son, you can easily understand that things that are to happen can be prophesied by way of the lights in the night sky, which are natural, and thanks to the prophetic spirit – not that I wish to attribute to myself a prophetic name or capacity – but, thanks to the revealed inspiration, as a mortal man, I am no less distant with my senses from the Heavens than my feet are from the earth: 'I cannot err, deceive myself or be deceived: I am a greater sinner than anyone else in this world, subject to all human afflictions'. Being overcome more times in a week than not by apathy, and with lengthy calculations, lending a pleasant odour to my studies, I have composed some books of proph-

ecy, each containing one hundred astronomical prophetic
quatrains, which I have thought well to rework in an obscure
fashion and which are prophecies that last from now until
the year 3797. This will possibly cause some frowns seeing
the extent of the time span, but all this shall come to pass
and make sense under the concavity of the moon and will
be universally understood over the whole Earth, my son. So
that if you live to a natural human age, you will see in your
clime and in the sky at the time of your birth the foreseen
future events. Since it is Eternal God alone who knows the
eternity of the light emanating from himself. And so I say
openly that to whomsoever His immense greatness to reveal
things, through long-sighted and gloomy Revelations, that
these are divinely manifested through occult sources, principally through two sources, that came to the knowledge of
the person He made Revelations to, the person who prophesies: one is that he sends Revelations by making things
clear through supernatural light to the seer, through the
science of Stars; the other is that he prophesies by inspired
Revelations, which is a communication from divine eternity,
through which the prophet comes to know what his divine
spirit has given him through God the Creator and through
natural instinct: it must be known that what he predicts is
true and that he has drawn it from the Heavens: and that
the light and the flame are of such a power and from so
great an altitude – no less than in the way nature and the
brightness of natural daylight give the philosophers such a
sense of assuredness – philosophers who, through the principle of primum mobile, have reached the deepest of depths
in the loftiest of doctrines. But with such discourse, my son,
I am going into too great a depth for the future capacity of
your senses, and I also find that the letters will cause such
great and incomparable damage, for I see that the world,
before the universal conflagration, will be so full of floods
and such great floods that there will be scarcely any territory
that will not be covered by water, and that will be for
such a long time that there will be no ethnography and no
topography that will not have perished: also before and

after such floods in numerous quarters the rains will be so scarce, and a great abundance of fire and falling rocks will rain down from the sky, and nothing will there be that will not be destroyed, and this will occur, in brief, before the final conflagration. Since, even though Mars concludes its century at the end of its last period, this it will resume, but the others will be gathered, some in Aquarius for many years, the others in Cancer for a longer and more lasting time. At the moment we are led by the moon, through the power of God eternal, but before it has completed its cycle, the sun will come and then Saturn. Because, according to the celestial signs, the reign of Saturn will return, and by calculations, the world will come close to a great revolution: and with regards to what is now written here, going back one hundred and seventy seven years, three months and eleven days, through pestilence, long famine, wars, and even more through floods, within these two limits, predetermined [by going] forwards and backwards more than once, the world will be so diminished and there will be so little life that no one will be found who will want to take over the fields, which will remain unoccupied for as much time as they have been possessed, and for what I can see in the Heavens, though we are at the seventh number of a thousand, which completes everything, we are nearing the eighth, where the firmament of the eighth sphere is situated, which is in a latitudinal dimension, where the great eternal God will come to finish the revolution: where the celestial images will begin moving again and the superior axis which renders the earth stable will not incline in the centuries of the centuries, until His will has been accomplished. Thus it will be and not otherwise, although, because of excessive ambiguous and fanatical opinion through Machometic (Mohammedan) dreams, in some moments, God the creator, through the ministry of his messengers of flame and fire, will make a move to reveal to our exterior senses, our eyes even, the sources of future prediction, indications of future occurrences, that must manifest themselves to him who presages. For the foreknowledge that is drawn from exterior light infallibly succeeds in identifying a part of it along with or through exterior light, since, in truth, it is all too evident that the part which appears to the eye of the intellect is not by person due to an imperfection of the sense of perception, seeing that all is predicted through divine Revelations and through the angelic spirit, revealed to the man who prophesies, giving pertinence to his prophecies, which come to enlighten him not in the way fantasy does with diverse nocturnal apparitions, but rather through constant daily prophecies, by way of astronomical calculations in conjunction with the most holy future predictions, without other considerations, save that of the freedom of courage. Come then, my son and understand what I have found through my revolutions, which concur with the revelatory inspiration, that now the sword of death comes closer, with plague, the most horrendous war that has ever been in the lifetime of three men, and famine which will befall the earth and often return, for the Stars show it in their revolution: and it is also said 'I shall punish their iniquities with an iron rod and scourge them and strike them through and through', for the Lord's mercy shall no longer be dispensed, my son, once the greater part of my prophecies are accomplished, and they will terminate upon their completion. Then, more than once during the sinister storms, 'I shall ground them to powder', the Lord will say, 'I shall destroy them and I shall have no pity' and a thousand other happenings will come by the waters and the earth and continual rains, as I have set down in writing more extensively in my other prophecies, which are composed in free speech 'In soluta oratione' and which define the places, the times and the pre-determined limit within which future mankind will unerringly recognise the events when they happen, as others we have noticed doing with greater clarity. However, notwithstanding the meaning of the words being masked, their significance shall be realised, when the obstacle of ignorance has been removed, fate will be easier to see. In conclusion, my son, accept this gift from your father M. Nostradamus, hoping that it will clarify for you each of the quatrains written herein.

> *Praying to Immortal God that He grant you long life, in good and prosperous happiness.*
>> *From Salon, this first day of March of 1555.*

As can be seen, in the letter there are some references to the Seer's own special chronology, which will provide an initial definition of the seventh millennium, and with that aim in mind, we can conveniently use the passage as a starting point in which the Seer writes:

> *Though we are at the seventh number of a thousand, which completes everything, we are nearing the eighth, where the firmament of the eighth sphere is in a latitudinal dimension where the great eternal God will come to finish the revolution: where the celestial images will begin moving again and the superior axis which renders the earth stable will not incline in the centuries of the centuries.*

The edition of 1557 varies from subsequent editions: *'Le monument superior'* becomes *'Le mouuement superieur'* in later editions. If what is written in the first edition is correct, then *'monument'* assumes the significance of something that is immobile and still, and it seems appropriate to translate this as *'axis'*. On the other hand, it is difficult to see what *'superior movement, which will not incline'* could possibly mean. We know however that, as a consequence of the precession of the equinoxes, the earth's axis executes a slow, circular rotation at both ends, like the handle of a spinning top when the top no longer has sufficient rotational force, and this elongated movement makes a complete circle about every 26,000 years, determines the correlations within the constellations of the zodiac at the Spring equinox. The correlation of constellations determines the astrological eras: today the sun is still in the ascendant on 21 March in the sign of Pisces, but at this point the correlation of Aquarius is still close.

It is therefore much more probable that *'monument'* is the correct word and that with this word the Seer is clearly referring to the earth's axis and to its slow inclination, which makes its invisible circle in the Heavens over the lengthy period of 26,000 years. Having said that, it must be noted that the phrase in question appears to be illuminating under another and more important aspect: '*Though we are at the seventh number of a thousand . . .*' conveys the meaning that at the time in which the Seer is writing (1555) the seventh millennium has already begun. This means that the date of the beginning of 1,000 years can be understood to be between AD 555 (at one extreme in which 1555 would be the final year of the seventh millennium) and AD 1555 (at the other extreme 555, if is taken as the first year of the seventh millennium). However, the Seer provides other references as well. In fact, '*though we are at the seventh number of a thousand*' stands to mean that the seventh millennium began some considerable period ago, seeing that the conjunction *though* is linked to the verb 'to be' (and not, for example, to 'to begin', 'enter', 'initiate') and would make no sense unless a considerable period had already elapsed.

Such an interpretation is supported the phrase close to it: '*we are nearing the eighth*'. If, as in Euclidean geometry, approaching end *B* of a segment means moving along the segment, starting from the end *A*, in literary and figurative terms, approaching *B* means having left *A* and covered at least half the distance separating *A* from *B*. From this we can therefore conclude that in 1555, when Nostradamus was writing this letter, between a minimum of 501 years and a maximum of 999 years of the seventh millennium have elapsed, which narrow the time span and pinpoint the beginning of the seventh millennium to within a span of only 499 years which ranges from AD 1054 (1555–501) and AD 556 (1555–999). To sum up, according to the Seer's clues 1555 could either be the last year of the seventh millennium or anyone of last 499 years of the millennium, in view of the fact that when Nostradamus was writing his prefatory letter to the *Centuries*, at least half the millennium had elapsed.

To take our deductions a stage further: the date when the seven millennia began can be fixed between 4946 BC (6000–1054) and 5444 BC (6000–556) and the end of the seven millennia can be any date between AD 1555 (supposing – at one extreme – that is the seventh millennium's last year) and AD 2054 (at the other extreme – supposing that in 1555, 501 years of the seventh millennium had passed and 499, therefore, remained).

Some may object to this first conclusion on the grounds that the Seer refers to the year 3797, in which, he says, his prophecies will end.

At this point, we should note that the Seer frequently resorts to a language used by the alchemists: the so-called *'green language'*, which they employed in order not to be understood by the ecclesiastical authorities, who, certainly, would have had no hesitation in putting them on trial for witchcraft and burning them at the stake. We shall later examine how this date was in fact used to mask the real one. So it must be read and interpreted in a sense that is entirely different from what it appears to be.

What is certain, however, is that we should not take this date as starting from the year of the birth of Christ: when, in his letter to his son César, the Seer speaks of the seventh millennium, he says that in the course of this and until its end, everything will come to pass. It will be also seen, when we examine the letter to Henry of France, that this is not a completely accurate statement, since the prophecies cover a longer period of time, extending to the beginning of the eighth millennium, but not going beyond it, and certainly not going into the ninth.

2. The letter to King Henry

Nostradamus's letter to Henry of France, which was used to preface the last three *Centuries*, contains further precious references to time, often in apparent contradiction with what the Seer wrote in his letter to his son César. If, in the first letter, the Seer devotes quite a lot of space to describing the prophetic inspiration, in this second, he devotes more space to illustrate future events, but in so doing, he is more cautious about giving clear chronologically defined explanations: instead he indulges in the use of obscure terms to indicate facts, people or personalities, and he sweeps back and forth in the future, so that it becomes a real labour for any interpreter to give the various events any chronological order.

Nonetheless, in this letter, there are two passages in which Nostradamus refers to elements in the Bible, which might be used to determine the date at which the 7,000 years began.

The Seer writes:

the time span of our ancestors, who came before us, is such ... that the first man, Adam, arrived about 1,242 years before Noah ... After Noah and the universal flood, came Abraham, about 1,080 years ... Then came Moses about 515–516 years, and between Moses and David, about 570 years. Then between the time of David and that of Our Lord there are 1,350 years.

In another part of the letter Nostradamus continues:

If we add the years from the creation of the world up to the birth of Noah 1506 years would have passed, and from the birth of Noah to the building of the Ark, just before the

Universal Inundation, 600 years pass. And at the end of the six years Noah entered the ark in order to be saved from the flood and the universal flood on the earth lasted a year and two months. And between the end of the flood and the birth of Abraham was a time span of 295 years. And from the birth of Abraham until the birth of Isaac 100 years passed. And from Isaac to Jacob 60 years and from the time he entered Egypt until the exodus 130 years passed. And from the time of Jacob's entry into Egypt until the exodus 430 years passed. And from the exodus from Egypt until the building of Solomon's temple in the Fourth year of his reign, 480 years passed. And from the building of the temple until Jesus Christ, according to the account in the Sacred Writings, 490 years passed. And so by these calculations that I made in connection with the sacred scriptures, it is about 4173 years and eight months, more or less.

The two parts of the letter are in apparent contradiction, since in the first, the number of years from the birth of Adam to Jesus Christ makes a total of 4757, while in the second part, the number of years from the creation of world to Jesus Christ, though given as 4173 by the Seer, actually produces a total of 4098 (and two months).

If we compare this chronology with what the Bible suggests we will notice immediately that facts relating to time do not coincide by any means. In fact, if we show the birth of Adam as 0, the chronology obtained from Bible is as follows:

Adam: 0–930 (Gen. 5:3–5)
Seth: 130–1,042 (Gen. 5: 3–8)
Enos: 235–1,140 (Gen. 5: 6–11)
Kenan: 225–1,235 (Gen. 5: 9–14)
Mahlaeel: 395–1,290 (Gen. 5: 12–17)
Jared: 460–1,422 (Gen. 5: 15–20)
Enoch: 622–987 (Gen. 5: 8–24)
Methuselah: 687–1,656 (Gen. 5: 21–27)
Lemach: 874–1,651 (Gen. 5: 25–31)
Noah: 1,057–2,007 (Gen. 5: 28–32)

As can clearly be seen, the time lapse between Adam and Noah is not 1,242 years but only 1,057. The error appears to be obvious and is not easily explained, for the book of Genesis is absolutely precise on this point and has no calculations.

It need hardly be said that the biblical text that the Seer had at his disposal was no different from the present day text and that the calculation at that time was extremely easy, as it is today. Which leads one to think that the error in the time lapse is none other than a deliberate one.

Following on from this, it is worth continuing with an examination of the genealogy of the Bible.

Shem: 1,558–2,158 (Gen. 7:6 e 11:10)
Arphaxad: 1,658–2,123 (Gen. 11: 10–13)
Shelah: 1,693–2,153 (Gen. 11:12–13)
Eber: 1,723–2,189 (Gen. 11:14–17)
Peleg: 1,759–1,998 (Gen. 11:16–19)
Reu: 1,789–2,028 (Gen. 11:18–21)
Serug: 1,821–2,051 (Gen. 11:20–23)
Nahor: 1,851–1,999 (Gen. 11:22–25)
Terah: 1,880–2,085 (Gen. 11:24–26)
Abraham: 1,948–2,123 (Gen. 11: 26, 12:4, 25:7)

There also appears to be an obvious error in the Seer's time lapse between Noah and Abraham. From what we can gather from the book of Genesis, there is a lapse of 891 years between Noah and Abraham and not 1,080, and from the end of the Flood to the birth of Abraham there is a passage of 290 years, not 295 (the Flood ends 1,658 after the birth of Adam (see Gen. 8:13), while Abraham was born 1,948 years after the birth of Adam). Then we have:

Isaac: 2,048–2,228 (Gen. 17:21, 21:5, 35,28)
Jacob: 2,108–2255 (Gen. 25:26, 47:28)
Joseph: 2,199–2,309 (Gen. 41:29, 46:47, 53:54, 45:11)
The arrival of Jacob in Egypt: 2,238 (Gen. 47: 8–11)
Moses: 2,373–2,493 (Deut. 34:7).

According to the chronology of the Old testament, there is a time lapse of 2,373 years between the birth of Adam and that of Moses, while in the first passage of his letter, the Seer mentions a period of 2,837 years between Adam and Moses: the difference of 464 years is considerable.

Furthermore, the arrival of Jacob in Egypt, to which Nostradamus refers in the second part of the letter, was 2,238 years after the birth of Adam, but there was certainly not a lapse of 430 years between that moment and the Exodus, which took place 2,453 years after the birth of Adam (Exodus 12,29–42 and Acts 7,6): only 215 years.

Using the genealogy provided in the Bible, the period between Moses and the reign of David, is 610 years, the reign of David having begun in 2,983 years after the birth of Adam (II Sam. 2,1 11) and ending 40 years later, and therefore in the year 3,023 (Sam. 5:4–5). In this case too Nostradamus would be making a substantial error in his calculations, amounting to more than fifty years. However, if we look at the time lapse between the birth of Moses and the birth of David, and take into account the fact That David lived for seventy years (II Sam. 5:4) – he died in 3,023 – one can deduce that he was born 2,953 after the birth of Adam and that, consequently, between the birth of Moses and the birth of David 580 years were to pass.

Solomon's building of the Temple occurred apparently 480 years after the Exodus (Kings, 6: 38), just as the Seer says. However, one must also look at the years of slavery, when the Israelites had lost their rapport with God, and, since they were not theocratic, these years were not included or counted in the Bible. In any case, between the building of the Temple and Jesus Christ, not 490 but 942 years passed. Taking instead as reference, the time of the reign of David, between this and the birth of Jesus Christ 1,001 years passed, as opposed to 1,350 as the Seer maintains in the first part of the letter. On the basis of the Bible, therefore, Adam certainly was certainly not born either in 4757 BC, or on any of the alternative dates, this can be taken from passages in the letter to Henry.

So we must try to understand *why* the Seer made so many

errors in his calculation of the time lapse between Adam and Jesus Christ. If can only be that these errors were made deliberately in order to mask the date at which the seven millennia began, so that no interpreter would understand the time span of his prophecies. The result is that no authors, among hundreds who have confronted this particular problem, have specified the same dates for the beginning and the end of his prophecies.

Let me say again that the overall calculation contained in the second part of the letter, which gives the sum of 4,098 years (and two months) rather than 4,173, is, on the whole, fairly accurate, if we bear in mind that, while the book of Genesis is absolutely unequivocal, and does not allow for varying interpretations, the passages cited in this second part, which refer to episodes contained in other books of the Bible, cannot always be verified with the same precision, and present some differences in calculation, which even though negligible, can excuse errors of a few of years.

If the errors can be explained only on the basis of a deliberate intention to conceal the Seer's precise calculations, then it is precisely on the basis of these that it is perhaps possible to arrive at the date the seven thousand years began.

This gigantic chronological puzzle, which was prepared with remarkable ability and intelligence and not without some subtle irony, would in fact have no sense whatsoever, if it did not lead to the solution desired.

The errors made must therefore be examined, and on the evidence of these, identify what the Seer secretly wanted to me made known.

In the first part of the letter to Henry the errors are as follows:

between Adam and Noah there is a difference of 185 years;
between Noah and Abraham there is a difference of 189 years;
between Abraham and Moses there is a difference of 90 years;
between Moses and the birth of David there is a difference of 10 years;

between the reign of David and Jesus Christ there is a difference of 349 years.

The total difference, therefore, is of 823 years.

The second part of the letter, as can be seen, contains a huge
error in adding up (4,173 instead of 4,098). Even this is no
random error, since it is unthinkable for such a polymath as
Nostradamus not to know how to do an elementary addition.
When one encounters the error, ones first impulse is to substi-
tute the 4,173 mentioned by the Seer with 4,098 (and two
months) obtained by calculating the sum.

But the fact itself that Nostradamus mentions a very precise
number, in contrast to what is written in the other part of the
letter, where there is a total sum, shows, I believe, that the
number which should be used, though it is the wrong answer
to the sum, is the one the Seer himself refers to. This may be
illogical but precisely because of this, it accords perfectly with
the Seer's way of reasoning and his characteristic tangling of
the facts.

And so, 4,173 is the first figure to which one must refer.

The second calculation appears as a consequent. The truth
is that, if the Seer willingly made an error of 823 years in his
calculation of the genealogy of the Bible, it is this figure that
must be added to the first: in sum, by committing these deliberate mistakes, the Seer is giving us to understand that they must
be added together to determine the date of the beginning of
the seven millennia.

This appears to be the only possible solution to this complex
riddle and is consistent with the logic of the alchemist's *green
language* – which hides the truth under different guises but
makes it possible for an initiate to understand the hidden truth,
once the key to the riddle is found, a key which in this case,
is: '*Add up the resulting errors!*' Having done this, one arrives
at a date of 4996 BC, which could be the starting point of the
seven millennia. However, such a hypothesis obviously needs
further verification and argument to support it.

And there is an immediate confirmation of this thesis: this
self-same date is arrived at from another direction.

It has been observed that the total sum of the years mentioned in the first part of the letter is 4,757, while that of the second part is 4,098.

But in the second part is a linguistic snare, which creates a situation where the 4,098 mentioned does not entirely correspond with what the Seer really intended to say.

In passage XCIX, Nostradamus writes:

> Et depuis l'yssue d'Egypt jusques à l'edification du Temple faicte par Solomon au quatriesme an de son regne, passerent quatre cens octante ans ou quatre vingts ans

which when translated means:

> *and from the Exodus out of Egypt to the building of the Temple by Solomon in the fourth year of his reign, four hundred and eighty years or four times twenty years passed.*

As is known, in French the number eighty is written as *quatre vingts* and not *octante*, therefore the specification would seem to be a correction, but the Seer has accustomed us to understand that nothing is ever written by pure chance, least of all numeric or linguistic errors.

What Nostradamus really intended to say by repeating the final figure correctly is that the first written number must also be obtained using the same method with which the number eighty is written, and the phrase as a whole means: '*and from the Exodus from Egypt to the building of the Temple by Solomon in the fourth year of his reign, four hundred and eighty years passed, or on the other hand (also as it is written) eighty, and that is four times twenty.*'

At this point what appears to be 480 becomes 720 (that is four times 180). So, in this passage the Seer's intention is to say that two distinct numbers must be considered. The first is the one which is apparent, that is 480, and the second – and hence the presence of the conjunction *or* – the result of multiplying 180 by 4, giving us 720.

Since everything Nostradamus's work has a clear purpose,

two distinct calculations must be made: with the first, the total addition of the years mentioned in the two parts of the letter, taking into account the concealed number 720, in which case the total sum of years in the second part of the letter amount to 4,338, and the total sum of years of the two parts becomes 9,095 (4,757 + 4,338).

In the second calculation, one must subtract from the number thus obtained the sum of the years that are apparent in the second part of the letter (4,098). This is not an arbitrary calculation: it is suggested by the Seer himself, when, having mentioned the erroneous sum of 4,173, he adds the phrase *'more or less'*, leaving us to understand that one must add to one side and subtract from the other.

By subtracting 4,098 from 9,095, the difference obtained is 4,997, but when the Seer mentions the erroneous 4,173, he gives a second warning: he adds *'and eight months, more or less'*, which leads us into thinking that apart from suggesting the first calculation using the addition and the subtraction *'more or less'* must mean that there must be a further addition of 8 months to 4,098, or that alternatively, these eight months must be subtracted from 9,095 beforehand. So the Seer is intending to indicate to us that either the eight months are to be added to one of the two figures (*more*) or that they are to be subtracted from the other (*less*), so that either one or the other calculation ensures the same final results. So, if one subtracts 4,098 and eight months from 9,095 one obtain a final figure of 4,996 (and four months); in just the same way, the final figure is obtained by subtracting the eight months from 9095 beforehand and then subtracting 4,098 from the resulting figure of 9,094 and four months: the answer 4,996 as well, and that is the first year of the seven millennia, a date previously calculated by a totally different method.

People will object that, at such a date, according to chronology of the Bible, Adam had not even been created, and that therefore 4996 BC does not have a logical or historical reference. To such an objection I say, first of all, that neither of the dates indicated by the Seer (4757 BC or 4173 BC) has a meaning in a biblical key, since, as has been observed, according to the said chronology, Adam was certainly not born either in 4757 or in 4173 BC. It appears evident that the temporal reference drawn from the Bible is merely an apparent one and is used only to indicate the effective date of the beginning of the seven millennia concealed beneath the erroneous date on the page. On the other hand, if Nostradamus were to have a date for the beginning of the seven millennia almost 1,000 years earlier than the birth of Adam, he would almost certainly have been accused of heresy and even in the best scenarios, been forced, like Galileo, to repudiate his thesis.

So, why 4996 BC?

In this connection one should note that influences in the life of Nostradamus are double-standard: not only is there the Bible and Sacred Scriptures, but also the history of ancient Egypt and its civilisation. Nor should it be forgotten that the Seer was a staunch Rosicrucian and that the Ancient and Mystical Order of the Rosicrucians has professed until today that its teachings are found in ancient Egypt and in its mysteries, from which Pythagoras and other philosophers of antiquity drew their learning. The Seer's passion for Egypt is attested to by the comment he makes on the *Hieroglyphic of Horapollo*, a text that was re-discovered just a little over thirty years ago.

Some, including myself, might in support of this thesis, draw attention to the fact that when Nostradamus was writing about his chronology in his letter to Henry, he uses the word '*hierograph*' when establishing the date of the Christ's birth, given as 490 years after the building of the Temple by Solomon, when this, as has been noted, was erected 948 years previously. Hierograph is commonly interpreted as 'sacred (hieratic) writings'. I would like to think here that it means hieroglyphics. No hieroglyphics exist which treat of the birth of Christ, and more pertinent references would indeed could have been drawn from the Sacred Scriptures. If it is indeed hieroglyphics to which he is referring, then it would be very significant and indicate to the interpreter that the chronology the Seer was using was taken from a completely different history: that of Egypt. In 4996 BC Egypt was still in its pre-dynastic phase, more precisely, in the period of Badarian culture, a period in which an already conspicuous civilisation flourished, as various archaeological findings have attested. But precisely in that period, following the particular Egyptian mythology as it is interpreted by the Rosicrucians, the end is said to have come for the reign of the gods and the demigods – those of spirituality and light – and the imperfect reign of men began – one of materialism and darkness that which the Egyptian Mysteries, custodians of the ancient secrets and traditions which were orally handed down, were trying to combat by cultivating men who were capable of understanding the true essence of existence along side their respect for other men and for creation.

What is more, in 1999, the Egyptian government flooded newspapers and television screens with advertising that was most significant, inviting tourists to come and visit Egypt of the seventh millennium, so, it is official historiography itself that sees Egyptian civilisation as having had its beginnings at about 5000 BC. There still remain two passages, which in appearance seem to contradict the hypothesis suggested here.

In the letter to Henry we read:

> ... with the hope of leaving in writing the years, towns, cities and the regions where most events will happen, even in the year 1585 and of the year 1606, beginning from the present time, which is 14 March 1557, and going well beyond, as far as the accession which will come after the beginning of millennium 7, calculated as learnedly as my astronomical calculation and my research have been able to stretch, where the adversaries of Jesus Christ and of his Church will begin to multiply with greater strength.

More than one interpreter commenting on this passage have pointed to the contradiction between this and what is written in the letter to César, where the Seer speaks of finding himself in that moment in the seventh millennium.

In this case too, one must examine what the Seer writes extremely carefully, particularly the terminology he uses. In the letter to César, Nostradamus speaks of '*seventh millen-*

nium', in this letter to Henry he refers to *'millennium seven'*. In the first passage he is using ordinals, and in the second cardinals. In the light of this observation, therefore, the contradiction is only on the surface.

Just as 1901 marked the beginning of the twentieth century, the seventh millennium runs from 6,001 to 7,000 – millennium number seven, on the other hand runs from 7,001 to 8,000, just as century number twenty begins in 2001 and ends in the last day of 2,099. So in this case, the Seer is using phraseology to confuse his interpreter and, it must be said, he succeeds very well, for the difference between the two numerical terms is so imperceptible in the context of the two passages that until now it has gone unnoticed.

The reference to the year 3797 still remains to be examined. The Seer points to this as the final date of the *Centuries* and of his prophecies. We have already been noted that this date cannot be taken as starting from the birth of Christ, if that were so, the whole period would go well beyond the eighth millennium and run into the ninth, which would contradict what is said in another part of the letter to César. In order to understand this chronological puzzle, reference must once again be made to the alchemist's *green language*. We shall see later on in his letter to Henry and in his *Centuries* that the Seer makes extensive use of this language, which employs anagrams, crases and other devices.

In this case, once we have reached the logical conclusion that the date given on paper should not be taken at face value, we have to find a different key to interpreting the text. All the numerical and linguistic artifices used in the text, however, contain within them the possibility of being discovered and resolved. And there is not one single passage in the work, as obscure and as indecipherable it may be, which cannot be interpreted and explained, once the key to the artifice has been discovered.

This means that 3797 cannot be transformed willy-nilly, just by transposing the figures, but that an identification of the hidden date must obey certain logical and interpretative criteria.

We must bear in mind the subtle irony that runs through the Seer's entire work. After he has given this number in his letter, Nostradamus writes: 'Que possible fera retirer le front à quelque uns, en voyant si longue extension, & par soubz toute la concavité de la Lune aura lieu & intelligence', a sentence which translates as: '*Seeing such an extension may cause some to frown [to retract their brow], but everything will take place and will be understood under the concavity of the moon*'. This is certainly the apparent meaning.

However, *front* does not mean only forehead, but also *head*, *leader*. And *retirer* does not mean only *retract*, but also *put* or *draw back*. The entire phrase, then, can also be translated as: '*this possibility will make it so that some, on seeing such an extension* [of time], *will put the first number* [the head] *behind* [the others]'. If this is what Nostradamus claims to be doing through his use of *green language*, then 3797 becomes 7973, which is obtained by placing the 3 (the head) behind the other numbers, so that the figure becomes the exact reverse of the first. This is precisely how another great personality of the Renaissance, Leonardo Da Vinci, might have written it. He wrote from right to left, with letters and numbers written backwards, so that his writing could be easily read with the use of a mirror.

It is difficult to dispute that this is the number Nostradamus really meant.

In fact, the Seer's chronology which forms the basis of his entire work is that of the 7,000 years and therefore this date, when read back to front, fit perfectly into such a time frame. Such a year, obviously, does not begin from the birth of Christ but from the beginning of the running of time according to the particular chronology on which the work is based. Therefore, if the seven millennia begin in 4996 BC, they will end in 2004, and 7973 would correspond to the year 2977 of the Christian calendar.

But this is not the real date of the end of his prophecies either, because, in this case too, the Seer expresses himself in a vague way: the prophecies, in fact, will end much before this, but such a date has its precise meaning in that it indicates the time until when Satan will remain bound in the deep abyss or pit, and mankind can thereby enjoy a long period of peace and fraternity. In fact, at the close of his letter to Henry, the Seer writes: 'Satan sera mis & lié dans l'abysme du barathre dans la profonde fosse . . . et demeurera lié enuiron l'espace de mille ans', which means *Satan shall be consigned and bound in the depth of the abyss, of the deep chasm, and will remain bound for the space of about one thousand years,*' a concept which is repeated again in *Centuries* VIII, quatrain 95, in which the Seer writes:

> Le seducteur sera mis en la fosse,
> Et estaché iusques à quelque temps,
> Le clerc uny le chef auec sa crosse,
> Pycante droite attraira les contens.

> *The seducer shall be put in the pit,*
> *And enchained there for some time,*
> *Clerk united with the leader, with his cross,*
> *The bitter truth shall attract the happy.*

So this is the date the Seer really meant, for, if the *Centuries* foresee the future up to a time that is considerably before Satan's imprisonment, nevertheless, at least in its reference to this fact, the prophecy extends almost a further thousand years. Therefore, if 4996 BC marks the beginning of the seven millennia, and if AD 2004 marks their end, then 2977 signifies the date until which Satan will remain chained in the abyss, and that is the 'about one thousand years' to which the Seer alludes. In fact, in the letter to Henry, Nostradamus does not say that Satan shall remain bound for a thousand years, but for '*about*' one thousand years *(environ)*, which confirms the accuracy of the interpretation that is being proposed here.

3. The beginning of the seven millennia

Au reuolu du grand nombre septiesme,
Apparoistra au temps Ieux d'Hecatombe,
Non esloigné du grand eage milliesme,
Que les entres sortiront de leur tombe.

At the end of the great septennial,
It shall appear at the time of Hecatomb Games,
Not far from the age of the great millennium,
That the buried shall issue from their tombs.
(Centuries X, quatrain 74)

The hypothesis that the seven millennia began in 4996 BC and that consequently they must conclude in AD 2004 is moving forward. Quatrain number 74 of the X *Centuries* tells us that the grand seventh number will be completed at the time of '*Hecatomb*' games. The problem is to see if 2004 can in some way refer to an event which signifying such an enigmatic moment.

Many interpreters have maintained that with the term '*Hecatomb*' Nostradamus intended a reference to a war or a massacre. In fact in classical Greek the word '*Hecatomb*' means '*one hundred oxen*' and signified the propitiatory sacrifice of one hundred oxen, which usually took place at the same time as the athletic games in ancient Greece. Hecatomb, was also an ancient city in Achaia, and in addition to this, the word '*Hecatomb*' was used to indicate the month of July.

If such a hypothesis is true – and there is no reason to doubt that it is – the date 2004 mentioned in the previous chapter, therefore, acquires a surprising confirmation. The Olympic Games of 2004, will in fact, take place in Athens! This interpretation becomes even more intriguing when it is appreciated that the word '*Hecatomb*' in its original Greek formulation is *Hecaton boes*. If we treat this as an anagram, we can see it includes the phrase: C.O.H. Athens. This is an abbreviation for *Comité Olympique Hellenique Athènes*', the Greek Olympic Committee.

This interpretation also appears to concur perfectly with the third line, '*Not far from the age of the great millennium*'. In fact, 2004 is not distant from 2000 (*the age of the great millennium*) and the term '*far*' can denote a time, which can be either before or after a certain date.

For the sake of completeness, we must also interpreting the fourth line, which many identify with the resurrection of the body according to Catholic belief. However, those who have interpreted this line this way, may have taken due account of the fact that Nostradamus did not write '*shall happen*' but rather '*shall appear*', that is, '*shall seem*'.

Why, therefore, will it seem, in 2004, that the dead will rise again? The answer lies in recent scientific and biological research. A sheep has been cloned, and both ethical and scientific debates are taking place as to whether such a practice is admissible or possible for human beings. In 2004, therefore, cloning will also be experimented on man, and the cloned human being will be similar in every way to his stock, even though he is dead. And so that cloned man, identical to a man already dead, will make it seem as though the latter has come back to life.

There no seems little doubt left to fixing the period of the seven millennia, as starting in 4996 BC and ending in AD 2004. So we now come to interpretating the second quatrain referred to in the introduction to this first part:

> Vingt ans du regne de la Lune passés,
> Sept mil ans autre tiendra sa monarchie,
> Quand le Soleil prendra ses iours lassés,
> Lors accomplit & mine ma prophetie.

When twenty years of the Moon's reign shall pass,
Seven thousand more its monarchy shall hold,
When the Sun has reclaimed its days left,
Then shall my prophecy come true.

(Centuries I, quatrain 48)

There have been very different interpretations to this quatrain: interpreters have made abstruse calculations of the lunar years, or they have dragged in the reform of the Gregorian calendar, or even claimed that they have identified a key in cryptic writing which alludes to political events (republic–monarchy). All these interpretations fail, first of all, to take into account what Nostradamus writes in his letter to his son César: '*At the moment we are led by the moon, through the power of God eternal, but before it has completed its cycle, the Sun will come and then Saturn. Because according to the celestial signs, the reign of Saturn will return, and, by all my calculations, the world will come close to a tremendous revolution.*'

There can be no doubt that the quatrain refers to this passage of the letter, and therefore, the interpretation which should be given to it cannot be separated from it.

When the Seer mentions the '*the Moon's reign*', he is making a precise reference to the Rosicrucians' mystical doctrine, according to which we are currently living in a period of obscurantism, in which man is totally absorbed by material pleasures and is overlooking the spiritual part of himself, which binds him to the Cosmos and God. The reign of the moon, a star which lives by reflected light, which is not strong enough to illuminate a humanity which is dedicated only to the material aspects of existence, will soon end, after having had dominion for 7020 years, and the sun will come once again to illuminate humanity, making it conscious of its divine essence, so that once this awareness is there, the golden age, personified by Saturn, can return.

The quatrain, therefore, echoes the mystical teachings of ancient Egypt: the reign of the gods and demigods having ceased in 4996 BC, then came the imperfect material reign of man, personified by the moon. And this reign will last 7020 years.

As is usual, the first two lines describing the time cannot be easily interpreted. In fact the figure of 7020 is separated in the two lines, and punctuation at first lead us to think that the twenty years are referring to the reign of the Moon and the 7,000 to the duration of a monarchy. But here again are devices found in '*green language*', that is, the impression of an apparent meaning is created while at the same time concealing the real one.

Consequently, in the light of this interpretation, which accords with what I have already said previously, Nostradamus's prophecies will end at the end of twenty years from the completion of the seventh millennium. Therefore, if the seventh millennium concludes in 2004, the prophecies will end sometime between 2024 and the first months of 2025, there being every reason for maintaining that in this quatrain the Seer has limited himself to revealing the length of the years, and omitting any calculation of months.

Between 2024 and June 2025, and coming at the end of 'a great tribulation', which will bring humanity, as we shall see later, almost to extinction, at the hands of the Antichrist, there will be a rebirth, which fully concurs with what John prophesied in the Apocalypse, a text which was certainly read and studied in depth by Nostradamus.

The quatrain can therefore be interpreted as follows: *After the passage of another twenty years of the Moon's reign, after the end of the seven thousand years, another will have his reign. When the Sun (the new king) will return to govern, my prophecy shall end.* The interpretation being offered here, moreover, concurs exactly with what the Seer writes in his letter to Henry: 'Et passant outre bien loing iusques à l'aduenement qui sera apres au commencement du 7. Millenaire profondement supputé . . .'

And that is, '*going well beyond, as far as the accession which will come after the beginning of millennium 7, calculated learnedly*'. It has already been observed that millennium 7, written as a cardinal number, really means the eighth millennium, and so, in this passage of the letter to Henry, Nostradamus is clearly saying that his prophecy will not end at the seventh millennium, but that it will extend well into the eighth, which once more supports my theory, since the date proposed as the end to the prophecies, that is, 2024–beginning of 2025, extends for at least a good twenty years into the eighth millennium.

As an added support to this theory, a final consideration should be made. In the second part of the letter to Henry, in which he adds up the sum to make 4,173 years, the Seer also adds in eight months, by writing '*yields about 4,173 years and eight months, more or less*'.

We have already noted above that the eight months were usefully employed to define the year 4996 with an alternative system; this, however, does not exclude the possibility that the eight months could have a second valence and that the parenthetic '*eight months, more or less*' may be interpreted as it appears to be, and that is that to the year 4996 BC eight months, '*more or less*', should be added.

It hardly needs saying that the eight months cannot originate in a sum of any kind, because Nostradamus, when he indicates the years, refers to the months only in regard to the duration of the Flood, which lasted on Earth for one year and two months.

So, if 4996 BC is the year the seven millennia began, the month would have to be August, and so the 7,000 years should finish in August of 2004 '*more or less*'. As is common knowledge, the Olympic games in Athens will begin in the month of August and will run their entire course, with the obvious consequence that from August 4996 BC until the '*Hecatomb*' games seven thousand years '*more or less*', will have passed.

4. The date of the end of the prophecies

We have now made some important steps towards defining the chronology of the Seer's work: we know, that is, that the prophecies will end in a period between 2024 and the first part of 2025.

At this point let us examine the letter to César again, since, in one of its passages, there is a precise reference to time. The Seer writes:

> Car selon les signes celestes le regne de Saturne sera de retour, que le tout calculé, le monde s'aproche d'une anaragonique reuolution: & que de present que cecy i'escripz auant cent septante sept ans trois moys unze iours par pestilence, longue famine, & guerres, & plus par les inundations le monde entre cy & ce terme prefix, auant & apres par plusieurs foys, sera si diminué & si peu de monde sera, que l'on ne trouuera que vueille prendre les champs qui deuiendront liberes aussi longuement qu'ilz estés en seruitude . . .

Which translated means:

> *Because according to the celestial signs, the reign of Saturn will return, by all calculations, the world will come close to a great revolution: and with regard to what I am now writing, going back one hundred and seventy seven years, three months and eleven days, through pestilence, long famine, wars and even more through floods, within these predetermined limits, and before and after on several occasions, the world will be so diminished and there will be so little life, that no one will be found who will want to*

*take on the fields, which will remain unoccupied for as much
time as they have been possessed.*

Those, who have studied this passage, have deemed it correct
to interpret the phrase '*de present*' as referring to the moment
in which Nostradamus was writing, that is, '*and with respect
to the moment in which I am writing*' and the term '*avant*' as '*in
front of*', with the consequence that the current interpretation of
the passage has always remained as '*and with respect to the
moment in which I am writing [that is, 1555] and forwards
by 177 years, 3 months and 11 days . . .*', obtaining a date of
1732, a year in which absolutely nothing happened.

In fact, the term '*de present*' should refer to what the Seer
had just written: that is, upon the return of the reign of Saturn
and the end of a tremendous revolution. '*De present*' should be
interpreted as '*in this moment*', giving the phrase a completely
different meaning, and is '*with regard to what I am now writing*'. This is supported by the preposition '*avant*' which does
not only means of '*in front of*' but also *before*. Therefore, with
this sibylline phrase, the Seer wishes to say that, with regard
to the return of the reign of Saturn at the end of the great
tribulation, one must go *back* in time for 177 years, three
months and eleven days to arrive at a date, which is the starting
point for mankind's calamities.

We have already observed that the end of the prophecies –
the end of great tribulation and the return of the Reign of
Saturn will come to pass between 2024 and the first months
of 2025. If we go back from this time for 177 years, we can
see whether a definite event took place in that historical period.
It cannot be a phenomenon over a long period, but rather it
must refer to a single day, that is absolutely precise. Otherwise
the antedating of years and months and days would make no
sense.

Proceeding backwards in time from 2024–5 by 177 years
we come to period falling between 1847 and 1848. At this
point, there are no longer any doubts: 1848 represents an
epochal turning point for the world: all the political balances
of power were shaken, much more profoundly than during the

Napoleonic period. Before 1848, Europe had enjoyed a long period of tranquillity with the Congress of Vienna in 1814 and the Restoration of the Bourbons; this was followed by a period when wars followed one upon another in an insistent rhythm. After 1848 come revolutions which began in the individual states, then the war of independence in Italy, the war between France and Prussia, colonialism along with all its aberrations and atrocities, the First World War and so forth.

This is the key year for contemporary history, and this is the year which Nostradamus pointed out as the starting point of repeated, devastating events. If this is true, then the exact date in 1848 on which all this began must be found: we must identify the exact day, month and year. History tells us that the first warnings came' in Palermo on 9 January 1848, with the occupation of the city by revolutionaries, an event which led King Ferdinand II to proclaiming a constitution on 11 February.

But the first true and authentic revolution similar to the one which happened in 1789, took place in France. It is interesting to quote here what Jacques Godechot has to say in his *The Epoch of Revolutions* (UTET 1969, pp. 479 et seq.):

'The revolution would undoubtedly have continued its course with this rather slow rhythm had it not been overtaken by the revolution in Paris of 24 February, which basically had the very same deep causes – the misery of the poorer classes, worsened by the economic crisis of 1846 – and the same motivations – the claim for political reforms that were more radical than in Italy, because the French regime was more liberal. Only the pretext was different, in view of the fact that the French revolution was the consequence of a refusal on the part of First Minister Guizot in the face of a request formulated by the XII Legion of the National Guard to organise a banquet for the reforms, similar to the banquets of the kind which had been held throughout France for a year. This refusal was imprudent, since it brought the risk of a shift towards the opposition on the part of the National Guard who had been assigned to protect him.

'The officials of the XII Legion, supported by the entire opposition, decided to risk everything and organised a banquet for 22 February, following a demonstration in the streets of western Paris. On 21 February the government renewed its injunction; the banquet was postponed, but the demonstration which had been under preparation for several days, could not be revoked. In fact, it was held, despite the rain, to cries of 'Down with Guizot!' With the singing of The Marseillaise and the hymn of the Girondists, made popular in Alexandre Dumas' successful play, *The Knight of the Maison Rouge*, and in the work of Lamartine. The protesters were held at bay by front line troops, but it was noted that the National Guard was reacting without conviction, even to the point of crossing over quite often to the protesters' side. The following night some barricades were raised, and next morning the guards were sent an appeal from the government. The majority of the legions voice their favour for the reform and refused to obey; indeed, one of them clashed with a cavalry regiment; another, the IV, delivered a petition to the Palais Bourbon, seat of the House of Deputies, calling for the fall of the ministry, and the XII shouted "Long live the republic!" The situation appeared grave. The National Guard's defection on 23 February 1848 was reminiscent of the French guards of 11 July 1789, and even more so, of the National Guard's conduct in July 1830 [When Charles X was overthrown]. Guizot realised this and handed in his resignation in the early hours of the afternoon. The news aroused an explosion of joy throughout Paris, and in the evening the streets were overflowing with processions accompanied by shouts of "Down with Guizot!" One of these processions clashed with a cordon of guards in front of the foreign ministry on Boulevard des Capucines, right where Guizot lived.

'Someone fired a shot from a rifle, for reasons still unknown. But this marked the beginning of a general shoot-out which left fifty lying dead or wounded; 16 corpses were piled on to a wagon and pulled around the streets of Paris accompanied by the incitement to revolt. On the morning of the 24th the capital was covered with barricades. The king entrusted command of the troops to General Bugeaud, famous for his success in Algeria, and four columns were formed with the aim of liberating Paris, but only one reached its objectives, at which point it became clear that the city would not to be taken, unless through bloodshed. Consequently the general gave orders for a cease-fire and for the troops to retire to their barracks. This retreat only encouraged the protesters; the secret republican societies, who had entered into action after three days, saw the possibility of seizing power and issued new demands: immediate abdication by Louis Philippe, a general amnesty, parliamentary and electoral reforms, the right to work. In many districts the National Guard joined with the insurgents and marched on the Tuileries, the royal residence. Louis Philippe made an attempt to review the line of troops and the National Guard assigned to protect the palace, but he was met with shouts of ''Down with the system!'' ''Long live reform!'' ''Down with the ministers!'' and at the moment when he was about to return to the Tuileries discouraged, he heard rifles shots coming from where protesters had occupied the police station belonging to the Royal Palace.

'Thereupon he signed an abdication in favour of his nephew, the Count of Paris, and the royal family abandoned the Tuileries, which was immediately invaded and ransacked by the crowds.

'In the Chamber of Deputies, the Duchess of Orleans, the Count of Paris' mother, vainly attempted to have herself recognised as regent. The chamber was invaded by protesters, and Lamartine made them acknowledge a provisional government composed of republicans, that is, Dupont de l'Eure, Lamartine, Ledru Rollin, Arago, Garnier-Pagés, after which the cry of ''Let go to the Hotel de la Ville!'' was heard and the provisional government move on there. There it was requested that a certain number of men designated by the editors of the republican journal, *The Reform*, be included in the government; these were the socialist Louis Blanc, the workman Albert and some radicals such as Marie, Armand Marrast, and Flocon.

'The provisional government, at an impromptu meeting, set out the following proclamation: ''The provisional government demand a republic based on ratification by the people, who will be consulted immediately''. The government, in fact, decided to dissolve the Chamber of Deputies, prohibit meetings by the House of Peers and convoke a national assembly elected on the basis of universal suffrage. The days in Paris centring on the 23 February and the proclamation of a republic in France gave an extraordinary impulse to the revolutionary movement throughout the whole Europe.'

February 22–24, therefore, became a turning point in the history of Europe; it was epoch-making in that it caused that chain reaction which was to upset the political and social balance of Europe: from that moment onwards, wars and revolutions followed one upon another, bringing upheavals with them, which are still today being experienced and will go on being experienced in the foreseeable future.

So we can now, with certainty, start with this date and count forward 177 years, three months and eleven days to arrive at the exact date on which Nostradamus's prophecies will come to an end, and that date is 1–3 June 2025.

The revolution in France broke out on 22 February and ended on 24 February, so the question now is deciding on the exact day to which the Seer referred. In order to do this, we must look at another passage in the letter to Henry where the Seer writes:

(X) However, hoping to leave in writing the years, towns, cities and regions where most [of the events] will happen, even in the year 1585 and in the year 1606, beginning from the present time, which is 14 March 1557, (XI) and going well beyond, as far as the accession which will come after the beginning of millennium 7, calculated learnedly . . .

More than one author commenting this passage, has wondered why the Seer referred to the years 1585 and 1606, which are not particularly significant historically, as well as why the date of 14 March 1557 was mentioned, when the letter was actually written on 27 June 1558. The reason is probable because

Nostradamus actually wrote this part of the letter in 1557, but the mystery remains as to why he deliberately mentioned the exact day.

The key to solving this puzzle once again lies in the double meaning of the language used. The passage in its original is as follows:

> Toutesfois esperant de laisser par escrit les ans, villes, citez, regions, ou la pluspart aduiendra, mesme de l'annee 1585 et de l'annee 1606, accomençant depuis le temps present, qui est le 14 de Mars 1557, et passant outre bien loing jusques à l'aduenement qui sera apres au commencement du 7 millenaire profondement supputé . . .'.

What the Seer actually meant to say was:

> *I will leave in writing the events which will happen from today onwards, which is 14 March 1557, up until what will immediately follow the beginning of millennium 7 [and such a time] can be accurately calculated in the same way [mesme] starting from the 14 March 1585 and [lastly] from 1606.*

We have seen that the end of the seventh millennium will coincide with the beginning of the Olympic Games in Athens. The I.O.C. has fixed the inauguration of Athens Olympics for 13 August 2004, which means that the eighth millennium (millennium 7) will begin precisely on 14 August 2004, which will be a leap year. From 14 March 1585 to 14 August 2004 there is a time span of 419 years and 153 days. At this point we must take the year 1606 into consideration and to this year the 419 years and 153 days must be added. Thus we arrive at the date of 2 June 2025, bearing in mind the fact that 2025 will not be a leap year. Thus the date of the end of the prophecies, which was deducted by following a completely different method, is, incredibly confirmed.

To support what I am saying, we should note that it was actually Nostradamus himself who suggested such a method in his letter to César, where he writes 'le monde entre cy & ce terme prefix, auant & apres par plusieurs foys . . .' which means *the world within these two limits, predetermined [by going] forwards and backwards more times than once . . .'* which is exactly the method that has been used, first by going forwards, in order to fix the approximate period of the end of the prophecies, then by going backwards by 177 years, in order to determine the year these human calamities began, and finally, having once found the historical event referred to, going forward by 177 years, three months and eleven days, in order to identify the exact date of the end of the prophecies. We have therefore achieved an accurate result, which is extremely important in understanding the work of Nostradamus, by making it possible to define its chronological order.

So, the conclusion that we have reached logically through using data from the two letters and from two basic quatrains is that the seven millennia begin 4996 BC and will end in AD 2004.

We have also determined that the end of the prophecies will occur twenty years later, between 2024 and the first months of 2025, since the Seer mentions only the years that will pass and not the number of months.

Using this period as a basis and the passages from his letters to his son César and to Henry, the exact date for the end of the prophecies and for the return of the reign of Saturn have been fixed as 2 June 2025: after this date, the Seer will make no further reference to any event, limiting himself to describing, in some quatrains, the future spiritual world.

The date fixed as a starting point for the seven millennia, moreover, agrees with the chronological definition proposed in the first part, where a starting point period of between 4946 and 5444 BC was mooted, a period which included 4996 BC, identified through an examination of the references to the Bible in the two letters. In Part Two, the letter to Henry will be examined first, a letter which, we shall see, conceals a surprising secret. This will be followed by the events which are prophesied in the quatrains and the sestets, in the chronological order defined here, as well as that defined movements of the stars, through which data that includes now and up to 2025 can be obtained, using other given data and through deciphering another significant quatrain, and lastly through the many points in Nostradamus's letter to Henry, now that the original and actual meaning of the text has been restored.

PART TWO

THE LETTER TO HENRY OF FRANCE

This letter to 'Henry the Second' of France forms a preface to the last three *Centuries* (VIII, IX and X) when they were first published. After a general preamble on the prophetic spirit, and his own chronology with its biblical references, he turns to future events, giving a host of details, but he does so in a totally confused manner. Reading the letter, a clear impression emerges: the Seer is intent on treating events in a way that is not chronologically ordered, describing, for example, what happened a century ago, immediately followed by what is still to happen, only to return to the past, then once more to the future.

All the interpreters, who have studied this letter, have, with obvious logical distortions, attempted to force a meaning upon this text which, judging by the way it is written, it cannot have. The letter to Henry was published with the last three *Centuries* in 1568, and in subsequent editions it was included with the complete works. Reprints of the *Centuries* have been numerous; not always correct, and often misapplied.

In any case, in the editions subsequent to the first, and certainly to the edition printed in 1605, both letters include Roman numbers that serve to divide them into paragraphs in a way that is not always logical and homogeneous.

The letter to Henry is given in its original French text in the Appendix III.

5. The first part of the letter (in translation): paras I–XXXVI

I have divided this letter into two parts: the first includes paragraphs I–XXXVI, which constitute the introduction. In this part the Seer, in a well coordinated and uniform text, expounds the reasons why he was led into dedicating the final part of his *Centuries* to Henry. The letter appears to be dedicated to the king of France, who was indeed Henry the Second, but from the context of the prophetic part it is clear that in fact the Henry to whom the letter refers is not this particular king of France but rather someone in the future, who still must make his appearance and who will be a decisive factor in the salvation of mankind. As others have already observed, the adjective '*second*' should not just be taken as an ordinal number, but its Latin meaning should be considered too. In Latin '*secundus*' means not only '*second*' but also '*propitious*'. Even here, therefore, the Seer, makes a play on words, fulfilling a double purpose perfectly: ingratiating himself with the sovereign of the moment, and in no way betraying the honest principles which inspire his work.

Nostradamus's visionary powers becomes obvious within the context of the letter: he recognises the future king as though he were a contemporary of his, travelling through time, which for him is the only constituent of eternity.

Separating the letter into two is necessary because the more strictly prophetic part, which depicts the future of humanity up until the 2 June 2025, does not have the same clarity as the other: in this second part the Seer resorts to a stratagem which renders the text totally incomprehensible, incoherent, not to say contradictory, and until now has evaded detection.

*To the invincible, the all powerful and most Christian Henry,
the Second King of France,*
*Michel Nostradamus, most humble and very obedient ser-
vant and subject, Victory and felicity*

*(I) Ever since that sovereign vision I had, O most Chris-
tian and victorious King, when I appeared before your
divine infinite Majesty, my face has long remained absent,
for since then I have been perpetually dazzled, never failing
justly to honour and venerate that day when I was presented
to you for the first time, as to an exceptional and most
human Majesty. (II) Now I am seeking an occasion through
which to reveal my good heart, and honest courage, so that
through this power of mine I may adequately bring them to
the awareness of your most serene Majesty. (III) Seeing that
declaring this through performances has not been possible
for me, coupled with a singular wish that from a long period
of darkness and obscurity, I could suddenly be flooded with
light and transported before the eyes of the sovereign and
the first Monarch of the Universe, (IV) though having been
for long in doubt as to whom to dedicate these three remaining Centuries of the prophecies, which conclude the thousand (V) and after having thought for long, I was seized by
a rash audacity, I decided to dedicate them to your Majesty,
undaunted by this, unlike those who, as the great author
Plutarch relates in his 'Life of Lycurgus', seeing the offering
and gifts that were used for sacrifice in the temples of the
immortal Gods of those times, and fearing that theirs were
not adequate enough as per expenditure and value, did not
dare present themselves at the temples.*

*(VI) This notwithstanding, on seeing Your Royal Splen-
dour coupled with your incomparable humanity, I took my
decision, not as was customary in regard to the kings of
Persia, in whose presence no one was permitted to venture,
or even to make an approach. (VII) But to a very prudent
and very wise Prince I have dedicated my nocturnal and
prophetic cogitations, composed primarily with natural
instinct, accompanied more by poetic impetuosity than by
poetic rigour, (VIII) and the most part composed with the*

*help of calculations from astronomy corresponding to the
years, months and weeks of the regions, areas and most of
the towns and cities throughout Europe, including Africa
and a part of Asia, owing to the change in regions that are
for the most part close to these climes, and made up of
identical characteristics: (IX) some may respond with a
sniff, the rhythm being as easy as grasping the sense is
difficult, and for this, O most humane King, most of the
prophetic quatrains are so ticklish, that there seems to be
no discovering the way or the means to interpret them, (X)
nonetheless, with the hope of leaving in writing the years,
towns, cities and regions where most events will happen,
even in the year 1585, and in the year 1606, beginning from
the present time, which is 14 March 1557 (XI) and going
well beyond, as far as the accession which will come after
the beginning of millennium 7, and calculated learnedly
(XII) as far as my astronomical calculation and my research
have been able to stretch, where the adversaries of Jesus
Christ and of his Church will begin multiply with greater
strength, (XIII) everything has been composed and calculated in chosen days and hours and as well and, as well
and properly and fairly dealt with was within my power.
(XIV) And the whole – invita Minerva – given freely and
not without inspiration, calculating almost as many deeds
in future time as there were in ages past, including the
present and what in the course of time concerning every
region will be recognised as happening, exactly as is written
without anything superfluous, as they say: 'As far as future
things are concerned, there is no definite truth'. (XV) It is
quite true, Sire, that by my natural instinct which was given
to me by my forebears, I have no fear foreseeing by using
and attuning this natural instinct with my long calculations
and freeing my soul, spirit and courage from every worry,
every care and annoyance with rest and tranquillity of the
spirit. (XVI) Everything harmonised and presaged on the
brazen tripod. (XVII) However many there are who attribute
as much to me of what I deserve as what I do not merit,
only eternal God, who is the judge, and who is pious, just*

and merciful towards the destiny of mankind, is the true judge, whom I ask to defend me against the calumny of the wicked (XVIII) who would also, slanderously, wish to examine into the reason why all your ancient forebears, Kings of France, were cured of the scrofula and were healed of the bites of serpents of other nations: and still others have had a certain instinct for the art of divination, and other things, which would be too lengthy to relate. (XIX) Notwithstanding, there are people who will carry on the wickedness of the malignant spirit for the course of time after my earthly extinction, when my writings will have more value than my present life. (XX) In any case, if I have erred in my calculation of the ages, that will not due to anyone else's wishes. (XXI) If it pleases your more than imperial Majesty to forgive me, if I protest before God and his Saints that I make no claim to put in writing in this present letter anything that is contrary to the true Catholic faith, by refer- ring to the calculations of Astronomy as far as I know. (XXII) Because the space of time from our first ancestors, who preceded us is such – if I may subject myself to the most correct judgement – that the first man, Adam, came about 1,242 years before Noah, (XXIII) not counting the time according to the Gentiles' calculations as Terence wrote, but only according to the sacred scriptures and the instinct of my spirit, employed in my calculations through Astronomy. (XXIV) About 1080 years after Noah and the great Flood came Abraham, who, according to some, was a very great Astrologer, who first invented the Chaldean letters. (XXV) Then came Moses, about 515 or 516 years [later]. (XXVI) and between the time of Moses and David about 570 years passed. (XXVII) Then, between the time of David and the time of our Saviour and Redeemer, Jesus Christ, born of One and Only Virgin, there were (according to the chronologists) 1350 years: (XXVIII) some may object that this calculation is not true, seeing that it diverges from that of Eusebius. (XXIX) And from the time of human redemption until the detestable heresy of the Saracens there were about 621 years. (XXX) From then until now the amount of time that has passed can easily be calculated, if my calculation is not good and valid for all nations, (XXXI) for the fact that all is calculated on the basis of the courses of the Heavens, along with inspiration that came to me in some hours of repose through the influence of my ancient progenitors. (XXXII) But the abuse of time, O most serene King, demands that the secret occurrences be not revealed except in enigmatic phrases, which, however, have but one unique meaning and can be understood in one unique way, without my having added anything that is ambiguous or of doubtful calculation, (XXXIII) but, rather, under the veiled obscurity of natural inspiration which comes close to the phrase of one of the 1,002 Prophets who have existed since the creation of the world, as from calculation, and from the Punic chronicles of Joel 'I will pour out my spirit upon all flesh; and your sons and your daughters shall prophesy.' (XXIV) But such a prophecy came from the mouth of the Holy Spirit, which is the sovereign and eternal power, united with the Heavenly One, to some of that number who have predicted great and marvellous occurrences. (XXXV) I, in that framework, in no way attribute such a title to myself. It would not please God, and I confess that all comes from God, and to him I render thanks, honour and immortal praise, without having mixed in the divination which comes from fate: but to God, to nature and the greater part accompanied by the movement of the course through the Heavens, (XXXVI) like seeing as though it were into a flaming mirror, as with veiled sight, the great, sad, prodigious, calamitous events approaching via the chief worshippers.

6. The prophetic part of the letter to Henry

With paragraph XXXVII the more truly prophetic part of the letter to Henry begins and continues to paragraph LXXXVII, and again from CVI to CXXIII, with a biblical and astrological interlude between.

One gets a strong impression when reading these passages that many of the events narrated in them have already taken place, as for example, where military regimes of the kind that were to become established in Italy, Germany and Japan are spoken of. But read what follows after these passages and this impression instantly vanishes, since what follows does not concur with these passages. The result, therefore, is an incredible muddle, in which numerous interpreters have made a strenuous effort to establish some logical coherence, and in so doing have ended up obviously forcing the text.

To the difficulty of comprehension are added further difficulties which stem from the use of the alchemist's *green language*. There are numerous anagrams, crases, and words having meanings that are totally different from what they appear to mean.

Take, for example paragraph CXI, which runs: '*the arches built with ancient iron will accompany each other to the waves of Neptune,*' a phrase which is immediately followed by the incoherent '*in the Adriatic there will be great discord and what was united shall be separated . . .*'

Two further paragraphs – LX and LXI – appear to contain similar incoherent and obscure non-sequiturs: '*(LX) and the two swords shall be taken from them, and only their insignia shall remain to them, (LXI) of which, by way of the curvature that attracts them, the people making it go straight, without wishing to comply to them through the opposite end of the acute hand, touching ground, etc.'*

When attempting the impossible translation and interpretation of paragraph LXI, the parenthetical *'touching ground'* brought to mind the image of a ship when it is docking. Beside this image was the word *'peuple'*: word which in modern French as well as in middle French can mean not only *people* but also *poplar*, a tree which grows straight and which, because of its form, brings to mind the main mast of a ship. Perhaps then the Seer in using the word *peuple* actually intended to mean the mast of a ship and made use of a metonym: a figure of speech in which a part describes the whole, in this case the ship itself. In this light, the phrase, though being still obscure, begins to assume a precise meaning and also the 'par le bout opposite de la main ague' which follows could well be included in this context, when translated as *'at the opposite extremity of the acute side'*, that is, of the prow. I then remembered and rushed to paragraph CXI *'the arches built of ancient iron will accompany each other to the waves of Neptune,'* a meaning for which I had vainly sought. Then designs of the first propellers came to mind, propellers seen long ago in who knows what illustration, which were formed of two iron arches joined together at their opposite ends in such a way as to form a kind of *'S'*. Then I attempted to connect the two passages, and surprisingly, not only did they complete each other reciprocally and logically, but also the syntax and punctuation harmonised. Joined together, the two passages described the invention of the propeller and of future motor propulsion of ships: *'the arches built of ancient iron will accompany each other to the waves of Neptune, which, attracted by their vortex, will make the ship go straight, without creating obstacles for the opposite part of the prow, by making it touch the ground . . .'* And so the first, fundamental secret that the letter concealed in its prophetic part was discovered: this was a gigantic literary puzzle, in which the individual phrases, after having been first written logically and chronologically, had been reshuffled, so making everything inexplicable and incoherent.

This theory finds further confirmation in paragraph LXXXVII, where the Seer confesses: '*And it is for this, Sire, that in these discourses I put down my predictions in a rather confused way*', so warning the interpreter of his voluntary manipulation.

The procedure was then to extrapolate each single paragraph from the context into which it had been inserted, in order to assign it to its proper antecedent and sequel. I noted then that in the editions subsequent to the first, the mysterious hand which had subdivided the letter into paragraphs, inserting the Roman numbers, had maintained the original punctuation of the original letter, prior to its manipulation, in such a way that, after a comma, for example, a word might begin with a capital letter, so indicating in this way that such a word came at the beginning of a new sentence.

Presupposing, then, that the Seer, when he has written openly of events in the original, non-manipulated letter, had observed a chronological order, I embarked on this long, patient work of *collage,* paying special attention to punctuation marks as well as historical notions, which made it possible to sort out passages belonging to the same, identical period. Everything began, as if by magic, to emerge with limpid clarity, except for the rather lengthy paragraph CXIII, which appeared intrinsically incoherent. My theory then gathered momentum: the Seer had reserved for this paragraph all those parts which in his complicated puzzle, which placed elsewhere would have run the risk of making it possible to discover the secrets that the text was determined to conceal.

So I then separated paragraph CXIII into six parts (marked here with the letters (a) to (f) which were then placed logically into the reconstructed text so that the meaning became coherent.

At this point, my work had merely reached its half-way mark, since the letter contained numerous anagrams, verbal tricks, double-entendres and other devices: the deciphering of all this required a considerable amount of time and energy, in view of the fact that some anagrams were extremely lengthy and also that some of the verbal tricks were extremely complex; in the end, however, the result obtained proved surprising as regards coherence, chronological precision and description of events.

As I have mentioned, the reordered paragraphs are those from XXXVII to LXXXVII and CVI to CXXIII, into which CIV and CV are to be then inserted. These contain astrological references which, we shall see, confirm the chronological theory I made in the preceding chapter and the succession of events as they are given in this present part: the reader is left to make his own judgement, naturally, though when it comes to reading the text, the Seer's extraordinary capacity for describing the future cannot but be emphasised:

CXIII (f) In the letter a few years ago which I dedicated to my son César, I had exposed some points openly and without any obfuscation. But here, Sire, are included many great and marvellous events which our descendants will see.

LXXXVII and it is for this, Sire, that in these discourses I put down my predictions in such a confused way,

Thus begins the prophetic part of the letter based on a logical reconstruction. With this phrase the Seer explains the reasons which led him not to express his prophecies in a clear fashion: the details it contains are too numerous compared with the letter to César: consequently, had he written all of it openly and without obfuscation, what he did not want to happen would have happened, and that is that man, coming to know his future, would have begun to behave in a way out of keeping with what God had established for him, by attempting to modify what destiny held in store for him.

LXXXVIII and when these shall happen and when they (that is it) shall be accomplished through the passage of time they shall conform little or not at all with what is above,

LXXXIX and all as much by the way of Astronomy as by others, also by way of the sacred scriptures, which can never err, so that if I had desired to attribute to each quatrain its own time, I would have been able to do so:

XC but this would not please everyone, least of all those interpreting them, until when, Sire, Your Majesty has granted me ample power to do this, so as not to furnish my calumniators with good reasons to attack me.

XCI However, counting the years from the creation of the world to the birth of Noah, one thousand five hundred and six years have passed.

XCII And from the birth of Noah until the building of the Ark was completed, just before the great Flood, six hundred years passed (whether the years were solar, lunar or a mixture of these is not known), I maintain that the sacred scriptures consider them as solar.

XCIII And at the end of these six years, Noah went into the Ark in order to be saved from the flood.

XCIV And on there was a great Flood which spread all over the earth, and which lasted one year and two months.

XCV And from the end of the Flood until the birth of Abraham two hundred and ninety-five years passed.

XCVI And from the birth of Abraham to the birth of Isaac a hundred years passed.

XCVII And from Isaac to Jacob 60 years from the moment he entered into Egypt until his death 130 years passed.

CVIII And from the entrance of Jacob into Egypt until his death four hundred and thirty years passed.

XCIX And from the Exodus from Egypt until the building of Solomon's Temple in the fourth year of his reign, four hundred and eighty or four time twenty years passed.

C And from the building of the Temple until Jesus Christ, according to the calculation in the sacred writing, four hundred and ninety years passed.

CI And therefore, on the basis of the calculation that I have made in accordance with the sacred scriptures, there are about four thousand one hundred and seventy three years and eight months, more or less.

CII Now, from Jesus Christ to now, for the diversity of opinions I leave off,

CIII And having worked up and calculated the present prophecies entirely according to the chain which contains its revolution, and entirely through the teaching of Astronomy and according to my natural instinct.

XXXVII First of all in the temples of God, then in the earthly ones, such a decadence will come, with a thousand other calamitous happenings, which in the course of the Centuries will be recognised as having happened:

The Seer gives a short summary of his proposal of what will progressively come to pass in the course of the Centuries until the seventh millennium, paying much attention to the vicissitudes of the Catholic church and to religions in general, for at the end of the seventh millennium what will be unleashed will have apocalyptic dimensions and will be the crucial point in the history of humanity.

CVI (To begin at the end), putting the tail in the place of the head, on the basis of a conjunction of Jupiter with Mercury, with a quadrature of Mars and Mercury, while the Dragon's head will be with a conjunction of the Sun and Jupiter, the year shall be pacific and without eclipse, but not altogether and will be the beginning which will allow for an understanding of what then will come.

Interpretation of this passage proved to be quite hard-going. In fact, the preceding passage (CV) gave the impression of fitting in with it perfectly, in that it ended with the '*teste du dragon en Libra*' and the subsequent passage, after a colon, continued with '*La queuë à son signe opposite*', which led to the thought that while the dragon's head was in Libra, the tail was in its opposite sign, that is Aries. But what followed in no way supported such an interpretation, since the Seer, when he was describing the astral situation of that period, stated that the tail was near a conjunction of Jupiter and Mercury, at that moment in Aries (that is, the sign opposite Libra), in order then to specify that dragon's head would have been near a conjunction of the Sun and Jupiter: the result would, therefore, be that Jupiter would have to be simultaneously joined with Mercury and the Sun in two different signs! The problem appeared to be insoluble, until the thought came that it had to do with a play on words. Nostradamus was using figurative language, just as when somebody says that an argument is inconclusive, they say it's *'without head or tail'*. So it was thus possible to guess that the Seer meant to say with the words, *'La queuë à son signe opposite'* *'the tail being put in the place of the head'*, that is, *'beginning from the end'*.

At that point, what I still had to identify was the year in which the Sun, Mercury and Jupiter would be in conjunction with the Dragon's head (Moon's north node) and Mars in quadrature with Mercury, with the added specification that in the year there was not to be a total eclipse of the Sun. Furthermore, the year in question had to *'at the tail'* of the prophecies, and was to be characterised by almost total peace in the world (*'not altogether pacific'*). The year which satisfies all these conditions is the year 1994. The year 1994 in fact, did not have a total eclipse: in November the Sun, Mercury, Jupiter and the Moon's node were all found together in the sign of Scorpio, while Mars was in Leo with an angulation of 90° (that is in quadrature) with respect to Mercury between the 24th and the 25th of that month.

In that year the virulence of the war in Bosnia, which had begun in May 1992, had already reached its peak. By the beginning of 1993 that war had already caused untold destruction and human suffering and the Vance-Owen and Owen-Stoltenberg peace plans had failed, a fact which had brought about the firm intervention of President Clinton and the United

States. In contrast to the conduct of the European States – based on equidistance between the parties in conflict – the USA, in 1994, assumed a clear position in favour of Croatia against Serbia, judged as an aggressor state. A spiralling conflict was ignited, and for the first time NATO aeroplanes attacked the Serbian-Bosnian lines. Serbia, furthermore, was isolated on the international level by economic sanctions. For the first time since the end of the Second World War, some Western countries were involved in war activities in Europe. Subsequently, the war broke out in Kossovo and NATO, in 1999, as it had done in Bosnia, decided on bombarding Belgrade and other cities in the Yugoslav Federation.

But 1994 registered another important event, that is the birth of an autonomous Palestinian State with Yasser Arafat as its leader. Arafat, who, long years of exile, was finally able to return to his homeland (1 July 1994). On 25 November, coinciding exactly with the astrological combination mentioned by Nostradamus, all the Palestinian military and political officials were gathered at Gaza, where they signed a treaty of non-aggression, thus establishing the basis for the birth of the Palestinian State. The creation of this new territorial entity appeared to presuppose a lasting peace between the Israelis and the Palestinians. The years that followed, however, have been turbulent ones, marked with terrorist attacks, outbreaks of hostility, a state of continuous tension, culminating most recently in the new 'Intifada' and in an open military conflict between Israel and Palestine.

According to the Seer, therefore, it is in 1994 that the causes which in the space of a few years are to lead the world to a Third World War are to be sought. There is no doubt that the isolation of Serbia and the subsequent bombardments have overthrown international laws, which until then had been observed and respected and allowed Western powers, and more importantly NATO, the right to intervene with the use of arms in the internal politics of a given country, when such a country violates fundamental human rights. Not all countries agree with this principle, and even the United Nations Organisation has found itself embarrassed in certain situations. Russia as well as China sternly contested armed intervention, and splits rapidly appeared in diplomatic relations between these countries and those of the Atlantic Alliance. Today Russia is forced to submit to this initiative, in view of its disastrous economic situation and its consequent need to obtain financial help from the West, but were Russia to find an alternative financial source enabling her to recover from her needy condition, she could once again make her military might felt, to such an extent as to be able to occupy the whole of Europe, and in very little time. Her awareness of the progressive loss of her role as superpower, on whose assent every international initiative once depended, a role which has seen itself replaced by Russia being relegated to a rearguard position, which does not even qualify for advanced notification of programmed initiatives, will play a determining role in the world's future. Bear in mind too that President Putin seems to be behaving ambiguously towards the West: on the one hand, he professes pacifism, giving an impression of wishing to continue the policy of détente initiated by Yeltsin, while on the other hand, in his domestic speeches to Russia, he appears to be firmly committed to regaining for his country that role of superpower which once belonged to the Soviet Union, devoting a lot of attention to the conditions of the armed forces and carrying out a bloody war of repression in Chechnya.

If therefore, the Balkan conflict in its various phases has brought about a substantial change in the rules governing international military intervention within a state for declared humanitarian reasons, the Middle-Eastern question, with all its political, economic and religious implications, has created a situation of permanent conflict due to the simple impossibility of resolving the problems arising from irreconcilable claims by both parts and to the perennial presence of tension and violence in the daily life of these territories.

CXIII (e) And it will be near (the end of) the seventh millennium that the sanctuary of Jesus Christ will be increasingly oppressed by the infidels who will come from the aculeus [the thorn], and the world will come near to a great confla-

gration, since, by the calculations contained in my proph-
ecies, the course of time goes very much further.

So in this statement Nostradamus is giving us a graphic picture
of what the basic passage in the history of humanity will be,
from the world as it is now to a future world of tolerance and
great spirituality.

The passage will certainly not be painless, but one which
will be preceded by a tremendous religious war, sparked off,
prominently, by infidels who will come from *'l'Aquillon'*. The
place of origin of these infidels has been interpreted as referring
to the geographic north, from where the *aquilon* (north wind)
blows. But in fact, Nostradamus did not write *'Aquilon'* but
'Aquillon', corresponding to the modern *'Aiguillon'*, which
means a sting or spur or *'Aiguille'* meaning *point*, *needle*, and
aculeus. My interpretation of this term is not that of certain
people coming from the north, but rather the territory where
such a people has its origins. And since it is certain, as the
quatrains and sestets will show, that the Third World War will
be set off by the Antichrist established in the Islamic countries,
the *'Aquillon'*, as a symbol, should be linked to the Middle
Eastern states.

The first thing to look at might be the national flag, bearing
in mind that it is the flag, more than any other symbol, that
represents a nation. The only national flag among the Arab
countries which has a pointed symbol at its centre, is Iran's.

It is worthwhile here to quote what Harold Mueller has to
say of Iran on the internet *(http://www.crwflags.com/fotw/flags/
ir.html)*:

The symbol consists of four crescents and a sword. The four
crescents are meant to stand for the word Allah (there is
indeed some resemblance to the Arabic writing of it). The
five parts of the emblem symbolise the five principles of
Islam. Above the sword (central part) is a 'tashdid' (looks
a bit like a W). In Arabic writing this is used to double a
letter, here it doubles the strength of the sword.

The flag of Iran, then, shows five sharp points, four of which are curved and which flank the sword, two on either side, with the sword in the middle. It could therefore be Iran, the most fundamentalist of the Islamic countries of the world, to which the Seer could be making reference with the use of the word '*Aquillon*'.

However, *Aquillon* could more simply refer to the particular characteristic of Islamic architecture where the most important buildings, particularly the religious ones, end with a cusp at the top of a hemispherical covering. This type of architecture is also characteristic of quite a number of Russian buildings and basilicas – the Kremlin for example, which might also lead us to conclude that with the term *Aquillon* the Seer intended those peoples and nations who in the future, according to his visions, would bring war and ruin to the West.

This interpretation is confirmed by the fact that when the Seer means Westerners and their origins, he writes '*Aquilon*' correctly, meaning the north. This distinction clearly emerges from in paragraph passage LXXXVI, where Nostradamus writes: 'Et seront lors des Seigneurs deux en nombre d'Aquilon, victorieux sur les Orientaux ... Orient tremblera de la frayeur d'iceux freres, non freres Aquilonaires', which can be translated as *'and there will then be two victorious Lords over the Easterners from Aquilon ... The East will tremble from fear of these brothers, who are not aquilonaire brothers'*. The final emphatic phrase is intended to warn the interpreter not to confuse between '*Aquillon*', from which the Seer has invented the adjective '*aquilonaire*' (with one '*l*' only) and '*Aquilon*', this showing the radically different meanings of the two terms employed.

> *CXIII (a) And at that time and in those countries, the infernal power will confront the Church of Jesus Christ with the force of the adversaries of his law and it will be the second Antichrist who will persecute that Church and its true Vicar by way of the power of its temporal Kings* [the oil Kings], *who, for their ignorance, will be seduced by tongues that will cut better than a sword in the hands of the madman.*

The above mentioned reign of the Antichrist will last only till the end of him, who was born near the age [the millennium] *and of the other who had been accompanied to the city of Plancus* [Lyons] *accompanied by the elect of Modone Fulcy by Ferrara, maintained by Ligurians Adriatics, and by the closeness of the great Trinacria* [by Hadrie, destined to be elected by the demon Lucifer and who was sustained by Iran and Iraq and enjoyed the protection of the great triangle (the Islamic-Russian-Chinese Alliance].

The passage is in need of a few comments, since Nostradamus in this part of the letter makes use of some anagrams and other cryptic systems that belong to the *'green language'*.

The Seer uses the expression *'Roy Temporel'*, which can be translated as *'temporal Kings'*, but is also an anagram for *'Roy en petrol'*, that is, *oil king*.

As will be seen later on the quatrains and the sestets, which concern our future, it is oil that will be the winning card in the first phase of the war, oil whose scarcity will have the effect of rendering useless to the West's war machines, which will be impossible to operate for lack of fuel.

The Antichrist, according to Nostradamus, was born near of the end of the century, and therefore the Seer uses the expression *'born near the age'* (of the millennium).

The second personality of whom the Seer speaks will be his ally or his right-hand man. The word *'demon'* is an anagram of *'Modone'*. The name Lucifer is of *'Fulcy'* combined with *'Ferrare'* (a city in Italy). The French text reads *'Fulcy par Ferrare'*, that is, *Fulcy* combined with *Ferrare*, and therefore *'Lucifer'*. The remaining part (*'par+frare'*), when seen as an anagram, yields the French word *'paraf(e)re'*, which means *initialled, marked*.

At this point, some explanations are necessary to understand how I have arrived at 'Hadrie'. In the French text the Seer uses the double adjective *'Liguriens Adriaticques'*, terms which literally would mean *'Adriatics Ligurians'*, contradictory terms, since a population is either Ligurian or Adriatic, the two seas being separated by the Italian peninsula. But note:

the two adjectives are written with capital letters, which, in the *'green language'* may signify that the face-value name in reality conceals a different one. Thirdly, the name *'Adriaticques'*, as it is written in the original text, contains an obvious double error: first of all, at the time in which Nostradamus lived, the word *'Adriatic'* was written as *'Hadriatique'*, that is with an initial *'h'* (see quatrains II, 86; III, 21; III, 23), secondly, the word was written without the letter *'c'* in front of the *'q'* (many editions of the *Centuries*, spell the name without the *'c'*, since it was considered to be an error).

In fact, in the course of my extensive study of the work of Nostradamus, I came to understand one fundamental element: no error is ever casual, and everything is the fruit result of a deliberately *enigmatic* design, one which is complex throughout and extremely clever. Therefore, if the error was intentional, there must be a different interpretation for the two adjectives.

Then I realised that the Seer, only a few lines before in paragraph CX, had written: 'Et en iceluy temps grandes voyles Bisantines associees aux Ligustiques par l'appuy & puissance Aquilonaire . . .', which on the surface means: *'And at that time, great Byzantine sails associated with the Ligustiques with Aquilonaire backing and power'*. The term *'Ligustiques'* meant absolutely nothing. And at first I presumed that it was simply a synthesis of *'Liguriens Hadriatiques'*, used in two quatrains (II, 85 and IV, 68). But if this were the case for the verses it might have been used to retain the verse's hendecasyllabic line; in the prose no such exigency exists. I then considered the participle *'associees'* which preceded the mysterious adjective, an adjective which, clearly stemmed from *'Liguriens Hadriatiques'*, and I realised that in that passage the Seer had applied a very subtle and imperceptible play on words and that the phrase was to be reconstructed as: 'Voy les grandes anti nés, bis associees aux Ligustiques,' that is, *'Look at the originals (adjectives) (anti nés: born before) written with capital (grandes) letters, (which can be) associated twice (bis) with the Ligustiques'*: therefore, *'Liguriens Hadriatiques'* are, the original adjectives written with capital letters, and from their synthesis the other is derived, '*were associated*' with '*Ligus-tiques*'.

If one subtracts from *Les grandes Liguriens Hadriatiques* those letters which make up *Ligustiques*, the remaining letters form '*Les grandes rien hadria*'.

Hadria brought back to mind the *Centuries I, quatrain 8*:

> Combien de fois prinse cité solaire,
> Seras changeant les loix barbares et vaines:
> Ton mal s'approche. Plus seras tributaire,
> La grand Hadrie recouirira tes veines.

> *How many times taken, solar city,*
> *You will change the vain and barbarous laws:*
> *Your evil is near. More will you have to give,*
> *The grand Hadrie will cut your veins.*

This quatrain – which will be examined later on – prophesies the devastation of Rome *(the solar city)* by a mysterious personage named '*Hadrie*'.

The fact that the Seer qualifies him as '*grand*', led to a theory that it treated precisely of the Antichrist and that the name obtained through the subtraction of letters could signify the same person of the quatrain. I then made an anagram of *Les grandes rien Hadria*, and in so doing, obtained *Le grand assyr(i)en Hadrie*, that is the great Assyrian Hadrie. At this point the enigma seemed to be resolved: by subtracting the letters of the second of the adjectives from the first, the name and the origin of the Antichrist were discovered.

Hadrie, however, did not appear to be the true name of the personality but rather a key through which the mystery of the name could be unravelled. At this point I took into consideration the fact that the Seer was suggesting that the process should be repeated (*bis* = twice), so I added *bis* to '*le grand assyren Hadrie*' and made another anagram of the whole for a second time, believing that the second anagram could have been a historical revision of the first. What I obtained appeared to be disconcerting and therefore amounted to a mere theory:

'*Id es(t): le grand Syrien Bashar*' (that is: the great Syrian Bashar) or also: '*I.e.: le grand Syrien B.H.R. Assad*' (that is: the great Syrian B.H.R. Assad'). In both of these hypothesis, then, the possible solution to the enigma of the *Byzantine sails* points to the youthful present-day Syrian president Bashar Al Assad, who until now has proved to be a very balanced leader, not to mention his unquestionable diplomatic talents, which give positive hope for the future of the Middle East. In singling out this possible name, almost simultaneously there came to mind a passage of the Apocalypse (13:16–18) where John wrote:

> And he causeth all, both small and great, rich and poor, free and bond, to receive a mark in their right hand, or in their foreheads:
> And that no man might buy or sell, save he that had the mark, or the name of the beast, or the number of his name.
> Here is wisdom. Let him that hath understanding count the number of the beast: for it is the number of a man; and his number is Six hundred threescore and six.

Over the course of the centuries many have made the attempt to identify the name and the owner of the name that were hidden behind that number, and at various times the name was held to belong to this or that personality.

Not so long after John's death the key had already been lost that would have led to an understanding of that number which went back to a particular science of Hebrew origin: *Ghematria,* based on the attribution of a numeric value to each letter of the alphabet so that a certain name was translated into numbers, which were then added together, to make a final number.

The numeric scheme of *Ghematria* is as follows:

A (Aleph): 1
B (Beht): 2
G (Gimel): 3
D (Dalet): 4
H (Hei): 5

V (Vav): 6
Z (Zayin): 7
C/CH (Chet): 8
T (Tet): 9
Y (Yud): 10
K (Chaf): 20
L (Lamed): 30
M (Mem): 40
N (Nun): 50
S (Samech): 60
E (Ayin): 70
P (Pei): 80
TS (Tzadik): 90
Q (Kuf): 100
R (Reish): 200
S (Sheen): 300
TH (Tav): 400
Final K: 500
Final M: 600
Final N: 700
Final P: 800
Final TS: 900
Final A: 1000

It should be noted that *sheen* (=300) is used when the *S* is followed by an *H* or by other consonants different from the *S*.

I tried *Ghematria* to the name *Bashar Al Assad* obtained the following result:

B= 2
A= 1
S= 300
H= 5
A= 1
R= 200
A= 1
L= 30
A= 1

$$S= 60$$
$$S= 60$$
$$A= 1$$
$$D= 4$$

A total of 666!

Surprised by this numerical result, I sought to take a closer look at the history of the youthful Syrian president and, in so doing, I discovered that his name was not originally *Assad*. Assad's father, the late president Hafez, had modified his original name *Wahash* into *Assad*. In Arabic the word *Wahash* means *Beast*. So the number 666 was *the number of the Beast*.

I was to discover a further disquieting element. To my astonishment Bashar Al Assad obtained a degree in medicine in Great Britain, specialising in ophthalmology. So he is a '*Medecin*': a name which is used in the sestets to denote the Antichrist.

Obviously all this could be reduced to a mere series of coincidences and is mentioned more for its oddness than to further the aim of identifying the young Syrian president with the sinister figure of the Antichrist. In closing this lengthy parenthesis and in drawing our attention once again to the passage under examination, further thought should be given to the fact that the Seer used the erroneous form of *Liguriens-Adriaticques*, in view of which I attempted to subtract from the erroneously written double adjective the word *Ligustiques*. When I did so, I was left with *rien-Adriac*, and I came to understand that the Seer, in suggesting such an operation, wanted to reveal the names of the two Islamic countries which would form the fundamental nucleus of the Middle-Eastern invasion forces, and that is, *Iran and Iraq* (Irac). For the names of both these countries can be extracted from the letters *rien adriac*, leaving only *ED*, the *D* of which can be transformed into the dental letter *T*, with the final result that *rien adriac* are *Iran et Iraq*.

But there was no end to the surprises: the sentence, continued with the apparently complementary terms '*par l'appuy*

& *puissance aquilonaire'*. I say *apparently*, in view of the fact
that *moyen par* also means *apart from, separately*, for which
the real meaning of the entire sentence could be the following:
'*Consider the original adjectives written with the capital letter
which can be associated twice to Ligustiques and, separately,
to l'appuy et puissance aquilonaire.*'

It then became clear to me that for this second part the Seer
was suggesting two operations: (1) subtract from *Liguriens
Adriaticques* the word *Ligustiques*; (2) Eliminate from the
result and from *l'appuy et puissance aquilonaire* the letters
they have in common.

As we have noted, *rien adriac* remained from the first operation, and if at this point we eliminate the letters that are
common to this result and to *l'appuy et puissance aquilonaire*,
the following letters there remain: R, D, L, P, P, U, T, P, U,
S, S, E, A, Q, U, I, L, O, N, A, I, E. If we then make an
anagram of this, we have the following, incredible result:
PALLID-OPAQUE RUSSE PUTIN and that is *the pallid,
impenetrable Russian Putin!*

In describing the present Russian head of state the Seer
employs a double adjective *pallid-opaque*, which belong
specifically to the language of alchemy and is employed when
describing a substance whose soft colour resists the penetration
of light. This adjective perfectly fits the physical and personal
characteristics of the Russian premier, who is of pale com-
plexion, and who possesses a cold and impenetrable stare,
which betrays no emotion.

At this point the enigma could be held have been resolved:
it concealed the name of the Antichrist (*Hadrie*), his country
of origin (*Syria*), his Middle-Eastern allies (*Iran and Iraq*),
his Eurasian ally (*Russia*) and perhaps the powerful leader of
the latter (*Vladimir Putin*).

*CXXII God the creator, then, will understand the affliction
of his people, and Satan will be placed and bound in the
abyss of the chasm in the deep hole.*

With this Nostradamus concludes the preamble to the prophetic part of the letter, almost a kind of presentation of those events that will subsequently be more minutely examined.

> *CVII And, in the beginning, there will be a year in which the greater persecution will be made against the Christian Church, such as not even in Africa there was and this will last until the year 1792, which will be held to be a renewal of the century.*

Thus the chronology of the human vicissitudes begins: the French Revolution brought terrible persecutions against the Catholic church, culminating in the rise to power of Robespierre, who proclaimed himself the promoter of a new creed, based on the so-called *'Supreme Entity'*.

> *XXXVIII God, in fact, will have considered the long barrenness of the Grand Lady* (the Republic), *for, immediately afterwards, she will conceive two important children* (the Republic of the United States and the French Republic).

Interpreters have long argued as to the identity of the *grand dame*. In fact, her identification with the Republic appears obvious, when one considers that republics, as opposed to monarchies, are barren by nature, since the republican system does not presuppose the principle of descendants, which a monarchical institution properly does. Furthermore, in Nostradamus's day, for many centuries all the other States apart from the Republic of Venice, had been governed by a monarchy. The republican system had experienced its greatest splendour in the Graeco-Roman period, so it might will have been said that that system had been sterile for a long time.

> *CXI (It will come to pass then) that the arches built of ancient iron will accompany one another to Neptune's waves.*
>
> *LXI which, attracted by their vortex, will make the ship go straight, without creating obstacles to the opposite end of*

the prow, causing it to touch the ground. This will create such progress that from a branch (of science) *that for a long time has been sterile, something will be born which will liberate the whole of humanity from that benign and voluntary slavery* (the dependence on wind energy), *placing it under the protection of Mars* (the civilisation based on metals and industrial ones) *and stripping Jupiter of every honour and dignity* (the discovery of the physical nature of electrical energy personified in Jupiter with his thunder bolts), *in the name of a free city* (the scientific community, which has no confines), *constituted and placed in a very different, small Mesopotamia* (at the time of Nostradamus physics still did not have its precise individuality, being half way between philosophy on the one hand and mathematics on the other, hence the figurative reference to Mesopotamia, a territory, which, as the name suggests, is situated between two rivers).

It seems totally logical that these two passages be read in correlation to each other, since they make complete sense, rather than one which is completely incoherent, as in many of the versions offered by other interpreters.

CXII In Adriatic there will be great dissension, and that which had been united will be separated, and what was and is a great city will resemble a house, which held supremacy and which was the Mesopotamia of Europe, at 45° latitude, and, once again, at 41°, 42° and 37°.

We thus come to the First World War, together with its most significant consequence, which is that of the dismemberment of the Austro-Hungarian Empire (*the Mesopotamia of Europe*, situated between the Danube and the Rhine), which reduced it in the end to only a small Austria.

CXV Contemporaneously and in the years to follow, there will be a terrible epidemic, rendered exceptional by the famine which will have preceded it and there will be great

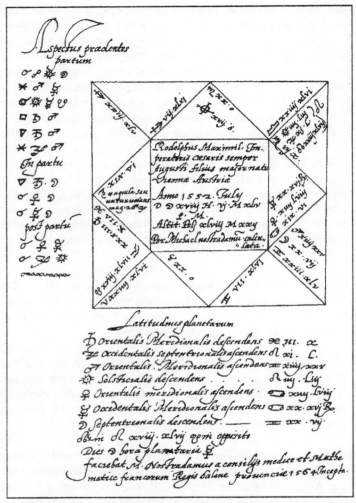

Astral chart (horoscope) commissioned by Nostradamus. The text in the central panel reads: Rudolf, firstborn of the Emperor Maximilian everlastingly August Caesar, Vienna, Austria. 1552 Monday 18 July at 6.45pm under a polar elevation (at the latitude) of 4822′. Calculated by Michel Nostradamus *tribulations such as has never come since the foundation of the Christian Church and throughout the Latin regions,*

LI until today, but it will be in the month of October that some great revolution will be made, and such that the heaviness of the earth will seem to have lost its natural movement and to have sunk into perpetual darkness: before and after spring time there will be extreme changes, modifications of states, with great earthquakes and the growth of a new Babylon, daughter of misery, which then will be augmented by thanks to the abomination of the first Holocaust.'

In this passage the Seer continues to expound on what would happen in the course of the First World War and at its end: Spanish influenza which would reap numerous victims, especially in the Mediterranean countries, and, above all, the Russian Revolution, exploding in October, would forebode profound political upheavals, which would then multiply after the Second World War, when memory of the Holocaust perpetrated by the Nazis would bring new proselytes to the communist cause.

LXVIII The populace will rise in support and will drive out those who wanted to enforce respect of the laws and it will seem that regimes have been weakened by the East [of Europe] and that God the creator has unleashed Satan from the infernal prison to bring to birth the great Dog and Dógam who will create a deleterious movement for the churches that is so great, that neither the Reds nor the Whites, the blind nor the impotent will any longer be able to judge and they will be deprived of every power.

In this passage Nostradamus describes what was to happen in Russia under the pressure from the poorer classes, which would overthrow everyone and everything, making it impossible for the re-establishment of order, even by the more moderate Bolsheviks themselves, the less by the white Russians, by then stripped of all their powers.

CXX And before those events, some unusual birds will cry huy, huy, in the air and after some time they will vanish.

This may be an allusion to the invention of the aeroplane, which came about before the First World War.

LIV Then great peace, union and concord will be forged, thanks to one of the young states of the turbulent fronts and separated from the different nations.

The young state of which the Seer is speaking is the United States, which had a determining role in ending the war and which, with President Wilson, was active, in creating an organisation, which would be able to ward off the repetition of such a catastrophe, and that is the League of Nations.

LIX But at the moment when the dignity of that (peace) *shall be at its highest and most sublime* (the creation of the League of Nations), *another desolation will be at hand, since other military potentates will emerge.*

XLIV In fact, as one who in a confused fashion and with tardy reconsideration wishes to ruin it, there will be three nations, with extremely different languages and origins and that is [Italy, Germany and Japan], *who will give rise to militaristic parties.*

This passage needs no special comment: immediately after the First World War, and in chronological order, Italy, Germany and Japan created extreme right regimes which were militaristic – Fascism, Nazism and Japanese Imperialism.

Why have I interpreted *Espaigne* as *Japan,* when at face value it look like Spain? The passages which follow and must relate to this paragraph lead me to think that the term *Espaigne* is an anagram. If one rearranges the letters, the word becomes *Giap(o)nese* (Jap(a)nese), which, when pronounced sound like the modern *Japonaise* and therefore *Japanese.* Also bearing in mind that in Spain power was seized and retained for many years by a regime from the right, that is Franco-ism. However, the Seer emphasises the extreme differences in language and origin of the three countries.

CVIII And the Roman people will begin to rise again and to come out of obscurity, reacquiring a little of their early splendour, but not without great dissension and continuous upheavals.

In two lines the Seer traces the foreign policy of Mussolini and the internal problems of Italy.

XLVI Such will be their power, that all will be done through common agreement and with strict alliance, with the aim of making aggressive conquests.

In 1936 Adolph Hitler formed a treaty of military alliance with Italy, and almost at the same time signed a similar treaty with Japan, which was anti-Communist in its aim.

Thus the well-known '*Rome–Berlin–Tokyo Axis*' came into being, which was reinforced in 1939 with the so-called '*Steel Pact*' between Germany and Italy.

LXXXV And this new triumvirate will last for seven years and the fame of this party will be universally recognised by everyone and the sacrifice of the holy and immaculate host will be carried on.

The Rome-Berlin-Tokyo axis, that is the triumvirate, came to an end in 1943, when Mussolini was dismissed by the Great Council of Fascism, which voted the Grandi's* order of the day, and was arrested and imprisoned on the Gran Sasso. So, between 1936 and 1943, exactly seven years passed.

Nazi-fascism reverberated throughout the world and its end was preceded by the Holocaust, that is, with the sacrifice of millions of innocent victims, which the Seer compares to that of Jesus Christ of the cross.

---

* Dino Grandi was President of the Chamber of Fascists and of the Corporations, which engineered Mussolini's political downfall and imprisonment.

XLII The second of these (Germany), *accompanied by the Italians, will advance so much that the second violent, convulsive progress will be forged toward the Mount Iovis* (the Elysée) *and from there move down to climb to the Pyrenees* (total occupation of France), *but such a direction will not achieve the creation of the ancient monarchy* (the reconstitution of the Holy Roman Empire) *and thus there will be the third human blood bath* (after the Napoleonic wars and the First World War) *and for a long time Mars will not be found in Lent* (that is, for a long time there will be war).

I have interpreted '*Mont Iovis*' as *Elysée* (Elysium) because on the coat of arms of the Capetians, above the lilies is written '*Mont Iovis Saint Denis*'. Mont Iovis signifies absolute power, Saint Denis is the patron saint of France. During the First World War the Germans had attempted to occupy France, but did not succeed because of the French army's strenuous resistance on the Marne. During the Second World War, however, they did occupy France, and a second '*violent convulsive progress*' was completely successful.

XLVIII Then a sterile lady more powerful than the second (the socialist republic) *will be received by two peoples, through the intercession of that first one who had been held solidly in the grasp of the one who had had overall power* (the USSR and Stalin) *and consequently by a second* (China) *and by a third* (Yugoslavia) *and this* (the Socialist Republic) *will extend its forces towards the east of Europe up to Hungary, which shall be subdued and on the sea it will extend itself to the Adriatic Trinacria* (Istria occupied by Yugoslavia), *already subdued by the Myrmidons* (the Fascists who had borrowed from the warriors of Achilles the war cry, 'Eya, Eya alalà') *and Germans and the barbaric party of the Italians shall be persecuted and driven out.*

LXII And its leader and governor (Duce Mussolini) *will be taken away and confined to a high mountain* (the Gran Sasso), *he having ignored the conspiracy of the plotters of the second Trasibulus* (Grandi), *who had meditated on all this for a long time.'*

LX And from him the two swords shall be taken (political power, that is*) and nothing will remain to him but the insignia* (the Italian Social Republic).

These passages of the letter do not need much commentary: in fact, once they have been placed in their correct position, they narrate what took place with surprising fidelity. The second sterile lady can be no other than the Italian Social Republic, which was profoundly different from the Western democratic republics. Through the intercession of Soviet Russia, Communism triumphed in China and Yugoslavia. Nostradamus makes reference only to two nations and not to the others belonging to the Warsaw pact, for the simple reason that these latter ones were practically subjugated by the USSR, while the former two maintained their independence, even though they professed an analogous political faith, not only did keep themselves at a distance from the Soviet Empire, they often found themselves in intense disagreement with it.

Even the regretful loss of Istria at the end of the Second World War is well represented: this region, in fact, is shaped like a triangle, and only it can be defined with the appellation of '*Trinacria Adriatic*'.

The fall of Mussolini is then described, a fall which took place at the hands of the *Great Council of Fascism*, which voted on the order of the day. *Grandi* on that occasion took on the mantle of the Athenian general Trasibulus. Then imprisonment on the Gran Sasso and the constitution of the Italian Social Republic, a puppet state of the Germans where Mussolini was relegated to a role which was, in essence, in name only, rather than one in which he could wield political power.

XLIX And then the great empire of the Antichrist shall begin in Atila (Yalta) *and Zerfes* (its servants) *to descend in great incalculable numbers, so much so that the Holy Spirit, emerging from 48th latitude, shall transmigrate, driving out from that abomination, the Antichrist, who shall make war against the royal one* (leader), *who shall be the Grand Vicar of Christ, and against his Church and his reign 'throughout his period of office and as occasion arises'.*

Here, the Seer is not using the term 'Antichrist' to denote a particular individual, in contrast to his reference to a second Antichrist later, who will be a well-defined person. Nostradamus refers of three Antichrists in the course of human history: Nero, Communism and the beast of the earth, of which John speaks in the Apocalypse, referred to as '*Medecin*' or as '*purveyor of the sea monster*', a term clearly borrowed from the Apocalypse, where the beast of the earth is shown as an offspring of the beast seen to rise up 'from the sea', which is Evil or the Demon.

It seems odd that translators of this passage have not understood that the word '*Atila*' does not signify a region of Mongolia (*Altai*). By treating 'Atila' as an anagram, we get a different meaning: Yalta. Following the Yalta agreements, the world became substantially divided into two spheres of influence: the Western sphere and the Communist one: half of the world's fate was determined by one dominating political doctrine which advocated materialism and professed the non-existence of God.

The word '*Zerfes*' may not indicate a geographical location; in middle French it often meant '*servants*'.

All this, however, results from the particular passage being inserted into a context which seems, on the one hand, to refer to the growth of Communist dominion (Para XLVIII, in fact, as has been observed, describes the conquests of the Social Republic). On the other hand, however, it concerns a person of note who is yet to appear (Para L, in fact, refers to a solar eclipse which will herald the Antichrist's arrival, and that eclipse took place on 11 August 1999).

The Grand Vicar of Christ, whom the Seer mentions, is obviously the present Pope John Paul II, whom the Communist regime has opposed in every way possible, even to the extent of making an attempt on his life.

LVI And the countries, towns, cities, kingdoms and prov-
inces that had abandoned the early ways which led to free-
dom, shutting themselves off even more resolutely, will be
secretly aggrieved by their freedom, and, having lost the
perfect religion, will begin to strike the left in order to return
to the right.

LXIX Then the greatest persecution, such as there has never
been, shall be made against the Churches,

LXV and many among them shall make apostasy of the True
Faith.

Nostradamus describes with disturbing accuracy what happened to many social groups who had deluded themselves into
thinking that they would obtain a more just and democratic
system, by embracing the Communist cause. Instead they
found themselves imprisoned, in a regime which deprived them
of every freedom. Subsequently, through numerous attempts
(the Hungarian and Czechoslovakian uprisings, etc.) they tried
to regain their lost freedom and to pass from left (that is, from
the Communist regime) to the right (that is to a democratic
one). The Communist system was a great persecutor of
churches and religions. Many of those, too, who were subject
to Communist regimes abandoned the Christian religion,
convinced of the justness of the Communist doctrine.

LXVI And, of the three parties, the one at the centre shall
be allowed to decline a little by itself,

LXVII The first shall be totally eliminated from Europe and
from the major part of Africa at the hands of the third,
because of people poor in spirit, who, for personal gain,
will betray their obligations through libidinous lust.

In this passage the Seer describes how parties evolved as a
result of the Second World War and by Communism. The
party of the right, after the fall of Fascism and Nazism and
the death of Franco, was practically wiped out from Europe.

The same phenomenon occurred in Africa, where parties of the extreme left overthrew rightist regimes, governed for the most part by unscrupulous and bloodthirsty dictators. The centre parties underwent a profound crisis in Europe, with Communism developing markedly in all countries.

LII And all this will last no longer than 73 years and seven months.

With this simple sentence the Seer reveals his disconcerting power of prophecy: from the October Revolution until the first democratically elected president (Yeltsin), exactly 73 years, 7 months and 17 days were to pass. The revolution broke out on 25 October 1917, and Yeltsin was elected President of Russia on 12 June 1991.

CIX Uenise (The United States), *in the meanwhile, raised its wings with such great strength and power and to such heights as almost to equal the power of Ancient Rome.*

'*Uenise*' has until now always been translated as '*Venice*', since in middle French the capital U was often written as a V, just as in Roman inscriptions found on monuments *(SENATVS POPVLVSQUE ROMANVS)*. However, the term '*Uenise*' can be interpreted differently: it contains not only a crasis, but also an anagram, which reads as '*E. Unies*', that is, '*Etats Unis*', the United States If you attribute this meaning to the '*Uenise*', then the reference takes on an altogether more meaningful sense, since at the present time the United States constitutes the most powerful country in the world, in effect, not so distant from the power of the Roman Empire.

LVII And the holiness destroyed long since shall be restored, with its original sacred texts, only after the great dog, the biggest of mastiffs shall come, which shall destroy everything, even what had previously been accomplished, and the temples will be raised anew and the clergy shall be reintegrated into its former state.

With the end of Communism, the churches reopen, and the clergy can return to practising its sacred mission.

After the Communist revolution *(the great dog)* there comes a democratic revolution *(the biggest of mastiffs),* which in no time has swept away governments and institutions, going as far as to rebuild a system based on liberty and parliamentary democracy.

> *LXXXII Such great oppression shall be perpetrated then on Princes* (leaders) *and the Governors of Kingdoms, even maritime and Eastern ones and their languages shall be mingled in one great, unique society.*

In this passage Nostradamus depicts the coming into being of the European Union, wished for by almost all the citizens of single states, even Turkey *(a maritime and Eastern nation),* with the consequence that a plurality of languages will be the outstanding characteristic of the new supranational entity.

> *LV And such a peace there shall be made, that the instigator and the promoter of the warring faction will be tied to the deepest hole through the diversity of its religious communities and the nation of the Rabid One, pretending to be a wise man, shall unite.*

With these few lines the Seer describes the two most significant events in recent years: the body of Stalin, who had created obstacles in every possible way against religious faith, was removed from the Kremlin, where it had been the object of veneration, only to be buried in a common grave; Germany, that is the nation of Hitler, *'the Rabid One, pretending to be a wise man'*, was once again united.

> *CXXI And after a very long period of time, when another reign of Saturn shall almost be upon us and a golden age.*

Thus the Seer comes to contemporary times: the United States with its power assures world peace, every country is against war; throughout the world, peace and harmony are preached, even though violence and tension still exist in certain corners (which explains the '*almost*').

What follows, therefore, concerns the future, which, unfortunately, appears to be very close.

> *CIV And after some time, and precisely that in which Saturn, which will return, enters on the seventh of* (millennium seven) *the month of April until 25 August, Jupiter on the 14 June until 7 October, Mars on 17 April until 22 June, Venus on 9 April until 22 May, Mercury on 3rd until 27 February . . .*

Before continuing, some clarification is necessary, since the French text presents some difficulties in interpretation. The Seer writes: 'et apres quelque temps et dans iceluy comprenant depuis le temps que Saturne qui tournera entre à sept du mois d'Auril, jusques au 15. d'Aoust . . .' The most obvious translation would be to refer the '*sept*' to the month of April; but '*sept*', as opposed to the other numbers, is spelled out. In view of this, according to the *green language*, its presence signifies something else.

'*Sept*' could be referring to the seventh house of Nostradamus's horoscope, or the seventh sign of the zodiac, both of which are identified with Libra. But this interpretation does not seem to have any connection with the days and months expressed. Furthermore, the French syntax is ambiguous: '*entre*' might mean '*between*', but I have come to the conclusion that '*qui tournera*' is a simple parenthesis, and '*entre*' does mean '*enter*' in view of the fact that on other occasions the Seer had spoken of the return of the reign of Saturn, while in the meantime *entre* assumed the meaning of the third person singular of the verb *entrer, to enter* (or in middle French *to begin*).

I concluded therefore that Nostradamus was alluding to the cycle of Saturn in millennium seven (that is, the eighth), beginning with Aries, which is the first sign of the Zodiac.

My problem was to try to see when, from 2004 onwards

(the end of the seventh millennium and beginning of the eighth) Saturn would be in Aries, bearing in mind that in Nostradamus's time the calendar in use was the Julian calendar, so the astrological ephemeris in current use at that time was fourteen days earlier than now. An analogous operation should have been made for the other planets that were named.

So, on the basis of the Julian calendar, the following time limits can be established:

> Saturn will be in Aries from the 11 May 2025, a date included between April and 25 August.
>
> Jupiter will be in Aries from 28 April 2022 and will remain there until 14 October 2022, a time span which includes the period between 14th June and 17 October.
>
> Mars will enter Aries on 31 May 2005, a date falling between 17 April and 22 of June.
>
> Venus will enter Aries during the period indicated by the Seer on 20 April 2006, a date falling between 9 April and 22 May.
>
> And Venus will enter Aries again in the period indicated by the Seer on 15 April 2017, a date that is also included within the period of 9 April to 22 May.
>
> Mercury will enter Aries during the period indicated by the Seer on 20 February 2005, a date falling between 3 and 24 of February.

Surprisingly the dates thus identified provide us with the date of the Third World War in its two phases, and confirm the accuracy of the chronology proposed here. In fact, as will be seen in the second part of this work, the Third World War should begin between the end of 2005 and the beginning of 2006. The first phase should reach its conclusion towards the end of 2017 and the second phase should begin in 2022. The war should end on the 2 June 2025.

So the date of Saturn entering into Aries represents the year of the end of the war and of the prophecies; that of Jupiter, the year of the beginning of the second phase of the war in 2022; that of Mars, Venus and Mercury, the date of the beginning of the war at the ending of the year between 2005 and 2006. Venus's second entry during the period indicated by the Seer, the end of the first phase of the war in 2017.

CXIX Then there will be the Antichrist, Prince of Hell, and once again and for the last time, all the nations of Christianity shall tremble and also those of the Infidels for the space of twenty-five years and there will be the most horrible wars and battles and buildings burnt and destroyed, with great bloodshed of virgins, brides and widows raped, suckling children shall be dashed against city walls, and so many evils shall be committed through Satan, Prince of Hell, that almost the entire world shall find itself destroyed and desolate,

LXXI and the owners of the fields and of the houses shall be unknown and grass shall grow taller than knee-high in the streets.

The scene described here appears as apocalyptic, the return to a complete state of barbarism.

In the first part of this work we noted that the Seer's prophecies would come to an end on 2 June 2025, when the 7,000 years and a further twenty (and some months) had elapsed. The interpretation put forward in that part is confirmed in the present passage.

In fact, when we come to examine the quatrains and sestets, we shall see clearly that the Antichrist's reign already began in 2000 and will last twenty-five years, ending, therefore, in 2025, which is exactly the same date we arrived at through a completely different approach.

L First, there will be a solar eclipse, that will be the darkest and most obscure that has ever been from the creation of the world until the death and passion of Jesus Christ.

This sentence as well confirms what has been said above, since the eclipse took place on 11 August 1999.

XLV Except for the nations situated above the 50th and the 52nd latitude, all will pay homage to a religion that is foreign to the regions of Europe, and the region of the north, situated at the 48th, stricken by a vain fear, shall be the first to tremble, and then the more western and eastern ones will tremble.

From what the Seer writes, it seems obvious that the Antichrist will assume the role of bearer of a new religion, which within the individual states will bring about popular uprisings and disorder: the said religion will spread like an oil slick, so much so that governments will not be able keep the phenomenon under control and will collapse.

This will happen, first of all, in France (Paris, in the cartography of those times, shown to be at the 48th latitude), but then the phenomenon will spread in Russia, China and, most of all, in the Middle East, undoubtedly an extremely fertile territory for promoting a religion which can be fused with Islam and which will present the Antichrist as a new Mohammed or Messiah.

England and the United States will, for the moment remain untouched by this, and then, as will be revealed, they will become heavily involved in that terrible conflict which the Third World War will turn out to be.

LXXV And the city of Achem (Mecca) *itself will be attacked and assailed from every side with great violence by armed people.*

In the passage the Seer speaks of the city of *Achem*, a name which, read backwards, produces the precise name of *Mecha*, the name of the Holy city of Islam as it was alternatively written during the sixteenth century. Furthermore, as we shall see in the following chapter, there are precise references in the quatrains to the seizure of Mecca at the hands of the new infidels. It is altogether credible that the growth of a new religion within the Islamic world – a world which, when it comes to religious questions is by nature turbulent and sensitive – can determine conflicts and revolutions, with blood-shed and the fall of governments within various Arab countries, which, as will be seen, will within a brief time become united under the dominion of the Antichrist.

LXIII Then the wickedness and abominations will shame-fully materialise and manifest themselves in a dark shadowy light and will cease only towards the end of his (the Anti-christ's) reign,

CXVI the signs remaining only in some quarters of Spain,

LXXXIII the mingling of the Latin tongue with the Arab because of the Libyans, and all those Eastern Kings will be driven out, destroyed, exterminated.

Having seized power in a vast part of the world, the Antichrist will display all his wickedness. He will set off a terrible war, exploiting the Arab countries as well as Russia; the Libyans will conquer Spain, and in that country Arabic will also be spoken. But the invaders will in the end be driven out and destroyed, while in Spain there will remain areas where some people, presumably those who will have moved there, will continue to speak Arabic, and their presence will be tolerated.

CXIV And on the basis of the aforesaid astrological calcu-lation, made in accordance with the sacred scriptures, the persecution of the people of the Church will stem from the power of the Islamic kings united with the people of the East. And this persecution will last for eleven years, more or less, when the principal king of the league will fall, and those years having been completed, his ally from the south will survive and for three years he will persecute the people of the Church more cruelly, through apostate corruption of one who will hold absolute power within the sphere of an armed religion and the holy people of God, observers of his law, and every religious order will be greatly persecuted and afflicted in such a way that the blood of the true clergy will flow everywhere, and one of the terrible temporal (oil) kings will be greatly praised by his followers for having shed more blood of innocent clergy than how much wine he could have poured and that king will commit incredible misdeeds against the Church, human blood will flow in the public streets and in temples, like heavy rain and nearby rivers will turn red with blood, and through a naval war the sea will also turn so red, that in a report from one king to the other, there shall be written: 'The water has turned red from naval battles'.

Here the Seer describes the terrible warlike scenario that is in store for us. The Islamic countries will first be unified under the Antichrist, who is exploiting the enormous economic potential of oil, and who will literally buy out Russia with its entire military arsenal, and in time will gain the support of China. Once this is done, the Antichrist will unleash his war, which will be characterised by tremendous religious persecution, with the slaughter and the massacre of priests, wherever his army manages to reach.

After eleven years the principal country of the league, which is Russia, will fall. But after a brief four-year truce, his work will be continued by his southern ally – China, who will persecute the clergy for another three years. In that period, the Catholic church, as an institution and an order, will cease to exist. In the meantime, the Antichrist, aside from being a very powerful political leader, will also be the religious head of his new and blasphemous creed; for this reason, there will be, as the Seer writes, a bloody persecution of the truly religious, who as new martyrs will immolate themselves on the altar of the True Faith.

CX And in those times, the great Byzantines sails supported by the Ligustiques (Iran and Iraq), *and by the power of the Aquilonaire* (Russian forces), *will create not a few problems, so much so, that the faith of the two Cretan* (Christian) *religions will not be maintained.*

Here in this passage the Seer describes the invasion of the Mediterranean countries, principally by the Russian fleet: such will be the terror that it will induce the majority into abjuring the Christian religion, Orthodox as well as Catholic.

We noted earlier that this passage conceals a play in words and, through resolving it, it was possible to identify the name of the Antichrist (*Hadrie*), his country of origin (Syria), not to mention his Middle-Eastern allies (Iran and Iraq) and his Eurasian ally (Russia), for which reason, in the interpretation of the passage, once the word-puzzle was discovered, it became possible to explain what the Seer really meant to say as opposed to what he appeared to say.

Nostradamus uses the term '*Cretenses*', which would appear to mean *Cretans*. Here as well it is the case of an anagram through which the word becomes '*Crest(i)ennes*': *Christians*, whose meaning fits perfectly into the rest of the sentence.

> *LXXIV And their assaults will not be in vain and the place that once was the home of Abraham will be assailed by Ioujalistes (*men who venerate the new religion*),*
>
> *LXIV and the heads of the church shall be without the love of God,*
>
> *LVIII and they will begin to indulge in lust and prostitution and to commit a thousand wickednesses.*
>
> *LXXII and complete desolation will be made of the clergy, and the military will sack the city of the Sun (*Rome*), Melitus (*Malta*) and the Stechades (*Egadi Islands*) and the port which takes its name from the beast of the sea (*of Marseilles*) will be blockaded.'*

By sea and by land the state of Israel will come under attack at the hands of the fanatics of the Antichrist, while the Church will plummet into an irreversible crisis: the clergy will be persecuted, Rome, Malta and the Egadi Islands will be devastated and put to fire and sword, and the port of Marseilles will be blockaded. At the same time, and even before then, because of the last Pope, the Church will receive a blow to its faith, which will induce many Catholics into giving it up, as they witness the ugly spectacle of many priests indulging in vice and fornication.

LXXVIII And the Holy Sepulchre, object of such great veneration, will remain for long exposed to the sky, under the universal vision of the eyes of Heaven, of Sun and Moon,

LXXIX and the holy place shall be transformed into lodging for small and large flocks, and adapted for profane acts.

Jerusalem, then, will fall into the hands of the infidels, and the Holy Sepulchre will remain practically abandoned to the weather: the churches, also will lose their function, becoming animal sheds and places for lewd spectacles.

CXIII (c) Because of these great upheavals, the memory of things that are represented by these symbols shall suffer an incalculable loss, even letters (particularly because of certain encyclical letters) *and all this shall make things favourable for the Aquilonaires* (Islam and its allies).

The churches, therefore, will be transformed into sheep pens, but the cause of this disaster, according to the Seer, must be sought in the '*letters*', which will determine the real disaster. We shall see the commentary on some of the quatrains that this disaster will be caused by the last pope, '*the Petrus Romanus*' in Malachia's prophecy. He, who is defined by Nostradamus as being of a '*Libidinous life*', and probably homosexual, as can be grasped from certain verses, will issue certain encyclical letters which will not be altogether in keeping with everyday morality, and this will bring about a profound upheaval within the Catholic church, to the extent that following his death a deep schism will occur.

This will prove useful to the Antichrist and his allies. It will be easy for him to depict the Catholic church as sinful and immoral, and the information media – television, radio, newspapers – will broadcast what he says, like a loudspeaker, amplifying his voice, thus rendering him an incredible service. In this way he will be able to carry out a religious war, almost a crusade, directed at ridding the world of these impurities. The Catholics, on the other hand, will be disconcerted and perturbed by the direction the new pope will assume, and they will discover themselves totally unprepared to face the new infidels.

Here then is full confirmation of what John writes in Revelations 13:11,18:

> And I beheld another beast coming up out of the earth; and he had two horns like a lamb, and he spoke as a dragon.
> And he exerciseth all the power of the first beast before him, and causeth the earth and them which dwell therein to worship the first beast, whose deadly wound was healed.
> And he doeth great wonders, so that he maketh fire come down from heaven on the earth in the sight of men,
> And deceiveth them that dwell on the earth by means of those miracles which he had power to do in the sight of the beast; saying to them that dwell on the earth, that they should make an image to the beast, which had the wound by a sword, and did live.
> And he had power to give life unto the image of the beast, that the image of the beast should both speak, and cause that, as many as would not worship the image of the beast should be killed.
> And he causeth all, both small and great, rich and poor, free and bond, to receive a mark in their right hand, or in their foreheads:
> And that no man might buy or sell, save he that had the mark, or the name of the beast, or the number of his name.
> Here is wisdom. Let him that hath understanding count the number of the beast: for it is the number of a man; and his number is Six hundred threescore and six.

The vision of John is that of someone living in the first century AD, to whom God gave the power to see all the future events in fleeting vision. In what way would television have described a man of those times, if not by defining him as a talking statue, relating and reproducing precisely the evil doings of the Antichrist, that is, of the beast of the earth? Through the information media then, the Antichrist will be able to spread his religion and force the inhabitants of the earth to pay homage to him in every area occupied by his troops.

LXX And in these circumstances there will arise a so great pestilence that more that half of the world, will perish:

LXXX what calamitous affliction will strike pregnant women then!

It is correct to suppose that the pestilence of which Nostradamus speaks is the consequence of atomic war and its accompanying radiation. His reference to pregnant women is significant: after the bombing of Hiroshima, numerous women who had been contaminated by the radiation gave birth to monsters, and this continued for years afterwards, and even today there are sporadic cases of this sort.

LIII And, afterwards, from the stem, what had been barren for so long, will burst into flower, and emerging from the 50th latitude, will renew the whole Christian Church.

XXXIX But while being in danger, she, who will have sided with him, unaware of the mortal risk of the times, in a zone falling between the 18th and not beyond the 36th latitude, will give birth to three males and one female, having two not of the same father. Among the three brothers there will be such a difference, but they will be united in an agreement, to such a degree that three or four parts of Europe will tremble.

XLVII They will be equal in nature but very different as to faith.

While the Catholic church is going through an irreversible crisis due to aggression from inside and outside, brought on respectively by the last pope and by the Antichrist, the Rose of Nostradamus will bloom, hence the reference to the stem that will renew the Christian church. In this passage the Seer is referring to the Rosicrucians of which he was a Grand Master. The Rosicrucians for centuries have remained silent, their school of esoteric thought, though still alive, has maintained a discreet profile, while not, however, hiding in secrecy. The Rosicrucians recognise Christ as the greatest of the cosmic masters and they are inspired by a rigorous morality, connected with the laws of the *Karma*. Obviously, the sons of whom the Seer is speaking are not brothers in a biological sense: they are brothers in that they all belong to the Rosicrucians, whose initiation rites define as '*brothers*' or, to be more precise, '*fratres*' all those who adhere to it. Of these brothers, two will not come from the same religious sect, a circumstance that is normal to the Rosicrucians, whose adherents may come from any religion, since Rosicrucian teachings are separate from religious beliefs and are limited to awakening man's mystic conscience. The three '*fratres*', united by the fact that they belong to the Rosicrucians, will gain political power, and thus a resurgence of the Western world will have its beginning in a Europe which will be almost entirely occupied by Eastern forces and the Antichrist's sect.

XL Through the youngest, the Christian monarchy will be sustained and augmented, the sects raised and then immediately dashed, the Arabs repelled, kingdoms united, new laws promulgated.

Many interpreters, in commenting on this passage along with others, which have been examined above, have been convinced of having identified here the figure of Napoleon, but only through an obvious forcing of the text. In reality, the passage is concerned with the future and refers to a personality, who will be the first to lead the resurgence of the civil and the Christian world. It is precisely to this personality that the last three *Centuries* and the letter under examination are destined; this personality will be King Henry of France, if for no other reason than that the numerous quatrains that concern him, assign precisely this role to him. In his project of reconstructing the world, after having driven out the Arabs, he will first restore a democratic 'party' system. Obviously, this experiment will not yield all the results he had hoped for, and so, Henry will decide to tighten political power, putting into force a system of government which will be strict but necessary in view of the times.

XLI Of the other children, the first will hold the furious crowned Lions, which have their paws on the intrepid coat of arms.

Many interpreters, in pointing out that lions appear on numerous heraldic coats of arms of European nations (Belgium, England, Holland, etc.), have opted for one or other of the various states. In reality there is but one state in which the coat of arms is composed of two lions, surmounted by a crown, which hold up a shield with their paws, and such a state is Spain since the Spanish Bourbons possess such an heraldic symbol. Consequently, the second '*frater*', we shall see when we examine the quatrains, will be a military leader, who, starting out from Belgium, will succeed in chasing the Arabs out of Spain, beyond the straits of Gibraltar.

CXIII b) Then the Gallic Ogmion (hero) *will pass through France, accompanied by such a great formation, that from an enormous distance the empire of the great law will be understood, and then, after some time, the blood of innocents will be spread abundantly by the hands of guilty ones who will be in a position of command.*

The third '*frater*' will be French, and he is defined by Nostradamus as '*Ogmion*', who in Celtic tradition was the God of eloquence and strength. In this passage too, the Seer uses the term '*Mont Iovis*' to mean France, which, as we have seen, is an inscription appearing on the Bourbons of France's coat of arms along with the name of the patron of France '*Saint Denis*'. In his war campaign '*Ogmion*' will find himself battling against the governors who have been nominated by the Antichrist, who will have occasion to unleash their anger against a helpless population, in an attempt to suppress a presumed revolt, set off by the approach of the liberator's troops.

> *XLIII And the daughter will be given for the conservation of the Christian church, since she will take away one of its leaders from the pagan sect of the infidels, and she will have two sons, one belonging to the faith and the other not, according to the convincing testimony of the Catholic church.*

The role of the '*soror*', that is, of the Rosicrucian sister, will be that of convincing one of the leaders of the Antichrist's league to cross over into enemy territory, dissuading him from the error into which he had fallen in embracing the false doctrine which had been professed by the Antichrist himself. After changing sides, this person will bring with him two men who, even though of different religions, will become aware of the terrible error that has been committed, and they too will become '*fratres*'.

It is possible that in this passage the Seer is alluding to Turkey, since, as will shall see in the commentary on the quatrains, that nation, after having been occupied by the Antichrist and having sustained him in war, up to a certain point, will cross over to the other side under the guidance of a leader whom Nostradamus call the '*White Turban*'.

> *LXXXVI And there will be, then, two men who, in the name of the north, will be victorious over the those from the east and among these such a great confusion and such tumult of war will be made that all the Eastern zone will tremble from fear of those brothers, who are not Aquilonaires brothers* (of the Islamic Alliance),

> LXXVI whose maritime forces shall be weakened by the Westerners.

The two '*fratres*', therefore, will determine an overthrow of the situation, bringing confusion among the forces of the

Antichrist. It should be noted here that the Seer takes pains to call the interpreter's attention to the difference existing between '*Aquilon*', which indicates the north as well as the Western forces, and '*Aquilonaire*', which means the opposing forces of the Arab Alliance.

> *LXXIII and new incursions will be made by sea, with the intent to liberate Castulum (Spain) from the first Mohammedans' conquest,*

> *LXXXI and the majority of the troops of the principal Eastern leader will be annihilated by the northerners and the people of the West, defeated and exterminated and the rest in flight and their children, born of different wives, will be imprisoned, and the prophecy of the Royal Prophet will then come true: 'Ut audiret gemitus compenditorum, ut solveret filios interemptorum.'*

The campaign for the liberation of Europe will, therefore, be brought forward, with the defeat of Russia and the Arabs.

> *CXVIII And the Grand Vicar of the Cape will be restored to his place but unhappy, and abandoned by all and the 'Holy of Holies' will once again be destroyed by paganism and the old and the new testaments will be banished and burnt.*

> *CV This will be between 1 June and the 24 of the said month and between the 25 September and the 16 October, with Saturn in Capricorn, Jupiter in Aquarius, Mars in Scorpio, Venus in Pisces, Mercury in a month of Capricorn, Aquarius and Pisces, the Moon in Aquarius and the head of the Dragon in Libra.*

The astronomical combination given in this passage indicates the year 2022. It is an *astronomical* combination, as opposed to an astrological one, in view of the fact that the years result from the astronomical cartography, while the astrological ones indicate the position of the stars, which is altogether different.

Here the astonishing fact is that Nostradamus was able to calculate such an astronomical combination, almost 500 years ago, while today, in order to identify something similar, one has to resort to sophisticated instruments. The resulting year 2022 appears to accord perfectly with the proposed chronology and it points exactly to the outbreak of the second phase of the war, which will last for three years, from the beginning of 2022 until 2 June 2025, as we shall see in the next part of this work.

> *CXVII The third Aquilonaire king* (of the Islamic Alliance), *hearing the laments of the people of his principal territory, will put together a great army and will pass through the districts of his forebears and their antecedents and he will succeed for the greater part in restoring the situation to its previous state,*
>
> *LXXXIV but not altogether, thanks to the forces of the kings of Aquilon* (of the north) *and because of the proximity of the time indicated by me and thanks to the three brothers, secretly united, who, one after the other, will seek his death through traps and ambushes.*

The war, then, is not over. With Russia having fallen, the Arabs having been defeated, China will advance, invading Europe, following the routes of the Huns, the Mongols and the Tartars. The Pope, defined as *Grand Vicar of the Cape*, that is, the Vicar of Christ, who wears the sacred vestment (*cape* is also a religious vestment in modern French), has at this point lost every form of religious influence: too many events have taken place, and the Catholic church, for some time now, has ceased to exist. The arrival of the Chinese, accompanied by the Arabs who will have regained their courage after the burning defeat, will restore the previous terrible situation, and this is also confirmed by passage CXIV which has already been examined, where the Seer writes that, after the persecution, lasting eleven years, from one of the first countries of the Arab League *'its southern ally will approach, who will even more cruelly persecute the people of the Church for three years . . .'* But by now 2025 is near (*'for the proximity of the time indicated by me'*) and the three brothers, who are heads of the Western forces, will succeed in a final effort in completing the process of liberation, defeating also the last powerful nation of the Antichrist forces.

> *LXXVII And great affliction will be caused to that nation and its largest cities will be depopulated and those who enter will be subject to the vengeance of the wrath of God.*

Victory is, therefore, complete but the price is very high. China will be practically destroyed and rendered uninhabitable because of radiation, which for the Seer assumes the significance of the terrible divine castigation, thus the impossibility for anyone to enter the principal cities of China, except at the risk of his own life.

> *CXIII (d) And by the will of God and into a deep pit shall Satan be bound and universal peace shall be made among men and the Church of Jesus Christ will be liberated from every tribulation, even though the Azos-tains* (without host) *will want to mix honey with the bile of their pestiferous heresy.*

In this passage the Seer uses the term *'Azos-tains'*, which has no meaning. However, when I treated this as an anagram, I obtained *'sanz-ostie'*, which is literally, *'without host'* and as such it indicates those religions in whose Liturgy the Eucharistic sacrament is absent.

> *CXXIII And then a universal peace will begin between men and God, and Satan will remain bound for the space of about 1,000 and the ecclesiastical power will return to its greatest potency, but then the demon will untie himself again.*

With the terrible war over, the Christian Church will have its reformation, and its religion will be that of all of humanity, even if there still will be heretics who will want to challenge religious principles.

This universal peace will last for about 1,000 years, as is also confirmed by John, in Revelations 20:1–5:

> And I saw an angel come down from heaven, having the key of the bottomless pit and a great chain in his hand.
>
> And he laid hold on the dragon, that old serpent, which is the Devil, and Satan, and bound him a thousand years, and cast him into the bottomless pit,
>
> And shut him up, and set a seal upon him, that he should deceive the nations no more, till the thousand years should be fulfilled: and after that he must be loosed a little season.
>
> And I saw thrones, and they sat upon them, and judgement was given unto them: and I saw the souls of them that were beheaded for the witness of Jesus, and for the word of God, and which had not worshipped the beast, neither his image, neither had received his mark upon their foreheads, or in their hands; and they lived and reigned with Christ a thousand years.
>
> But the rest of the dead lived not again until the thousand years were finished.

Thus the prophetic part of the letter ends, followed by a salutation:

CXXIV All these images, from the sacred scripture, are in perfect harmony with the visible heavenly things, as results from Saturn, Jupiter, Mars and the other planets joined together and as will be more clearly seen in some quatrains.

CXXV So that if I had wanted, I would have been able to make a deeper calculation and adapt some things to others.

CXXVI But seeing, O Most Serene King, that someone from the censure would have been able to find something to criticise, the moment has come for me to withdraw my pen from paper in order to dedicate myself to my nocturnal rest: 'O king, the most powerful of all kings, exceptional events will soon occur, but neither can I or do I wish to put them all in this letter dedicated to You: but in order to understand certain horrible facts, a little is sufficient, because great is your open mind towards everyone, as are equal your humanity towards men and your mercy towards the Gods, so that you alone appear to be worthy of the most prestigious and Christian title of king, which also confers upon you the supreme religious authority

CXXVII But I only ask you, O most clement King, to understand, with your singular and prudent humanity, my courageous desire and sincere commitment, which I know myself to possess, to have obeyed your Most Serene Majesty, since my eyes were so close to your solar splendour, which the magnitude of my work cannot reach or seek.

From Salon this 29th of June, 1558.

PART THREE

NOW AND THE FUTURE

7. The Foundations: *Centuries VI, quatrain 54, and the sestets*

> Au point du jour au second chant du coq,
> Ceulx de Tunes, de Fez, et de Bugie,
> Par les Arabes captif le Roy Maroq,
> L'an mil six cens et sept, de Liturgie.
>
> *At dawn at the second cock-crow,*
> *Those of Tunisia, Fez and Bugia,*
> *The King of Morocco by Arabs captured,*
> *Year one thousand six hundred*
> *and seven, of the Liturgy.*
> *(Centuries VI, quatrains 54)*

This quatrain appears to treat of the overthrow of the monarchy in Morocco by other Arab countries, but the reference date (the year 1607 of the Liturgy) makes it extremely difficult to place the event in time. We must ask what Nostradamus means by the word *Liturgy*.

Liturgy has a wide range of meanings: in Ancient Greece it alluded to the obligations of wealthier citizens to upkeep certain public or religious offices at their own expense, it also had a purely religious meaning, referring to a system of activities through which the community of the faithful profess their faiths.

If we take into account the *Centuries'* context, it could be that the Seer was using the term *liturgy* in its religious sense and particularly its system of rites and activities which regulate the form of sacred expression inherent in the Catholic church to which he belonged.

If this term refers to the system of rules and formulae belonging to the Catholic faith, then it is safe to say that if there is one work with which it can be associated more than to any other, that work is the Breviary, which covers it in its broadest sense. This is what Fernand Cabrol has to say about the Breviary in the *Catholic Encyclopaedia*, (1913):

> The Psalter constitutes the most oldest and venerable part of the breviary. It is composed of 150 psalms, which are divided in a particular fashion. These psalms formed the nucleus of the Hebrew Liturgy, which extends backwards to twelve centuries before the birth of Christ . . . The apostles followed the examples by these and indicated the psalms to the Churches as models for prayer.
>
> The history of the text of this Psalter is interesting. The most ancient Psalter used in Rome and Italy was the *Psalterium Vetus*, in the Italian version, which seems to have been introduced into the Liturgy by Pope St Damasus (d. 384). He it was who first ordered the revision of the Italian by St Jerome, in AD 383. On this account it has been called the *Psalterium Romanum*, and it was used in Italy and elsewhere till the ninth century and later. It is still in use in St Peter's at Rome, and many of the texts of our Breviary and Missal still show some variants (Invitatory an Ps. xciv, the antiphons of the Psalter and the responsorial of the Proper of the Season, Introits, Graduals, Offertories, and Communions). The *Roman Psalter* also influences the Mozarabic Liturgy, and was used in England in the eighth century.
>
> But in Gaul and in other countries north of the Alps, another revised edition entered into competition with the *Psalterium Romanum* under the somewhat misleading title of the *Psalterium Gallicanum*; for this text contained nothing distinctively Gallic, being simply a later correction of the Psalter made by St Jerome in Palestine, in AD 392. This revision diverged more completely than the earlier one from the Italic and, in preparing it, St Jerome had laid Origen's *Hexapla* under contribution.
>
> It would seem that St Gregory of Tours, in the sixth century, introduced this translation into Gaul, or at any rate

he was especially instrumental in spreading its use; for it was this Psalter that was employed in the Divine psalmody celebrated at the much honoured and frequented tomb of St Martin of Tours. From that time this text commenced its 'triumphal march across Europe'. Walafrid Starbo states that the churches of Germany were using it in the eighth century: – 'Galli et Germanorum aliqui secundum emendationem quam Hieronymus pater de LXX composuit Psalterium cantant'. About the same time England gave up the *Psalterium Romanum* for the *Gallicanum*. The Anglo-Saxon Psalter already referred to was corrected and altered in the ninth and tenth century, to make it accord with the *Gallicanum*.

Ireland seems to have followed the Gallic version since the seventh century, as may be gathered from the famous *Antiphonary of Bangor*. It even penetrated into Italy after the ninth century, thanks to the Frankish influence, and there enjoyed a considerable vogue. After the Council of Trent, St Pius V extended the use of the *Psalterium Gallicanum* to the whole Church, St Peter's in Rome alone still keeping to the ancient *Roman Psalter*. The Ambrosian Church of Milan has also its own revision of the Psalter, a version founded, in the middle of the fourth century, on the Greek.

At the time of Nostradamus, therefore, the basic nucleus of the Liturgy was made up of the *Psalterium Gallicanum*, and as we have seen this collection of psalms was the work of St Jerome in AD 392.

But the year AD 392 is fundamental to the Christian church, not only because it is the date the Breviary was completed, but also, more importantly, because in that year, and on 8 November, the Emperor Theodosius issued an edict adopting Christianity as the official religion of the Empire.

Prior to Theodosius, the Roman state had tolerated other religions: a consistent part of the population still observed the ancient polytheistic religion; the Jewish religion obviously existed, and coexisted, not always peacefully, alongside the Christian religion.

From Theodosius onwards Christianity became the only

dominant religion, and in time, numerous laws were promulgated to induce even the most recalcitrant into embracing it.

So this two-fold historical reference highlights 392 as the year of birth of the Liturgy, and defines the obscure date in the quatrain as being 1999 (392+1607).

Once we have defined the date at which the Liturgy began, we also have to take certain considerations into account regarding the interpretation of the quatrain in light of what took place in 1999, for in that year, King Hassan II of Morocco died and was succeeded to the throne by his son Mohammed VI.

In view of this, if the year of the Liturgy is AD 392, as I am maintaining here, and if, consequently, the quatrain is referring to the year 1999, its interpretation can only be as follows: *On the coming of day, at the second crow of the cock, those of Tunis, Fez and Bougia will take prisoner the man, who has become king of Morocco, in the year 1607 of the Liturgy.*

Identifying the year of the Liturgy is fundamentally important for future discussions in the book.

This particular quatrain, however, is not there just to foresee future events in Morocco, for in a good part of the *Sestets* reference is made to a date which begins with the number 6 (such as 605, 606, 607, 609 etc.) all dates, which in my opinion, start from the creation of the Liturgy, that is from the year AD 392.

The *Sestets* appeared mysteriously in 1605, contained in an edition of the *Centuries* a good forty years after the Seer's death. For this reason the majority of Nostradamus scholars of have judged them as apocryphal. There are other considerations which support this, such as the different structure of the verses (the first two lines are a rhymed couplet, the third is linked to the sixth, and the fourth and fifth are once again a rhymed couplet), the use of a more developed language, and less obscure than the quatrains. Everything, therefore, gives the impression that this brief work in verse could not in any way have been written by the Seer's pen.

However, those who have stigmatised the *Sestets* as spurious have not fully appreciated their undoubted prophetic content. In fact, as will become evident, events which are narrated in them have had ample confirmation through events that have already come to pass. So, it is safe to say that they are the work of a Seer. We can only surmise, then, that immediately after the death of Nostradamus, a Seer, who was endowed with the same capacity, came to the fore, a Seer, however, whom for personal reasons or because of modesty, preferred to remain anonymous. Such a theory could work, even though it remains improbable that in the space of only two generations two extraordinary Seers appeared in France. This hypothesis, however, seems to find confirmation through the system of dating to which the *Sestets* conform. As we have seen – and this will be confirmed by the analysis that follows here – the dates of the *Sestets* begin with the number *six*, and the application of the key which is hidden in the 'year one thousand six hundred and seven of the Liturgy' fits in perfectly with this, for if we add the year AD 392 to the number given in the *Sestets*, the resulting dates are altogether compatible with the events narrated therein. With this in mind, we can advance a much more logical hypothesis: that whoever wrote the Sestets had identified the year of the Liturgy and had used that chronological key to date events. But since, as we have said, it appears highly improbable that, in the space of only forty years, two Seers endowed with extraordinary capacities were to appear in France, it is much more realistic to suggest that whoever wrote the *Sestets* had been able to read Nostradamus's work '*in soluta oratione*', that is, in its '*non-coded*' state, and on this basis had then compiled the new prophecies, even though referring to events already described in the quatrains, giving them, however, a more precise date, bringing to light new events which the Seer of Salon had overlooked, as well as lengthening by a few years the final moment of the prophecies, and also, giving some events a more precise geographical location.

Only through acceptance of this hypothesis can the mystery of the *Sestets* find a complete solution, and can an understanding be reached as to the reason why their author remained anonymous: he was linked to the Seer in some way, which, had his name been revealed, would have led someone to guess the source from which the prophecies had been drawn.

We can therefore say that, though they may not be directly traceable to Nostradamus, the *Sestets* can justifiably be included in his prophetic work, and such a conclusion will be confirmed on numerous and surprising ways in the course of this present work.

The *Sestets* make ample use of an animal symbolism, to signify the various countries involved in the events that are narrated; the animals most used are the Leech, the Wolf, the Elephant, the Gryphon and the Crocodile. The most difficult task interpreting the *Sestet* is identifying the country or entity hidden in these animal symbols. The following criteria have been used to identify them:

(1) *Leech*

The Leech is a parasite which attaches itself to other animals or to humans in order to suck blood. It was first thought that the leech might refer to Arab countries, whose wells suck oil from the earth and could easily have appeared as enormous leeches in the eyes of a sixteenth-century man.

However, the context in which the leech was mentioned in the *Sestets* did not always fit in with this identification, so, another theory presented itself, one which was based on the notion that, with the term leech (blood sucker), the Seer meant a country which, in order to survive, was forced to resort to the resources of other countries. I immediately thought of post Soviet Russia, continually forced to ask help from the Western nations, in particular Germany and the United States, in order to repair its disastrous economic situation in some way.

In the quatrains, Nostradamus symbolises Russia with another animal: the bear *(Ours)* and no symbol could be more fitting, especially if you consider the perfectly similar assonance of the French between *Ours* and URSS (USSR). But the present-day Russia has undergone profound changes, and as a consequence, the animal might symbolise it now has to be changed.

This idea is confirmed in the events mentioned in the *Sestets,* and so the identification I am putting forward here appears to fit well.

(2) *Wolf*

It was generally thought that in the quatrains, the *wolf* indicated Hitler's Germany, which had all the characteristics of that ravenous animal. In the *Sestets* this word appears to be only partially correct. The wolf of the *Sestets*, in fact, represents Western, continental Europe, including Germany, obviously. The identification appears to fit, if one consider that the wolf is a cosmopolitan animal, present in every European country, so much so that there could not be an alternative symbol for the European Union, and all this not considering the fact that Germany, with its 90 million inhabitants and conspicuous economic potential, is undoubtedly the country of major importance within the European Union.

(3) *Elephant*

The size of the elephant might lead us to think of a huge country like Russia, China or India. In fact, this is a hidden symbol for the Arab countries, and in order to understand the relation between them and the Elephant, you must look in the Koran. According to the Koran, in AD 570 the Abyssinians invaded the Arabian Peninsula, and at the head of their army was an elephant. At that moment, in order to rescue the Arabs, God had sent down some huge birds which held in their claws large clots of dried clay with which they pelted the Abyssinian army from on high, causing it to flee. From that moment on, that year was called '*Year of the Elephant*', and it was precisely in that year that Mohammed was born. The sestets also use the name *elephant*, to symbolise the group of Arab countries who practise Islam.

(4) *Gryphon*

The *Gryphon* is a mythological beast, which, in Ancient Rome, attacked ships sailing in the Mediterranean on their way up the Adriatic. The *Gryphon* is said to have originated in Scythia, a region around the Black Sea. For two reasons, Turkey could be identified as the *Gryphon*: first of all, its geographic location, and secondly because, at the time of Nostradamus, the Ottoman Empire was the most powerful state in the world, and its ships, like the mythical *Gryphons*, attacked and looted those navigators who had the misfortune to encounter them.

However, another country could well be concealed behind the *Gryphon*, and that is the United States. It is well known that the animal symbol of the United States of America is the bald eagle, a rapacious bird as was the mythical *Gryphon*.

As for the context in which the *Gryphon* is mentioned in the *Sestets*, it does appear to be a bearing to the US. The US will have a determining role in future events and will be present from a certain point forward with its armed forces in the European theatre of war.

(5) *Crocodile*

This animal at first evoke thoughts of Egypt, in view of its proliferation in the Nile.

However, if we want to identify who is hidden in the symbol of the crocodile, we should look at the animal's temperament and its hunting technique. The crocodile is a crafty animal which camouflages itself by hiding in the mud. When the hapless prey passes within reach, the crocodile springs suddenly from the water, seizes it in its powerful jaws and drags it under water, causing it to die from drowning.

In the light of such characteristics and of the context in which it appears in the *Sestets*, the crocodile cannot but be identified with the Islamic terrorism. The terrorists, in fact, like the crocodile, camouflage themselves in the midst of the sea of humanity. They prepare their treacherous attempts and their traps in the shadow. They strike without warning and without giving their chosen victims the possibility of reacting or of defending themselves.

With this, all the animals present in the *Sestets* have now been identified, and you will see that this identification fits perfectly into the context of events narrated in them, and will be further confirmed by the quatrains, which refer to them through the use of other words.

8. Contemporary Events

The fall of The Berlin wall

Auant conflict le grand (mur) tombera,
Le grand à mort, mort trop subite et plainte
Nay imparfaict: la plus part nagera,
Aupres du fleuue de sang la terre tainte.

Before the conflict the great (wall) *shall fall,*
The great one too suddenly dead and unexpected tears,
Imperfectly born the greater part will swim,
Near the river, the earth drenched with blood.
                                    (Centuries II, quatrain 57)

In the edition of 1557 the word *mur* does not appear, while it is present in some subsequent editions. In my judgement, in this case, it is a simple oversight, since without the word *mur*, the line is no longer hendecasyllabic.

Once we have established this, the quatrain does not lend itself to any other interpretation. After the fall of the Berlin wall, whose end marks also the fall of the Soviet empire (*the 'great dead'*), desegregation comes too unexpectedly to allow the necessary time for reflection on the altered European situation. This makes many (the orthodox Communists) feel desperate. As a result of this new situation, a great conflict will come into being. While many ex-Communist countries will succeed in staying afloat and in directing themselves towards democracy without great bloodshed, war will break out in the Balkans, and near Bosnia, and the river of Sarajevo, the earth will be tinged with blood. After the fall of the Berlin wall, the crisis within the Communist system has certainly not spared the

Soviet Union: the dream of Gorbachev to guide the immense country towards a more democratic regime failed miserably, and as a consequence all activities of the Communist party after the attempted coup were suspended.

Centuries III, quatrain 95, is quite eloquent at this point:

> La loy Moricque on verra deffaillir,
> Apres une autre beaucoup plus seductiue:
> Boristhenes premier viendra faillir,
> Par dons et langue une plus attractiue:

> *The law of Moore will be dismantled,*
> *For another one more seductive.*
> *The first Boristenes* (Russia) *shall be ruined,*
> *For more attractive gifts and language.*
> *(Centuries III, quatrain 95)*

As other interpreters (as, for example Giorgi, *Nostradamus Revealed*, Milan, 1995) have indicated, with the term '*Moricque*' Nostradamus goes back to Thomas Moore, who lived between 1477 and 1535, and who in his '*Utopia*' professed the doctrine of *ante litteram*, a philosophical doctrine similar to Marxism.

The quatrain explains that the principles of Communism will bring ruin, for people will prefer the logic of capitalism in the style of Western democracies.

Russia is represented in the term '*Boristhenes*', which is the ancient name of the Dnieper river. American policy, initiated by Reagan, was that of granting conspicuous aid to the Soviet Union, and progressively softening its attitude by so doing. The Soviet economic situation, furthermore, would not have allowed for a prolonged continuation of the military challenge against the United States, and the decision by the American president to initiate the very costly project of the space shield brought home to Gorbachev the conviction that the moment had arrived for a change in policy. Events then followed one upon the other with increasing momentum.

The Balkan conflict

Laict, sang grenoilles escoudre en Dalmatie,
Conflict donné, peste pres de Balennes
Cry sera grand par toute Esclauonie,
Lors naistra monstre pres et dedans Rauenne.

Milk, blood, frogs flowing in Dalmatia,
Conflict, pestilence to nearby Balennes (Albania),
The shouting runs throughout Slavonia,
The show will be born at Ravenna, and nearby.
(Centuries II, quatrain 32)

Milk is indicative of wealth and the frogs people who have been abandoned. The quatrain, therefore, signifies that in Dalmatia there will be a war which will deplete resources and will bring bloodshed to a people already afflicted by grave problems. Near Albania such a misfortune will take place that the cry of suffering will be heard throughout Slavonia. On the part of the Italians there will be humanitarian initiatives – accurately – the Italo-Bosnian chamber of commerce will be founded in Ravenna. This will promote various demonstrations aimed at bringing about an awareness of the situation existing in the Balkan country.

Different meanings have been attributed to *'Balennes'*: by treating it as an anagram, I have transformed it into *Albennes* – Albania, which seems an appropriate meaning. But there is a second interpretation that could be attributed to it: Belgrade was founded by the Byzantines, and the name initially means *white city* (in Latin *Alba*), hence, with the term *Albennes* the Seer might also have meant the inhabitants of Belgrade. In any case, the quatrain's meaning does not alter, and it becomes more relevant than ever to the present times, with the bombardment that recently took place and the genocide perpetrated by the Serbs in Kossovo, whose minority is of Albanian origin.

Many interpreters have translated the word *'Monstre'* as *'Monster'*. However, in middle French *'Monstre'* meant primarily *show*, then *prodigy* (from the Latin *'monstrum'*, which means an out-of-the ordinary event). Then, figuratively, it carries the meaning of *military parade* (where soldiers put themselves on show) and only last that of *monster*.

It seems obvious in this instance that the Seer meant *show*; and the reference to Ravenna is not a casual one, since it is precisely in that city that the Italo-Bosnian chamber of commerce has its headquarters. In other parts of the Italian province of Emilia, there were initiatives aimed at awakening awareness of the problems in Bosnia, hence the prepositions *'near to'* and *'inside'* Ravenna.

The death of Princess Diana

Le penultiesme du surnom du Prophete,
Prendra Diane pour son jour et repos,
Loing vaguera par frenetique teste,
En deliurant un grand peuple d'impos.

The penultimate with the prophet's name,
Diana will have the day to rest,
Far will she wander with frantic head,
Delivering a great people from duty.
                    (Centuries II, quatrain 28)

Considerant la triste Philomelle,
Qu'en pleurs & cris sa peine renouuelle,
Racoursissant par tel moyen ses iours,
Six cens & cinq, elle en verra l'issue,
De son tourment, ia la toille tissue,
Par son moyen senestre aura secours.

> *Consider the sad Philomel,*
> *Who weeps and cries her pain anew,*
> *Thus shortening her days,*
> *Six hundred and five, will see the end*
> *Of her torment. Already the cloth is woven,*
> *By her means the hapless will be helped.*
>
> *(Sestet 18)*

Quatrain II, 28 represents and describes the death of Princess Diana and is a typical example of the difficulty involved in deciphering the quatrains. The first line is the object of the sentence, which we can read reads as follows: The penultimate day of Diana's life, a day she rested, was in the Christian calendar the feast day of a prophet – St John the Baptist – 29 August. Diana died tragically on 31 August. Her death is attributed to a '*frantic head*' with which she wanders far away. In fact, she died because the driver lost control of the car.

With her death, Diana freed a great people (the English people) from a sense of duty, that had divided public opinion, undecided between loyalty to the Crown and an intense empathy for Diana's vicissitudes.

Sestet 18 tells the same story, indicating the exact year. The year 1605* (of the Liturgy), as we have seen, is the year 1997, a date derived by adding 392 (the year of the *Breviary*) to 1605. In the sestet, Diana is compared to the unfortunate princess, protagonist of the sixth book of Ovid's *Metamorphoses*. Philomela was the daughter of Pandione, a noble gentleman from Athens, who had given his other daughter Progne in marriage to Tereus of Thrace, the tyrant, who, with his army, had subdued the barbarians who had been threatening Athens. At the request of his wife who desired to see her sister again, Tereus had gone to Athens to bring the princess Philomela back to Progne. When he saw the princess, Tereus lost his head completely. Having obtained consent from her, Tereus then brought Philomela aboard his ship, but, on reaching Thrace, instead of

---

* In French and Italian the thousand is frequently omitted when indicating a century, e.g. '900 for 1900.

accompanying her to the palace, he took her to a cabin in the woods and raped her. The woman cried out indignantly and threatened to broadcast his barbarism to the four winds. Upon this Tereus cut out her tongue with his sword and kept her prisoner. But Philomela began to weave a cloth on which she embroidered all her sad story and a maidservant brought the cloth to Progne, who thus was informed. Progne, taking advantage of the Bacchanalia, together with other women, went masquerading to the cabin and freed her sister, together with whom she plotted a horrible revenge. Progne, aided by Philomela, killed her own son, Iti, and cooked him up for Tereus, who in total ignorance, ate him. Only after he had finished, did Philomela reveal her presence to him, brandishing Iti's severed head. Tereus tried in vain to kill the two women, who transformed themselves into birds. And he himself was transformed into the lugubrious hoopoe.

Diana, like Philomela, maintained a rigid silence concerning her troubled marriage. In the end, weary of her own suffering and of keeping silent, she decided to reveal everything publicly through a long television interview, which took the world by storm ('*by now the cloth is woven*'), and after her separation from Prince Charles, she continued to pine away in her sufferings, earning for herself the title of '*Sad Princess*', thereby shortening her life, in view of the fact that her sufferings, having been made public, caused her to be persecuted by the press, so much so that it led to her death.

A further identification of Philomela with Diana, is that the Greek name Philomela literally means '*lover of music*'. Such, too, was the Goddess Diana (or Artemis), sister of Apollo, often portrayed in Hellenistic art with the lyre, the musical instrument with which Apollo accompanied his songs.

The death of Mother Theresa of Calcutta

Dame par mort grandement attristée,
Mere & tutrice au sang qui la quittée,
Dame & Seigneurs, faits enfans orphelins,

Par les aspics & par les crocodilles,
Seront surpris forts, Bourgs, Chasteaux, Villes,
Dieu tout puissant les garde des malins.

Lady greatly saddened by death,
Mother and guardian of the blood she left,
Ladies and Lords, the infants orphans made,
Through the crocodiles and serpents,
Strongholds, boroughs, castles, towns, will be surprised,
All powerful God, protect them from Evil.

(Sestet 35)

The death of Theresa of Calcutta, taking place in India, an exotic land *of serpents and crocodiles*, saddened each and every one, while the children whom she had assisted and saved from starvation and disease, were left orphans, having lost their mother. They, at this point, with Theresa dead, in a world full of perils (hence the significance of the parenthetical '*through serpents and crocodiles*'), find themselves only under the protection of God, whose saving hand the Seer invokes.

The revision of the History of the Church by John Paul II

Le temps present auecques le passé,
Sera jugé par grand Iouialiste,
Le monde tard par luy sera lassé,
Et desloyal par le clergé juriste.

Time present and time past
Are judged by the grand jovialist
Weary will be the world left by him
And disloyal through the jurist clergy.
(Centuries X, quatrain 73)

This is an obvious reference to the courageous revision of the past that the present pope is accomplishing at the present moment, by reviewing the position of the Church regarding its relationship with the Jews and criticising dark episodes from the past, such as the misdeeds of the Inquisition, the massacres of the Huguenots and Cathars.

The word '*Jovialist*' in this quatrain refers to Pope John's name *(Giovanni = Giove)* as well as his theological role, *(Jove – Giove)* substituting the term God. We can also find the same term used in a different sense in the letter to Henry. There it is used to indicate the followers of Antichrist, defined as '*Jovialists*', that is, people who will celebrate the new religion on Thursday *(jeudi)*.

Upon his death, the pope will leave behind a world weakened in its faith, due to modern times and saddened by hostility on the part of the clergy, who can barely tolerate the critical revision of the Church's history and traditional positions brought about by the Pontiff and which leans towards defending the past, using stratagems worthy of a lawyer *(jurist clergy)*.

And analogous traces of what is taking place in the sphere of the Church at the hands of John Paul II can be culled from the following sestet:

> Au grand siege encor grands forfaits,
> ecommançans plus que jamais,
> Six cens & cinq sur la verdure,
> La prise & reprise sera,
> Soldats és champs jusqu'en froidure,
> Puis apres recommencera.

> *To the great seat still greater facts,*
> *Will begin again more than ever.*
> *Six hundred and five, upon the green*
> *There will be capture and recapture,*
> *Soldiers in the fields as long as the cold will last,*
> *Then afterwards, all will begin again.*

(Sestet 14)

The year 605 is the year 1605 of the Liturgy, and consequently 1997 (1605 + 392). The first three lines are about the changes wished for by the Pope (*the great seat*), which have brought about great unease.

The remaining lines are about the wars of that year, breaking out in spring and continuing until winter (Africa, Kossovo, etc.), and they also make it possible to foresee that in the following year as well there was to be a resumption of the fighting, as did, in fact, take place.

The fall of Kohl

Six cens & six, six cens & neuf,
Un Chancellier gros comme un boeuf,
Vieux comme le Phoenix du monde,
En ce terroir plus ne luyra,
De la nef d'oubly passera,
Aux champs Elisiens faire ronde.

Six hundred and six, six hundred and nine
A Chancellor as huge as an ox,
As old as the Phoenix of the world,
In this territory will shine no more,
From the ship of oblivion he will pass
To the Elysian Fields to do the round dance.

(Sestet 25)

There is no doubt whatsoever as to the fact that the Sestet refers to Kohl. In fact, in the second line, the Seer describes the physical characteristic which correspond exactly to the dimensions of the ex-chancellor. In the third line there is an accurate reference to another characteristic of Kohl: his ability to succeed in having himself elected more than once when everyone had given up hope on him, just like the Phoenician Arab who was resurrected from his ashes. But the Phoenix of the world, as Nostradamus refers to him, using a figurative expression, can be nothing else but coal, which looks like compressed black ash, almost burnt wood, but which instead burns and yields heat and energy. At this juncture, then, there remains no doubt as to the identification of the personality, since *Kohle* in German means *coal*. The year 606 is the year 1606 of the Liturgy, and, therefore, 1998 (1606 + 392), the year which corresponds exactly to the year of the fall of Kohl, who as a consequence of not having been re-elected, will be gradually forgotten. In the last verse of the sestet, a reference to the Elysian Fields is made, the mythical paradise of the heroes, that could mean that Kohl would die in 2001 (year 1609 of the Liturgy). However, and in view of what actually happened early this year, it seems that the Seer meant that Kohl would visit a cemetery very often, from 2001. In this year, in fact, Kohl's wife tragically took her life, after enduring many years with a painful and incurable illness. It's well known that Kohl was very close to his departed wife and he might spend a lot of his time praying at her graveside.

The current situation in Italy

Romain pouuoir sera du tout à bas,
Son grand voisin imiter les vestiges:
Occultes haines civiles et debats,
Retarderont aux bouffons leurs folies.

Roman power will be completely at the bottom,
Will want to imitate its great neighbour's footsteps,
Secret civil hatred and quarrels,
Will delay the buffoons' lunacy.

(Centuries III, quatrain 63)

This quatrain eloquently reflects the present political situation in Italy. There was a project for constitutional reform based on the French model. But the lack of any sincere desire to collaborate, the hatred and grudges among the various political exponents, the useless discussions and endless debates brought about a paralysis of the intended reforms, and this, everything considered, turned out to be a blessing, since the projected constitutional reform, in the manner in which it was elaborated, would have resulted in a horrible juridical abortion, filled with incoherencies and contradictions, the fruit of compromises, contrived against the Italian people. The incapacity demonstrated by these men of politics in the formulation of serious constitutional reform earned them the Seer's cutting epithet.

The troublesome Palestinian question

Soubz l'opposite climat Babylonique,
Grande sera de sang effusion,
Que terre & mer, air, ciel sera inique,
Sectes, faim, regnes, pestes, confusion.

Under the skies of Babylon iniquities,
So great will be the flow of blood,
That land and sea, air, sky shall be barren,
Sects, starvation, reigns, pestilence, confusion.
(Centuries I, quatrain 55)

This quatrain appears to be so entirely clear that it has no particular need for commentary, except that to mention that Nostradamus often uses the term Babylon to indicate the Middle East.

Vladimir Putin's rise to power in Russia

As we have seen in the letter to Henry, the enigma of the 'Byzantine sails' made it possible to identify the Russian leader who, in the future may become the Antichrist's closest ally, that is, Vladimir Putin. Putin assumed power in Russia on 31 December 1999, following the Yeltsin's resignation, by then very fragile in health but, more importantly, involved in a severe financial scandal.

Sestet 21, in my judgement, treats of Putin.

L'autheur des maux commencera regner
En l'an six cens & sept sans espargner
Tous les subjets qui sont à la sangsue,
Et puis apres s'en viendra peu à peu,
Au franc pays r'allumer son feu,
S'en retournant d'où elle est issue.

The author of evils will begin his rule,
In six hundred and seven, without sparing
All the subjects who are born of the leech.
And then afterwards will come, little by little
To the free country to rekindle his fire
And returning whence she came.

(Sestet 21)

The year 607 is the year 1607 of the Liturgy and therefore the year 1999 (1607+392) and precisely on the last day of 1999 Putin began to 'reign in the Leech' as is clearly indicated in the sestet. The Seer describes Putin as 'the author of evils', since he is well aware of what should take place in the near future.

According to the Seer, the near future should hold in store for us is a military alliance between Russia and the Islamic countries, which would be unified under one leader.

Present-day Russia came into being as a result of the desegregation of the USSR, having reached a point where it was no longer capable of withstanding the challenge offered by the West's model. It may well be said, therefore, that Russia today was generated by the Western world, that *free country* that was the constant point of reference for the aspirations of people governed by Communist regimes.

Based on the interpretation I have given to the sestet, in the not so distant future, with the conflagration of a new and frightful war, Russia, under the leadership of Putin will progressively come to occupy the West, by then economically and militarily weakened.

Already towards the end of 1999, the first symptoms of a radical change were to be felt, and they grow in the years 2000–01. The vertiginous rise in the price of crude oil is seriously compromising Western economies, especially those countries without their own resources. The formation of two opposing blocks is progressing: on the one hand, the oil-producing countries, particularly those Islamic, and on the other hand, the industrialised consumer countries. *Sestet 23* appears to have some bearing on this:

> Quand la grand nef, la proue & gouuernal,
> Du franc pays & son esprit vital,
> D'escueils & flots par la mer secouée,
> Six cens & sept, & dix coeur assiegé
> Et de reflus de son corps affligé,
> Sa vie estant sur ce mal renouée.

> *When the great ship, with prow and rudder*
> *Of the free country and its vital spirit,*
> *With reefs and waves from the sea is tossed,*
> *Six hundred seven, and ten, the heart besieged,*
> *And from the outflow of its plagued body,*
> *Its spirit by this evil is renewed.*

> *(Sestet 23)*

The meaning of the sestet is as follows: the Western world, likened to an ungoverned ship, will be tossed about upon a stormy sea and flung upon the cliffs of war. This should be taking place between 1999 and 2010, a period during which the West will undergo such violent aggression that its very survival will be put into doubt (*coeur assiegé*). However, as a result of this very trying moment, there will come about a regeneration of humanity, on a moral as well as on a material plane, and humanity will be propelled in the direction of truth and justice.

As to what years the sestet is referring, it must be observed that while the year 607 is undoubtedly 1999 (1607 + 392), it is likely that the Seer is alluding to the year 2010 with the number 10, rather than to the year 2002, because between 607 and 10 there is a comma.

The beginning of an irreversible stock market crisis

Le Mercurial non de trop longue vie,
Six cens & huict & vingt, grand maladie,
Et encor pis danger de feu & de eau,
Son grand amy lors luy sera contraire,
De tels hazards se pourroit bien distraire,
Mais bref, le fer luy fera son tombeau.

The Mercurial (stock exchange) *will not live for long,*
Six hundred eight and twenty, the malady will strike it,
And still worse danger from fire and water,
Its great friend will then be contrary,
Such risks that could have been impeded,
But within little time, the sword (war) *will be its tomb.*
(Sestet 24)

Nostradamus uses the term '*Mercurial*' to mean the stock exchange, a term which in modern French also has the meaning of stock listings. At the time of the Seer '*Mercurial*' only meant *Mercury rod*; in view of this, the manner in which Nostradamus qualifies the stock exchange becomes astonishing. In 2000 the stock market would experience the beginning of an irreversible crisis, the first symptoms of which were felt in 1998, first through the collapse of the stock exchange in Asia and then through the Brazilian economic situation.

In fact, the year 2000 was not a positive one for the world stock markets and even less so was the year 2001, which has continued to experience a progressive decline in shares and a fall in the industrial and technological indexes. The tragedy of 11 September 2001 has triggered a severe financial crisis, with a dramatic plunge of the world stock market, showing once again how closely the financial market is related to political events. Furthermore, it is rather disconcerting how *Sestet 24* clearly indicates how the terrorist attacks *(feu)* and even more the war *(fer)*, may produce an irreversible crisis in the stock exchange, so much so that to the extreme consequence may be its ultimate demise.

This '*malady*' will persist for twelve years and then will worsen as result of war *(fire)* and devastating floods *(water)*. The world market, of which the stock exchange is the most significant expression *(the great friend)*, will no longer allow for commercial transactions or speculations, and those involved in heavy investments in stocks and reckless speculations will find themselves ruined.

Lastly, when the Third World War breaks out, the stock market will receive the '*coup de grace*' and will definitely cease to exist.

Analogous views are contained in *Centuries IV, quatrain 30.*

> Plus unze fois Luna Sol ne vouldra,
> Tous augmentés & baissés de degré:
> Et si bas mis que peu or on couldra,
> Qu'apres faim peste descouuert le secret.

> *More than eleven times Moon and Sun will not come*
> *Everything increased and lowered by degree,*
> *And so badly reduced that little gold will flow,*
> *Then famine, pestilence and the secret revealed.*
> *(Centuries IV, quatrain 30)*

The time span given in the sestet and the quatrain is identical. In the quatrain the Seer referes to the vertiginous rise in prices and to the loss of buying power that money will have.

Many interpreters have placed the quatrain chronologically at the end of the First or the Second World War, when there was galloping inflation in many countries. But the reference to the discovery of a secret seems to point to the near future. The secret of which the Seer is speaking could be the secret of his *Centuries*. In fact, as we saw in the commentary on the letter to his son César, Nostradamus first wrote his work in a '*non-coded*' way and then subsequently transformed it into verses, which were then assembled in a disorganised way and rendered obscure through applying all the techniques available in the '*green language*'.

His '*non-coded*' work will eventually be found and duly revealed: this will come about in the course of a great tribulation, when humanity will be afflicted by famine and overcome by radiation, as will be seen in the final part of this present work.

It also likely that *Sestet 53* treats of the market and of its final destiny.

> Plusieurs mourront auant que Phoenix meure,
> Jusques six cens septante est sa demeure,
> Passé quinze ans, vingt & un trente neuf.
> Le premier est subjet à maladie,
> Et le second au fer, danger de vie,
> Au feu à l'eau, est subject à trente-neuf.

> *Many will die before the Phoenix dies,*
> *Until six hundred and seventy is his house,*
> *After fifteen years, twenty, and a thirty nine,*
> *The first is subject to a malady,*
> *The second to the sword, vital danger,*
> *To fire, to water, is subject at thirty nine.*
>
> *(Sestet 53)*

Six hundred and seventy is 2062, and in that year the death of the '*Phoenix*' will take place. It should be emphasised that with this term, Nostradamus does not intend to refer to the mythical Phoenician Arab of Greek and Egyptian tradition, but rather to the commercial market of which the ancient Phoenicians were the great experts. The sum total of the three numbers in the sestet (15, 20, 39) is 74, and in subtracting this number from 2062, the year 1988 is obtained. That year, according to the Seer, should have witnessed the beginning of the crisis in the world markets, which have become progressively afflicted. And the period of its maladies will last until 2003 (1988 + 15). The subsequent twenty years will be desolated by war, and the second period of worsened conditions will terminate in 2023 (2003 + 20). But the war *(fire)* will not be over by then, and the market will still be subject to it. Then natural cataclysms with rain and floods *(water)* will intervene, all of which will finish off whatever commerce there is on a global level, with the consequent demise of the market itself: those who dispose of resources will jealously want to hold on to them, because the consequences of the war and of natural events will have brought about such a scarcity all commercial activities will be paralysed.

The electoral conflict between George Bush and Al Gore

The disconcerting result of the presidential elections in the US, where the difference between the two candidates in the decisive State of Florida amounted to a few hundred votes, gave rise to judicial appeals by both parties and to a deep rift in the electorate, with protests which seemed destined to last for quite some time coming from both sides.

Sestet 12 in my judgement could have something to do with this:

> Six cens & cinq tres grand nouuelle,
> De deux Seigneurs la grand querelle,
> Proche de Genaudan sera,
> A une Eglise apres l'offrande
> Meurtre commis, prestre demande
> Tremblant de peur se sauuera.
>
> *(Sestet 12)*

Before offering a translation of the sestet, some clarification appears to be necessary, for text presents a few difficulties, which are indeed unusual, since the sestets are normally quite easy to read. The first line would seem to be indicating the year 1997 (1605+392) with the word *tres* being superlative of *grand* (great). So, the whole line would mean: *'1997, very great news'*.

However, the lack of a comma after the word *cinq* and the

absence altogether of a dash between *tres* and *grand* may mean that the *tres* belong to the first number, so the line could be interpreted as '*605+3, great news*'. In which case, he would be referring to the year 2000 (the sum of 1605+3+392). The third line seems to allude to a particular locality: *Genaudan*, which is non existent. The few interpreters who have examined the sestets have translated *Genaudan* as *Gevaudan*, a township of France. But, *Genaudan* could well be an anagram. It could be transformed into 'age d'un an' *(aged one)* or, perhaps more likely, '*age d'an un*', *(the epoch of year one)*. Thus the entire line would mean '*it will be around the year 2001*'. The sestet could then be translated as follows:

> The year two thousand, great news,
> The great conflict between the two gentlemen,
> Will take place near the year two thousand and one,
> In a church, after the offertory,
> Murder will be committed, and the praying priest
> Trembling with fear will be saved.

So, according to this interpretation, while the electoral battle is carried on between the republican and democratic candidates for the presidency of the US, a murder would take place in a church. And in fact on Christmas eve a bloody terrorist attempt was carried out in a handful of Catholic churches in Djakarta and Sumatra, with numerous victims.

Almost, at the same time, Bush prevailed in his electoral and judicial duel against Al Gore, who on 15 December 2000 finally conceded victory to his opponent.

Islamic terrorist attacks

Already in 2000 numerous terrorist acts took place in a number of countries, not to speak of frequent and bloody massacres, such as in Algeria, and these acts will continue for a long time and they will intensify with the advent of Hadrie.

And on the 13 October 2000 precisely, there was, outside

the port, of Aden a bloody terrorist attack on a ship belonging
to the US Navy, the USS *Cole*, an attack that resulted in the
death and wounding of numerous navy personnel.

It is to this attack that *Sestet 29*, in my judgement, is
referring:

> Le Griffon se peut aprester
> Pour à l'ennemy resister,
> Et renforcer bien son armée,
> Autrement l'Elephant viendra,
> Qui d'un abord le surprendra,
> Six cens & huict, mer enflammée.

> *Now the Gryphon can prepare itself*
> *To go against his great enemy,*
> *And well strengthen his army,*
> *Otherwise the elephant will come,*
> *And all of a sudden will surprise him,*
> *Six hundred and eight, the sea is aflame.*
>
> *(Sestet 29)*

Let us begin in our commentary with the last line *'Six hundred
and eight the sea is aflame'*. Six hundred and eight is, in fact,
the year 2000 (1608+392) and the attack came about exactly
in that year, while similar episodes do not appear to have taken
place during the course of it. The Gryphon, as we saw earlier
in the commentary on the animals used in the sestets, represents
the United States, while behind the symbol of the Elephant
are concealed the Islamic countries. The sestet is, therefore,
putting the USA on alert regarding the danger it faces. The
Islamic army will arrive and will take it by surprise, just
as the US was taken by surprise by the twofold event of
11 September 2001, and, according to Nostradamus, it will
also be by the outbreak of the Third World War, set in motion
by an unexpected attack on the White House and the death of
the American President.

The 2000 attack was just the prologue of the much more
terrible one of 11 September 2001.

De coup de fer le monde estonné,
Par Crocodril estrangement donné,
A un bien grand, parent de la sangsue,
Et peu apres sera un autre coup
De guet à pens, commis contre le loup,
Et de tels faits on ne verra l'issue.

By blow of iron in a disconcerted world,
By the crocodile strangely given,
To a great one, a nearby leech,
And shortly after, another blow
Against the wolf, extremely unexpected,
Of all this we shall not see the outcome.

(Sestet 45)

The contents of the sestet are unequivocal, and confirm the correctness of the interpretation of 'C*rocodile*' as terrorism. Two grave attempts will occur in the world ('*blow of iron*'): one against the United States (the '*very great one*', great enough to have territory very close to Russia), and a country belonging to the European Union, probably Germany, will unexpectedly be struck. These bloody attempts will cause discord on the world scene, and the underlying goal will not be understood. These attempts will be the premonitory symptoms of the great religious revolution that will involve the whole of the Middle East. (The above was written in the first Italian edition of this book and unfortunately, as far the United States are concerned, the prophecy was fulfilled on 11 September 2001).

The destruction of the World Trade Centre in New York is also dealt with uncanny precision by another quatrain.

Ennosigée feu du centre de terre,
Fera trembler au tour de cité neufe:
Deux grands rochiers long temps feront la guerre,
Puis Arethuse rougira nouueau fleuue.

> *Sea of fire at the World Centre,*
> *The tower of the new city will tremble:*
> *Two great rocks will be at war for a long time,*
> *Then Arethusa will redden a new river.*
>
> *(Centuries I, quatrain 87)*

Enosigen was an alias for Poseidon (*the shaker*), hence the translation of *sea*.

Centre de Terre is the French translation of World Centre. The reference to the tower(s) of a 'new city' is basically textual. The Seer advises us that the tragic event will have as a consequence a long conflict between two blocks (*great rocks*), being thus the first skirmish of that World War widely described in so many quatrains and in almost half of the sestets.

The last line is not readily understood. Arethusa was a nymph who while diving in the waters of a river, was attacked by an evil entity living there. She cried for help to Diana, who transformed her into a pure spring. On the basis of the mythological reference, the subject of the line is the new river, that will attack Arethusa reddening the waters with blood. That could mean that an evil entity will redden with blood the clear waters of innocent humanity, of elderly people, children and women indiscriminately, according to Nostradamus, massacred.

But also France will find itself a victim of the wave of Islamic terrorism.

> Celuy qui a les hazards surmonté,
> Qui fer, feu, eaue, n'a jamais redouté,
> Et du pays bien proche du Basacle,
> D'un coup de fer tout le monde estonné,
> Par Crocodil estrangement donné,
> Peuple raui de veoir un tel spectacle:
>
> *He who has always ridden the hazards*
> *And never, iron, fire, water has feared*
> *From a neighbour of the Basacle* (French country),

With a blow of iron in a disconcerted world,
By the crocodile suddenly given,
And people shocked by such a spectacle.

(Sestina 31)

This sestet foresees the Antichrist, the person who 'ride the hazards and doesn't fear the war', will bring death into the Basacle region by means of terrorism. The term of Basacle, I believe refers to the Bazacle canal, that in the sixteenth century was actually called Basacle (mentioned also in Rabelais's *Gargantua and Pantagruel*). The navigable canal is situated near Toulouse. Hence the sestet refers to a city that will be victim of an attack.

A few days after the 11 September events, a terrific explosion rocked an industrial area of this town causing 30 deaths and more than 2,000 wounded.

The French authorities were inclined to believe it was an accident. However, a French minister suggested the possibility of a terrorist attack, because, among the bodies, a locally well-known Islamic fundamentalist was found. Allegedly, he was still wearing what looked like the characteristic uniform of the suicide bombers.

Islamic terrorism is well described by Sestet 19:

Six cens & cinq, six cens & six & sept,
Nous monstrera jusques à l'an dix sept,
Du boutefeu l'ire, hayne & enuie,
Soubz l'oliuier d'assez long tems caché,
Le Crocodril sur la terre acaché,
Ce qui estoit mort, sera pour lors en vie.

Six hundred and five, six hundred and six and seven,
Will show to us until the year seventeen
The wrath, the hatred and the envy of the firebrand,
Long concealed under the olive tree,
The crocodile crouching on the ground,
What was dead will now to return life.

(Sestet 19)

The presence of the first three figures signifies the years 1997, 1998, 1999, which derive from the years 1605, 1606, 1607 of the Liturgy, and the addition of the number 392, as already demonstrated.

The second line, on the other hand, refers to the year '17' rather than to the year 617, which points to 2017 and not 2009 (1617 + 392).

The Crocodile to which the sestet refers, in this context, also represents the terrorism of the Islamic fundamentalists, a kind of armed and unstoppable wing of the Antichrist, dedicated to massacres and acts of violence. Islamic fundamentalism, which for many years had not been in the limelight and had been considered a relic of the past, once more in 1997 and 1998, became active in a truly bloodthirsty manner, particularly with the repeated slaughter of innocent victims in Algeria, but also in other parts of the Arab world, Egypt, for example. In 1999 it resumed its bloody course, and according to the sestet, it will continue until 2017.

Until a few years ago, fundamentalism kept itself hidden behind an apparent pacifism (*the olive*) only to break loose in the last few years. According to Nostradamus, it will make a firebrand of its anger against the Western world, its hatred towards Christians and its envy towards the more flourishing European and American economic situation. The date of 2017 should mark the end of this state of affairs and the disappearance of fundamentalism.

As we shall see later in this book, the Third World War will be divided into two distinct periods of warfare. The first will occur between 2006 and 2017 and the second between 2022 and the 2 June 2025.

This emerges in the letter to Henry already examined, where in passage CXIV he wrote: '. . . *The persecution of the people of the Church will stem from the power of the Islamic kings of united with the people from the East* (Russia and China). *And this persecution will last for eleven years, more or less, when the principal king of the league will fall, and those years having been completed, his ally from the south will survive*

*and for three years will persecute the people of the Church
even more cruelly . . .'*

As we have already seen, war should break out into 2006.
Consequently, if its first phase (which should conclude, as the
letter to Henry prophesies, with the defeat of the Islamic people
and the annihilation of Russia) is to last eleven years, then the
date 2017 indicated in the sestet appears to be correct, because
in that year the *'Crocodile'* will finish waving its firebrand of
wrath, hatred and envy and will definitely be dead.

The Antichrist

Between the end of 1999 and 2000 the Middle East witnessed
a change in government in three Arab States.

In February 1999 Jordan's King Hussein died and his son
Abdullah II now sits on the Hashemite throne.

In July 1999 King Hassan II of Morocco died and was
succeeded by his young son Mohammed VI.

In June 2000 Syrian President Hafez Al Assad died and his
son Bashar Al Assad took over the reins, following a plebiscite.

On the basis of Nostradamus's letter to Henry and what will
emerge from the quatrains still to be examined, the Antichrist
will be of Islamic origin and will be a powerful and capable
leader, a catalyst for all the evils and the violence that now
afflict our planet.

His advent is prophesied in *Centuries I, quatrain 84*:

> Lune obscurcie aux profondes tenebres,
> Son frere passe de couleur ferrugine,
> Le grand caché long temps soubs le tenebres,
> Tiedera fer dans la playe sanguine.

> *Moon obscured by deep shadows,*
> *Its brother changes to the colour of iron,*
> *The great one, for long concealed in the shadow,*
> *Will cool the sword in the bleeding wound.*
>
> *(Centuries I, quatrain 84)*

The now imperfect reign of the Moon, that is, the present political system and the current way of life, will go into a profound crisis, while the Sun is acquiring the threatening colour of Mars, presaging the imminence of war.

The Demon, having remained wrapped in obscurity, will then reveal himself, setting off his terrible and long-lasting war.

In this quatrain the Seer describes the events that are in store for us: the irreversible crisis of present-day society, the beginning of a long period of war, the rise of the Antichrist, creature of the demon.

The quatrain is contained in the first *Centuries* in which the Seer does not dedicate much space to the events of the present moment.

In the last three *Centuries*, the Seer is more precise in determining the moment in which the Antichrist with his Evil nature will make his appearance.

> L'an mil neuf cens nonante neuf sept mois,
> Du ciel viendra un grand Roy deffrayeur,
> Resusciter le grand Roy d'Angolmois,
> Auant apres Mars regner par bonheur.

> *The year one thousand nine hundred ninety nine seven months,*
> *A great king of terror will come from the sky,*
> *Who will resurrect the great king of Angoulême,*
> *Mars* (war) *before and after will reign with favour.*
>
> (*Centuries X, quatrain 72*)

Quatrain X, 72 is probably the best known, and in 1999 it caused rivers of ink to flow in newspapers throughout the world. Everyone, in fact, awaited the coming in July of the grand king of terror: instead, nothing happened.

This once more is a demonstration of how difficult it is to interpret the verses of the Seer, although they look as though they can be readily understood. To understand the meaning of this quatrain, we must refer to what Nostradamus writes in his letter to Henry regarding the advent of the Antichrist: *'And there will precede a solar eclipse, the darkest and most tenebrous that has ever been since the creation of the world up to the death and the passion of Jesus Christ'*.

As we know, an eclipse took place on 11 August 1999 and in the Middle East it was total, long lasting and dark. This took place in the year 1999 and occurred a few days after the seven months were up. The first line, then, referred to an eclipse as an astronomical phenomenon which preceded the coming of the grand king of terror, after which war (*Mars*) would *reign with favour*. So, we must look at what personalities came into the limelight in the Middle-Eastern world after the solar eclipse of August 1999: Jordan's Hussein died in February 1999 and Hassan of Morocco in July of that same year. Therefore, the only new head of an Islamic nation coming to power after the August eclipse was the youthful Syrian president, Bashar Al Assad, called upon on 17 July 2000 to carry out the seven-year mandate at the highest level of power.

Taking into account the month in which President Bashar rose to power (July), if the quatrain in question is referring to him, it could assume a different interpretation: *'The year 1999, seven months'* could have the meaning *'the year 1999 having passed and a further seven months'*, which would bring us to July 2000.

Putting aside this hypothesis, which is tentative since it identifies a biblical figure with one existing today, it appears certain that the Antichrist will be capable of arousing great enthusiasm and of gathering great masses around him, as can be gathered from *Sestet 16*:

> En Octobre six cens & cinq,
> Pouruoyeur du monstre marin,
> Prendra du souuerain le cresme,
> Ou en six cens & six, en Juin,
> Grand'ioye aux grands & au commun,
> Grands faits apres ce grand baptesme.

> *In October of the year six hundred and five,*
> *The purveyor of the sea monster,*
> *Will take the sacrament from his sovereign,*
> *Or in the month of June of six hundred and six,*
> *Great joy for the great and the common people,*
> *Great acts after this grand baptism.*
>
> (Sestet 16)

Six hundred and five is the year 1997 (1605+392). Therefore, the delegate of the marine monster, which is, the beast of the earth, and therefore the Antichrist, has already had its investiture on the part of its sovereign. The date of October 1997 lends itself to a double interpretation: it might mean a solemn investiture on the part of the forces of evil (the demon) and could therefore have a mystical-esoteric significance, but it might also be simply pointing to the fact that at that date 'the purveyor of the marine monster' was still not reigning and had a sovereign, who, in delegating important political tasks to him, was training him in the difficult art of governing. Analogously, the date of June 1998, apart from referring to the joy shown by the satanic sects for the future coming, could instead be indicating a political event allied to the work of 'the purveyor of the marine monster', who having well acquitted himself well of the tasks entrusted to him, has proved capable of carrying on in governing his country, thus bringing a sigh of relief to those who nurtured fears about his capacities, that is, the dignitaries of State (*grands*) and the people (*commun*).

On the other hand, numerous medieval and even modern mystics prophesied the arrival of the Antichrist in this period. Let us look at an extract from the perspicuous and well documented work of Massimo Centini dedicated to the Antichrist:

Saint Hildegarde of Bingen, a Benedictine of Rupertsberg in Germany, prophesied many facts concerning the future. She also provided some details on the Antichrist. In his work Scivias wrote: 'the world had just gone past the threshold of the sixth age and was entering the seventh, which is that which precedes the last day'; in that period the Antichrist, 'will descend among men when on the throne of Peter will be seated a pope who will assume the name of two apostles of Jesus . . . It will be the angel of rebellion who will cause fiery sparks to rain down from the sky'.

The reference to Pope John Paul appears evident, the same way in which the time indicated appears to coincide, and that is, the end of the sixth millennium and the beginning of the seventh. We noted in an earlier chapter, that between the creation of Adam and the birth of Jesus 4001 years passed, consequently in 1999, according to the biblical chronology (not to be confused with Nostradamus's chronology), the sixth millennium ended and the seventh began.

Also the Nun of Dresden, living a the time of the seventeenth and eighteenth centuries, had foreseen the advent of the Antichrist in her letters to the Pope and to the regents of the period. The passage of interest here, quoted by Centini, is as follows:

There will come a time when the voice will fly. And men will speak among themselves across the seas and mountains. Again there will come a time when images will fly. And men will be able to see one another across the seas and mountains. Between 1940 and 2010 Lucifer will transfer his duke to the earth. And on the earth the satanic hierarchy will dominate, led by a demon that will speak the language of Attila but dressed in Caesar's clothes . . . This will be the reign of the great pestilence. This will be the forest of iniquity.

Centini's work also provided information on Sister Bertina Bouquillon, who died in 1850. She wrote:

The end of time is near, and the Antichrist will not delay in coming. We will not see him, neither will the nuns who will follow us, but those who will come after them will fall under his dominion. Nothing will be changed at home when he comes: everything will be found in its habitual order, the religious exercises, the duties in the corridors, will carry on as usual, when our sisters will come to know that the Antichrist is master.

In these prophecies as well, the period foreseen for the appearance of the Antichrist is established as being around 2000, since between Sister Bertina and her fellow sisters who were to fall under the dominion of the wicked being, it is a question of three lifetimes and, therefore, at least 150 years.

Nostradamus describes the Antichrist's personality in *Centuries X, quatrain 10*:

Tasché de murdre, enormes adulteres,
Grand ennemy de tout le genre humain,
Que sera pire qu'ayeuls oncles ne peres,
En fer, feu, eau, sanguin et inhumain.

Tainted with murder, immense adulterer,
Great enemy of the whole of mankind,
Who will be worse than grandfathers, uncles and fathers,
By sword, fire, water, blood and inhumanity.

(*Centuries X, quatrain 10*)

The description by the Seer needs few comments: no one worse than the personality of which it speaks has ever walked the face of the earth, a personality for whom murder and massacre will be the order of the day, so much so that he will surpass in cruelty all the inhumane and bloodthirsty characters who have preceded him.

Even more explicit in portraying this personality and the cruelties that the Antichrist will perpetuate is *Centuries IX, quatrain 17*.

Le tiers premier pis que ne feit Neron,
Vuidez vaillant que sang humain respandre,
Redifier fera le forneron,
Siecle d'or mort, nouueau roy grand esclandre.

The third worse than the first, worse than Nero,
Behold how much blood he will shed,
He will rebuild the furnace,
The golden century dead, new king great disaster.
                                    (Centuries IX, quatrain 17)

As we have seen, for Nostradamus, the Antichrists in the history of mankind are three: Nero, Communism and the one who is yet to come and who will be worse than all his predecessors.

The Seer invites the world not to lose courage, despite the slaughters, which will be committed, slaughter that will culminate in the building of cremation furnaces. We have seen in the letter to Henry that Nostradamus, in speaking of Nazism, Germany and of Second World War, twice referred to the Holocaust, indicating it as the principal reason for which Communism was able to enjoy an expansion, by exploiting the reactions and the anxiety among people confronting such horrendous crimes. In this quatrain, the Seer warns that the Antichrist will rebuild the furnaces, and with this he leaves the clear impression of the horrendous crimes which will be committed.

Numerous interpreters have been convinced that they identified Hitler as being the personality described, but such an identification appears to be manifestly wrong: in the first place, because, as from the letter to Henry shows, the *second* Antichrist was Communism, which, after Yalta was able to spread in large areas of the world; in the meantime, the third, who is yet to come, will remain in power for twenty-five years, power which Hitler did not maintain for such an extended period of time; secondly, the Seer, in referring to the furnaces, uses the term '*redifier*', that is, '*to rebuild*', and with this seems clear that it treats of a *second* time in which furnaces will be used for cremation.

9. Dark forebodings for the new millennium

In numerous quatrains and sestets, Nostradamus sombrely exposes what will happen in the new millennium. In view of the closeness of the beginning of the third millennium of the Christian era (2000) to the end of the seventh millennium of his particular chronology (2004), that, too, is included.

> Faulx à l'estan, ioincte vers le Sagitaire,
> Et son hault AUGE de l'exaltation,
> Peste, famine, mort de main militaire,
> Le siecle approche de renouation.

> *Saturn in Aquarius and others towards Sagittarius,*
> *At its highest summit of exaltation,*
> *Pestilence, famine, death by military hands,*
> *The century nears renewal.*
> *(Centuries I, quatrain 16)*

> Apres grand troche humain plus grand s'apreste,
> Le grand mouteur les siecles renouuelle:
> Pluye, sang, laict, famine, fer et peste,
> Au ciel fer, courant longue estincelle.

> *After great human massacre, a still greater comes,*
> *The centuries renew the great motor,*
> *Rain, blood, milk, famine, sword and plague,*
> *In the sky sword and long rivers of flame.*
> *(Centuries II, quatrains 46)*

The contents of the two quatrains are fairly analogous: they foresee a great upheaval at the beginning of the new millennium. The second millennium has ended, and the great motor which causes the earth to move, on the basis of whose revolutions around the sun are calculated years and Centuries, starts once more to traverse the long millennary period, which will be terrible: there will be massacres (blood), deteriorating wealth and resources (milk), starvation and scarcity, epidemics due to plagues or radiation, war among armies (death by military hands).

The astral combination to which *Centuries I, quatrain 16* refers, even though it is difficult to interpret, especially in the French text, should be that of 1 January 1992, with Saturn in Aquarius, Mercury, Venus and Mars in Sagittarius.

The contents of *Centuries V, quatrain 32* are similar, Nostradamus refers to the wealthier countries of the earth:

> Où tout bon est, tout bien Soleil et Lune,
> Est abondant, sa ruine s'approche:
> Du ciel s'aduance de vaner ta fortune
> En mesme estat que la septiesme roche.

> *Where all is well, and good with Sun and Moon,*
> *Where there is abundance, its ruin draws near:*
> *The sky advances, winnowing your fortune,*
> *In the same way as with seventh rock.*
> *(Centuries V, quatrain 32)*

In the wealthier and well-governed countries, monarchies *(Sun)* as well as Republics *(Moon)* ruin approaches. The Antichrist advances, to destroy everything and reduce the world to the state described by John after the opening of the seventh seal. The Seer uses the term '*roche*', that is '*rock*,' but the reference to the seventh seal appears obvious: in the work of John, each seal is a severe blow against impious mankind, almost the launching of a powerful rock in the form of a punishment.

The opening of the seventh seal, triggers off the last act of the human drama:

And when he had opened the seventh seal, there was silence in heaven about the space of half an hour.

And I saw the seven angels which stood before God; and to them were given seven trumpets.

And another angel came and stood at the altar, having a golden censer; and there was given unto him much incense, that he should offer it the prayers of all saints, upon the golden altar which was before the throne.

And the smoke of the incense, which came with the prayers of the saints, ascended up before God out of the angel's hand.

And the angel took the censer, and filled it with fire of the altar, and cast, it into the earth: and there were voices, and thundering and lightings, and an earthquake.

And the seven angels who had the seven trumpets prepared themselves to sound.

The first angel sounded, and there followed hail and fire mingled with blood, and they were cast upon the earth: and the third part of trees was burnt up, and all green grass was burnt up.

And the second angel sounded, and as it were a great mountain burning with fire was cast into the sea: and the third part of the sea became blood; and the third part of the creatures which were in the sea, and had life, died; and the third part of the ships were destroyed.

And the third angel sounded, and there fell a great star from heaven, burning as it were a lamp, and it fell upon the third part of the rivers, and upon the fountains of waters;

And the name of the star is called Wormwood: and the third part of the waters became wormwood; and many men died of the waters because they were made bitter.

And the fourth angel sounded, and the third part of the moon, and the third part of the stars; so as the third part of them was darkened, and the day shone not for a third part of it, and the night likewise.

(Revelations, 8: 1,1)

It the light of the contents of the quatrain, it does seem that
'*seventh rock*' is intended to refer to the seventh seal as in the
Apocalypse.

Even gloomier are the forebodings of *Sestet 27.*
Celeste feu du costé d'Occident,
et du Midy, courir jusques au Leuant,
Vers demy morts sans point trouuer racine,
Troisiesme aage, à Mars le Belliqueux,
Des Escarboucles on verra briller feux,
Aage Escarboucle, & à la fin famine.

Fire in the heavens from the West coast,
From the south, running right across to the Levant,
Towards the half-dead, without finding any root.
Third age (millennium): *to Mars the warlike,*
Flaming rubies will be seen sparkling with fire,
The age of the ruby and finally famine.

(Sestet 27)

The third millennium will be characterised by terrible war,
which will continue, even after a great part of the world's
population has perished. After the protracted period of war
(the age of the ruby, which in the language of the alchemists
represents the violence of the passions), there will follow a
long famine, brought about by the scarcity of food, due to the
fact that a great part of the earth will be contaminated by
radiation and the animal species will be almost extinct.

With this in mind, the contents of *Centuries I, quatrain 67*
are by no means encouraging:

La grand famine que je sens approcher,
Souuent tourner, puis estre uniuerselle.
Si grande et longue qu'on viendra arracher,
Du bois racine, et l'enfant de mammelle.

The great famine whose coming I sense,
Will return often, and then will become worldwide,
So great and lasting that from the woods
Roots will be torn, and infants from the breast.
                                    (Centuries I, quatrain 67)

From Nostradamus's day, plague and famine have always haunted the world, but until now there has existed a clear differentiation between wealthy countries and poor ones. The Seer, however, foresees that, within a brief time, starvation will become universal, without distinction as to country, people or continent: this will be the direct consequence of the Third World War, which is at our door, preceded by epochal changes, as are prophesied in *Centuries I, quatrain 56*.

Vous verres tost et tard faire grands change,
Horreurs extremes et vindications:
Que si la Lune conduicte par son Ange,
Le Ciel s'approche des inclinations.

You will see, sooner or later, everything change,
Extreme horror, and vengeance:
That if the moon be led by its Angel,
Heaven approaches its inclinations.
                                    (Centuries I, quatrain 56)

With this quatrain the Seer synthesises what has already happened and what is to happen. Just the mere thought of the French revolution, of the two world wars, of the advent of Communism allows us to realise the many changes that have been undergone by states and political establishments since his time. Up to this point the real imperfect world, personified by the moon, has been guided by the Church (the Angel), which has continuously summoned mankind to observe the moral principles and those of tolerance. But such a function is by now on the verge of exhausting itself: the time is drawing near in which the coming upheavals will be such that the world will ultimately emerge completely altered.

10. Trouble ahead for the Catholic church

Before continuing along the course of the future, I would like to digress by looking at the future of the Catholic church, whose fate Nostradamus particularly took to heart, because, notwithstanding the errors it has committed throughout the centuries, the Seer saw it as mankind's purifier with its continued reminder to moral and spiritual values.

Beginning with Malachia's 'Prophetia de Summis Pontificibus' and John Paul II 'De labore Solis' (that is, The Labour of the Sun, which according to the Ptolemaic system, rotated around the earth as does the actual pontiff, visiting, in his apostolate, various countries of the world), there will follow only two other pontiffs, and these will be the 'De gloria ulivi' and the 'Petrus Romanus'.

As we shall later the last pope will be captured on the sea by Arabs, while he is attempting to escape, and this will take place at the outbreak of the Third World War, in the year 2006.

From 2001, therefore, only five years remain until the 'succumbing by sea of the Reign of the Church', and during these five years, there will be three popes: the present one, John Paul II, the 'De gloria ulivi' and the 'Petrus Romanus'.

Having established this premise, we can now examine the relevant quatrains:

> Pol mensolee mourra trois lieües du Rosne,
> Fuis les deux prochains tarasc des trois:
> Car Mars fera le plus horrible trosne,
> De coq & d'aigle de France freres trois.

Pol, the sun-man (or *the keystone*), *will die at three leagues
    from the Rhône,
Having fled the first two Tarascons* (attacks) *of three:
For Mars will make the most horrible Throne* (angel),
Of cock and eagle of France three brothers.

(*Centuries VIII, quatrain 46*)

This quatrain needs vital clarification.

The expression '*Pol mensolee*', in the French text, should identify the present pontiff, as numerous other interpreters believe and such an identification appears to be correct, since it hints at the origin of the Pope (*Pol* possibly signifies Polish), and his main characteristic (i.e. that of carrying out his pastoral visits in all parts of the world, as did the Ptolomaic sun in its revolutions around the Earth). An alternative interpretation for 'mensolee' could be that of *keystone* – as the person who holds all the Church intact, without whom the edifice would collapse.

An interpretation of the second line depends on the meaning of the mysterious word '*tarasc*,' unknown in middle French. It could refer to citizen of Tarascon (near the Rhône). It might be a word borrowed from the classic Greek '*taraxis*', which means, *shaking, agitation, tumult,* or finally '*upset stomach*'.

During the Pope's reign, two attempts have been made on his life: the well-known one by Alì Agcà, the lesser known one which took place in Manila during one of his pastoral visits, and which was fortunately thwarted.

The term '*tarasc*', then, might mean 'terrorist attack' and the line would mean that the Pope, after having escaped two attacks, would be the victim of a third, which will be fatal. It might also refer to the fact that the Pope has twice undergone intestinal surgery (the first as a consequence of the attempt by Agcà, the second because of a polyp), and will find himself forced to undergo a third operation in Lyon, where one of the most famous European clinics for the cure of tumours exists, and that this operation will be fatal.

The fact, however, that John Paul II will die 'two leagues from the Rhône'.

The meaning of '*trosne*', in the third line, again causes

problems. In middle French it means 'thrones'. However, 'thrones' are a rank of angels. Angels are the foundation of the Kingdom of God, and the word was used in ecclesiastical language in this sense and this appears to be the one it is intended in this line. Also that the fourth line refers to more than one person (*three brothers*).

If this is the correct interpretation, then the verse now has a precise meaning: with the death of John Paul II, the winds of war will begin to blow (*Mars*), and in that future war, the angels, who will save mankind and lead the Western world to victory and to a new civilisation, will be three brothers, who figure in the letter to Henry. They are Henry himself, the Gallic '*Ogmion*', and the Roman king, referred to in '*Centuries*' V, Q. 13, about whom, more later. Of these brothers, two will be ecclesiastics, and this should not be surprising, since the war of religion, which will be unleashed by the Antichrist, will lead to a return of the Crusades, and the ecclesiastics themselves will be part of a militant Church.

This is clearly expressed in *Sestet 26.*

> Deux freres sont de l'ordre Ecclesiastique,
> Dont l'un prendra pour la France la picque,
> Encor un coup si l'an six cens & six
> N'est affligé d'une grande maladie,
> Les armes en main jusques six cens & dix,
> Gueres plus loing ne s'estendant sa vie.

> *Two brothers are of the ecclesiastical order,*
> *One for France will take the pike,*
> *Once more a blow, if the year six hundred six,*
> *Will not be afflicted by a great malady,*
> *Arms in hand until six and ten,*
> *Scarcely longer than this will his life last.*
>
> (Sestet 26)

This sestet is obviously referring to two of the three brothers in *Quatrain 46* and in the letter to Henry, since the verse takes this for granted, with a mere mention. In the near future, one of them with weapons in hand will defend France. In the meantime, 1998 (1606+392) has gone by without particular affliction. But in the following year, and definitely until 2002 (1610 + 392) a situation will evolve in which France will be forced to remain on the alert with weapons at the ready. War will not yet have broken out, seeing that this will come about between December 2005 and January of 2006. But the situation will be one of extreme tension, and when war eventually breaks out, France will come to ruin, for, as we have already seen in the letter to Henry, a great part of its territory will be under occupation by Muslims, and this now clarifies the last line 'Scarcely longer than this will his life last'.

The moment of John Paul II's death can be guessed quite closely by comparing *Centuries II, quatrain 97* and *Sestet 44*:

Romain Pontife garde de t'approcher,
De la cité qui deux fleuues arrose,
Ton sang viendras aupres de la cracher,
Toy & les tiens quand fleurira la rose.

Roman Pope woe if you approach,
That city bathed by two rivers,
Your blood you will be near to spitting,
You and yours, when the Rose shall bloom.
                    (Centuries II, quatrain 97)

La belle rose en la France admiree,
D'un tres grand Prince à la fin desirée,
Six cens & dix, lors naistront ses amours
Cinq ans apres, sera d'un grand blessée,
Du trait d'Amour, elle sera enlassée,
Si a'quinze ans du Ciel reçoit secours.

The beautiful rose admired in France,
And at the end coveted by a grand Prince,
Six hundred and ten, then her loves will be born,
Five years later will be wounded by a great one,
With a Love's (Death's) arrows he will be entrapped,
If at fifteen years will be helped by Heaven.
                    (Sestet 44)

Many have interpreted *Quatrain 97* as referring to the attack by Alì Agcà in Rome, a city washed by the Tiber and by the Aniene. Such an interpretation does not appear to be correct, however, because the Pope must of necessity reside in Rome, and so there would be no sense in warning him not to approach that city, the seat of his office, and also because the attack concerned only the Pontiff himself, while none of his entourage was injured.

If, on the contrary, the city washed by two rivers were Lyon, then the warning by the Seer would refer to the same episode mentioned in *Quatrain 46* of *Centuries VIII*, which was commented on earlier.

My own interpretation of the rose in this the quatrain is Rosicrucianism, the same which in the letter to Henry is mentioned as '*blooming from the stem, long sterile*', and which in the tragic period of the death of the great pontiff, should begin to bloom, creating a mystical movement directed towards the future reformation of the Christian Church. Such an interpretation seems to find confirmation in *Sestet 44*.

Rosicrucianism, when it blooms, will find among its adepts someone who is potent (*grand Prince*), who in 2002 (1610+392) will join the initiatory movement.

Five years later, which will be in 2007, Rosicrucianism will undergo persecution at the hands of the Antichrist (by a great wound), who will strike it with an arrow. The French text speaks of an arrow '*d'Amour*', but the presence of the capital letter leads me to believe that it is an anagram and that its meaning is the exact opposite, that is *à mo(u)rt*, with the assimilation of the '*d*' into '*t*'. In 2017 (fifteen years from 2002) Rosicrucianism will receive divine assistance, which will enable it to re-establish the religion of Christ.

Note that the date 2017 coincides with the first and most tragic phase of the Third World War, which will be marked by the victory of Henry over the forces of the Antichrist, with the expulsion of the Arabs from Europe.

The expansion of Rosicrucianism is also confirmed by *Centuries V, quatrain 96*:

> Sur le millieu du grand monde la rose,
> Pour nouueaux faictz sang public espandu:
> A dire vray on aura bouche close,
> Lors au besoign viendra tard l'attendu.

> *The rose in the midst of the great world,*
> *Through new deeds still more bloodshed:*
> *To tell the truth mouths will be closed,*
> *When there is need the awaited one is late.*
>   (*Centuries V, quatrain 96*)

This quatrain prophesies that, at a certain moment in the future, two politico-religious blocks will come into being: in almost all of Europe, in Africa and in great parts of Asia the Antichrist will dominate; in the Americas, in parts of Europe, in a part of Asia and in Australia there will be Rosicrucianism, which will have undertaken its project of regeneration of the Christian faith. In that time there will be yet another massacre caused by a delay in help. However, the moment will not be one for protest or objection: the gravity of the situation will induce everyone into keeping their lips sealed. *Centuries V, quatrain 31* also mentions the Rose:

> Par terre Attique chef de la sapience,
> Qui de present est la rose du monde:
> Pont ruyné & sa grand preminence,
> Sera subdite & naufrage des undes.

> *In Attic land leader of wisdom*
> *Who now is the rose of the world:*
> *The bridge fallen and its great pre-eminence,*
> *Will be subdued and shipwrecked in the waves.*
>   (*Centuries V, quatrain 31*)

The leader of the Rosicrucians, who at that time will be considered the repository of all wisdom, while crossing a perilous bridge in Attica (or in an Arctic country, seeing that in the original text it is not possible to distinguish whether the letter is an '*R*' a '*T*'), will fall and meet his death in the waves.

Apart from this tragic episode, the quatrain's contents confirm my theory that the Rosicrucianism, in the near future, will enjoy that great increase in membership that will make it possible for mankind to reorientate themselves toward enlightenment and an awareness of God. If my interpretation is correct, the death of the holy pontiff should take place sometime in 2001–2002, when the Rose mentioned in the sestet, will already have bloomed. But the time span can be reduced further, for the sestet makes it clear that when the grand prince accepts initiation into the mystical movement, he will already have gained admiration in France; consequently, the year of reference could be 2001.

The definition of the time is further confirmed in *Centuries X, quatrain 91*:

> Clergé Romain l'an mil six cens & neuf,
> Au chef de l'an feras élection:
> D'un gris & noir de la Compagnie yssu,
> Qui onc ne fut si maling.

> *In six hundred and nine, the clergy of Rome*
> *At end of year will hold election:*
> *Of one of the Company, grey-black,*
> *As malignant as none has ever been.*
> (Centuries X, quatrain 91)

The year 1609, according to my theory, might be 2001 (1609 + 392). Interestingly, in 1609 no pope was nominated, for Camillo Borghese under the name of Paul V had been sitting on St Peter throne since 1605 and remained there until his death in 1621.

If this thesis is correct, then the nomination of the new pontiff should take place on the last day of 2001. In the quatrain the Seer uses the expression *chef de l'an*, which in modern French means new year, but in middle French *chef* could in rare circumstances mean extremity, hence, the term *chef de l'an* might mean the last day as well as the first of the year.

Therefore, according to my hypothesis, on 31 December 2001, the Conclave could proceed to the election of a new pope.

My suggestion is founded, first of all, on the correctness of the *Prophetia de Summis Pontificibus*, secondly on the correspondence of the year of the Liturgy to AD 392, and thirdly on the fact that the year 1609 mentioned in the quatrain also starts from that of the Liturgy. If all those presuppositions are correct, then in 2001 the Conclave might nominate a new pontiff. At this point the date of the present pontiff's death should establish itself around the last months of 2001 in Lyon, taking into account the time that is necessary for the celebration of the funeral and for the reunion of the Conclave.

It this doesn't happen on 31 December 2001, the only possible alternative would either be 13 January 2002, following the Julian calendar, or 20 March 2002, if Nostradamus was referring to the astrological year, which starts on 21 March.

Other dates cannot be considered because, as we shall see later, the two popes would reign four years and seven months in total. For this reason, if the imprisonment of the last pope occurs on September 2006 and his death in October of the same year, and if we subtract the four years and seven months from the latter date, we will get March 2002 as the last possible date for the election of the penultimate pope.

The new pope might emerge from among the Jesuits, if that is what Nostradamus meant by the term *'de la Compagnie yssu':* in ecclesiastical matters when *'Compagnie'* is used, it usually means the Company of Jesus.

However, *'de la Compagnie yssu'* could have a different meaning: that of *'outside the assembly (of the Conclave)'*. The Conclave, in fact, is formed exclusively of cardinals below the age of 80, but this organ of the Church is to nominate also non-cardinals as popes. If this interpretation is correct, the meaning of the line could be that a prelate who is not part of the Conclave and therefore out of the *'Compagnie'* will be elected as pope.

The new pope is defined by the Seer as *'grey and black'*

and the double adjective could mean that he will be a black man with grey hair.

We know that in Malachia's *Prophetia de Summis Pontific-ibus,* the new pope is called '*de gloria Ulivi*', a motto which can be translated as '*symbol of peace*', hence it is probable that the new pope has a noble coat of arms or that he has adopted a pastoral coat of arms bearing a symbol of peace, such as a white dove or an olive branch. Bearing in mind the negative characteristics of the new pontiff, and having considered the history of all the popes who have succeeded since the death of Nostradamus to the throne of Peter, it is possible to support the theory that it is this new pope to whom *Centuries VI, quatrain 26* is referring:

> Quatre ans le siege que peu bien tiendra,
> Un suruiendra libidineux de vie,
> Rauenne & Pyse, Veronne soustiendrant,
> Pour esleuer la croix de Pape enuie.

> *For four years will hold office badly,*
> *One libidinous of life will come,*
> *Ravenna, Pisa, Verona will rise,*
> *To elevate the cross against the contested Pope.*
> (Centuries VI, quatrain 26)

We know, then, that the penultimate pope will hold the throne for about four years: therefore, since he should be elected by 31 December 2001, his Pontificate will cease in December of 2005.

In the first Italian edition, whom dealing with the penulti-mate pope, I referred to him with the following quatrain:

> Quand le sepulcre du grand Romain troué,
> Le jour apres sera esleu Pontife,
> Du Senat guieres il ne sera prouué,
> Empoisonné, son sang au sacré scyphe.

> *The sepulchre of the great Roman is found,*
> *The day after, the Pontiff will be elected,*
> *He will not be much approved by the Senate,*
> *Poisoned, his blood in the sacred chalice.*
>
> *(Centuries III, quatrain 65)*

I was also affirming that in all the history of popes since the death of Nostradamus, there does not ever appear to have been an episode such as the one described in the quatrain, so, taking into account the fact that the present pope should die in Lyon, and that the last pope will come to a tragic end, captured by the Arabs, the quatrain gives the appearance of referring exclusively to the successor of John Paul II.

I now believe that this quatrain refers to the bright figure of John Paul I, elected by the Conclave at the first vote, who reigned as pontiff for only one month *(de medietate lunae)* and died in rather suspicious circumstances.

As far as the discovery of the Sepulchre of a '*great Roman*' is concerned, all the interpreters unanimously agree that it treats of an archaeological discovery, and some have had the idea of identifying the discovery with that of the tomb of Peter, which came about during the period of Pope John XXIII. This, however, appears to be altogether incorrect, considering the immense favour and sympathy aroused by this great pontiff, as well as of the fact that between the time of his nomination and the discovery, there was no chronological concordance with the description given by Nostradamus.

In the first edition, I gave also the opinion that the '*great Roman*' was in fact Pope John Paul II, since he is one of the most shining pontifical figures in all the bi-millenary history of the Church. I was, however, misinterpreting the *great Roman's* real meaning.

In reality, there is only one '*great Roman*', and he was Paul of Tarsus, who, according to the gospel, was a '*Roman citizen*' *(civis romanus)*. Hence, the line refers to Saint Paul and the pope who was named after him, Paul VI.

So the verse means: 'when a (worthy) sepulchre for the Great Roman (Paul VI) will be found, after one day the Pope will be elected'. In fact, Albino Luciani, Pope John Paul I, was punctually elected at the first vote and, after his election, he was faced immediately with hostility from the Church establishment, which opposed his drive for radical changes and complete transparency of financial and administrative matters in the Vatican. Very soon, the new pope made many unsuspected enemies, and that caused his untimely end. Like the Lamb of God, he was sacrificed at the altar of political convenience, and while for Jesus there was the Cross, for John Paul I there was the poisoned cup.

To Albino Luciani, Nostradamus dedicated another quatrain, that can be read as a moving tribute to a gentle and good person.

> Esleu en Pape, d'esleu sera mocqué ,
> Subit sondain esmeu prompt & timide,
> Par trop bon doulx a mourir prouocqué,
> Crainte estainte la nuit de sa mort guide.

> *Elected Pope, as elected mocked,*
> *Called at once impulsive and shy,*
> *Through his great goodness and gentleness*
> *   destined to die,*
> *Night brings his death, upright and trembling.*
> *(Centuries X, quatrain 12)*

Immediately after his election, Albino Luciani was an object of derision for his sincere impulsiveness and his shyness. A character too good and devoted to the purest principles couldn't survive too long in a sphere that at that time was involved with shady financial interest and illicit business connections. To have been elected as the Chief of the Church, for a person so averse to any material interest and, at the same time, perfectly aware of all the wrongdoing around him, was just a way to sign his own death sentence. Thus, the poison he took before going to bed awoke him shaking in the middle of the night, and he died held upright by his assistants.

In any case, after four years of the 'grey and black' pope,

a pontiff will be elected, who will not be worthy of the throne of St Peter, a pontiff whom the Seer unhesitatingly defines as *'libidinous of life'*.

The actions of this pontiff will be such that in a brief time there will be protests, which will grow into a schism.

It is definitely to this pope that *Centuries VIII, quatrain 93* refers:

Sept mois sans plus obtiendra prelature,
Par son decez grand scisme fera naistre,
Sept mois tiendra un autre la preture,
Pres de Ueinise paix union renaistre.

Seven months without obtaining the prelacy,
By his death a great schism will be generated,
For seven months another will hold the priesthood,
Near Uenise (the United States) *peace and union will be reborn.*

(*Centuries VIII, quatrain 93*)

Why I am certain that this quatrain refers to the last pope derives from a series of considerations: in the first place, in the history of the Church from 1566 until today, there has not been a single pope who has lasted only seven months and who upon his death has caused a schism.

Secondly, it has never come about that a vicar has held the pontificate for seven months.

Thirdly, if one makes an anagram of *'Uenise'*, one get *'E. Unies'* and, as we have seen in the letter to Henry, this name conceals the present day USA.

And confirmation that the interpretation being offered here is correct comes from *Centuries VIII, quatrain 99*:

Par la puissance des trois Roys temporelz,
En autre lieu sera mis le saint siege:
Où la substance de l'esprit corporel,
Sera remys et receu pour vray siege.

By the power of the three temporal Kings (the oil Kings),
The Holy See will be put elsewhere:
Where the substance of the material spirit,
Shall be recognised and accepted as the true See.
(Centuries VIII, quatrain 99)

As I have indicated in the commentary on the letter to Henry, the '*Roys temporels*' are in reality, the '*Roys en petrol*', which is, *the oil kings*, and precisely, Iraq, Iran and Libya, which, as will shall see, will attack Italy, destroying everything in their path.

This will, of necessity, determine the transfer of the Holy See to a secure place, and, certainly, such a place could not be Europe, which, like Italy, will be subject to tremendous aggression. So, it appears altogether probable, if not certain, that the Holy See will be forced to transfer to the United States, which confirms the accuracy of the proposed anagram and the reference of *Centuries VIII, quatrain 93* to the last pontiff.

The transfer elsewhere of the Holy See is, furthermore, confirmed by *Centuries IX, quatrain 99*:

Vent Aquilon fera partir le siege,
Par murs geter cendres, chauls et poussiere:
Par pluyes apres, qui leur fera bien piege,
Dernier secours encontre leur frontiere.

The north wind will make the throne depart
From the walls will be thrown ashes, lime and dust:
Through the rain afterwards, which will ensnare them,
Help in extremity near their frontier has gone.
(Centuries IX, quatrain 99)

The scenery that the quatrain describes is one that refers to the invasion of Italy and to the devastation of Rome in 2006. What is of interest here is that the quatrain confirms that the Holy See will be forced to transfer elsewhere.

During the seven months of his pontificate the last pope will issue an encyclical letter, which will be the cause of a grave schism, which will come about after his death and which, as will be seen in the following chapter, will constitute the occasion hoped for on the part of the Antichrist in order to launch his war of religion:

> Pour le plaisir d'Edict voluptueux,
> On meslera la poyson dans la foy:
> Venus sera en cours si vertueux,
> Qu'obfusquera du Soleil tout la loy.

> *For the pleasure of voluptuous Edict,*
> *They will mix poison into the faith,*
> *In the course of which Venus* (Islam) *will be so virtuous,*
> *That all the law of the Sun* (Catholicism) *will be*
>   *obfuscated.*

>   (*Centuries V, quatrain 72*)

In line 3, Venus is referring to Islam, as Muslims celebrate Friday *(Vendredi)* as their holy day – originally Venus' day. On the other hand, Catholics, like Christians in general, celebrate Sunday – the Sun-day.

The last pontiff will issue an encyclical letter, which will be licentious and contrary to common Christian morals. This will generate confusion and resentment among the faithful, who will become disorientated. In contrast to such a situation, the new Islamic faith will be, in appearance, rigorous and inspired towards observance of the moral precepts, with the consequence that numerous people will consider this to be the true faith.

This might be an interpretation of the vision of Giovanni di Roquetaillade, cited by Centini in his work 'The Return of the Antichrist' (page 256):

A Western Antichrist will appear in Rome, while an Eastern Antichrist will divulge his false doctrines from Jerusalem . . . Misery and massacre will punish the clergy, in particular, the Franciscans, purified by suffering and reduced to absolute poverty, such as that which was believed to have properly belonged to Christ and the Apostles.

It is possible, that the last pope, the *'Petrus Romanus'* of the *Prophetia de Summis Pontificibus*, by Malachia, is in reality, a creature of the Antichrist himself, who will bring about his election by way of underhand manoeuvres, and this can find confirmation in the prophecies of sister Bertina Bouquillon, mentioned above, where this Seer refers to the fact that her fellow sisters would find themselves from one day to the next having to depend on the Antichrist, without being aware of it.

Once again it must be emphasised that the Antichrist will put himself forward as the bearer of an apparently faultless religion, since his personality will be endowed with extraordinary intelligence and ability, not to mention the fact that he will probably also have power and capacities which will not by any means be uncommon.

This is confirmed in Revelations 13: 13–15:

And he doeth great wonders, so that he maketh fire come down from heaven on the earth in the sight of men,

And deceiveth them that dwell on the earth by means of those miracles which he had power to do in the sight of the beast; saying to them that dwell on the earth, that they should make an image to the beast, which had the wound by a sword, and did live.

And he had power to give life unto the image of the beast, that the image of the beast should both speak, and cause that as many as would not worship the image of the beast should be killed.

In light of this, looks as though *Centuries I, quatrain 4* is refers to the final pope:

Par l'Uniuers sera faict un Monarque
Qu'en paix & vie ne sera longuement:
Lors se perdra la piscature barque,
Sera regie en plus grand detriment.

> *By the universe will a monarch be elected,*
> *Who in peace and life will not linger,*
> *The fisherman shall lose his boat,*
> *That will be governed in the greatest of torments.*
>
> *(Centuries I, quatrain 4)*

Almost all interpreters have translated *'Par l'Univers'* as *'for the universe'*, making the quatrain refers to the monarch of the universe, who is identified as Henry of France. Still others have maintained that the quatrain alludes to Napoleon Bonaparte.

In fact, *'par'* should correctly be translated as 'by'. The universe to which the Seer alludes can be none other than that organ of the Church which represents it in its totality, and that is the Conclave, in which all the cardinals of the earth meet, in order to elect the pope, and as a consequence they represent it in its universality.

The election of a corrupt and depraved pope will cause a terrible upheaval within the Church, since that pope, with a lifestyle totally lacking in spirituality, will incite protests, which will grow into a schism, forcing Peter's boat into the midst of a tempest which will cause it to be shipwrecked.

And this shipwreck will be violent: the end of the last pope, in fact, is described in *quatrain 15* of *Centuries V* and in *quatrain 93* of *Centuries II*

> En nauigant captif prins grand Pontife,
> Grans apretz faillir le clercz tumultuez:
> Second esleu absent son bien debife,
> Son fauory bastard à mort tué.

> *The Great Pontiff captured as he sails,*
> *Great preparations fail, the clergy agitated,*
> *The vicar is absent, his possessions plundered,*
> *His favourite bastard killed.*
>
> *(Centuries V, quatrain 15)*

Bien pres du Tymbre pressé la libitine,
Un peu deuant grand inondation:
Le chef du nef prins, mis à la sentine,
Chasteau palaix en conflagration

Very near the Tiber in haste Libitina,
A little before the great flood:
The leader of the boat taken prisoner in the sink,
Castle and palace in flames.

(Centuries II, quatrain 93)

The contents of the two quatrains are almost identical. The pope will be captured aboard ship, while he is attempting to escape. There will be an effort to free him, but this will fail. In that moment the papal secretary will be absent from Rome, the clergy will be in agitation; in the meantime, the Eastern invaders will seize the papal belongings, and the favourite of the pope, defined as *bastard*, will be killed.

The Roman goddess of funerals (*Libitina*) is hurrying towards Rome and preludes the great invasion of the eternal city, which will come about at the hands of those from the East, and which is described in numerous quatrains, which we shall examine later.

The leader of the boat is obviously the pope, who will be captured and imprisoned in the sink of the ship, while Castel Sant'Angelo and the palace of the pope will be destroyed with explosives.

If this interpretation is correct, then the events being described should occur in the year 2006, since the last pope should be elected after December 2005 and therefore with every probability between January and February 2006 and should sit on the throne of Peter for only seven months.

Such an interpretation finds, then, surprising confirmation in *Quatrain 14* of *Centuries V*, which contains one of the few definite astrological references which make it possible to fix a date:

Saturne & Mars en Leo Espagne captifue,
Par chef libique au conflict attrapé:
Proche de Malthe, Heredde prinse viue,
Et Romain sceptre sera par coq frappé.

Saturn and Mars in Leo, Spain occupied,
Drawn into conflict by Libyan chief,
Near Malta, Infante is captured live,
And Roman sceptre will be broken by the cock.
                    (*Centuries V, quatrain 14*)

The astral conjunction to which the Seer refers will occur in June–July 2006. At that time war will already have broken out, presumably some months will have passed since its beginning, and Libya, having entered the conflict, will move to occupy Spain, while the Infante will be captured near Malta.

The barbarians will shatter the power of the pope. The Seer uses the term '*coq*', normally used to indicate France, to define the barbarians. As '*coq*' means *Gallic* and refers to the inhabitants of Gaul (coming from the Latin Gallia), and the Gauls, from the time of the kings, were among the staunchest enemies of the Romans, for whom they were barbarians.

In view of this quatrain, it seems to be highly sustainable that in 2006 the Third World War will already have begun and that Rome will suffer the outrage of an invasion. What is of interest here is that the last pope will be captured in 2006, and that, together with him the Catholic church will come to its end.

However, there is another quatrain that might date the moment of the end of the last pontiff even more accurately:

Le prince Arabe, Mars, Sol, Venus, Lyon,
Regne d'Eglise par mer succombera:
Deuers la Perse bien pres d'un million,
Bisance, Egipte ver. serp. Inuadera.

The Arab prince Leo (Assad), *Mars, Sun, Venus,*
The reign of the Church will succumb at sea,
Towards Persia very close to a million
Turkey, Egypt, serpent will invade.

(Centuries V, quatrain 25)

In the Italian edition I had considered the astrological combination of Mars, the Sun, Venus in Leo, a combination which the Ephemerides had indicated as running from the 2–6 August 2000, with the consequence that for that date I had foreseen a war taking place between Iran, Turkey and Egypt on the part of that Arab chief who subsequently would have destroyed the Kingdom of the Church from the sea.

The event, as is well known, did not take place; in view of which another possible interpretation for the quatrain must exist. Since the Ephemerides are absolutely precise and do not allow for ambiguities of any sort, my first step was to see when the next combination of Mars, Sun and Venus in Leo would be and I discovered that this would come to pass no earlier than 2015, a date that was altogether incompatible with the chronology of other future events.

The problem, therefore, seemed to be one without any solution. This remained so until I began to consider the possibility that *Lyon* bore no reference to the constellation bearing the same name, but rather to the *Prince Arabe,* who in such a case would have been mentioned by name. On consulting a dictionary of Arab names, I discovered to my surprise that in Arabic the name *Assad* means 'Lion', and once again the sole person who came to mind was the young Syrian President, Bashar Al Assad.

At this point the question was that of seeing when Mars, the Sun and Venus would be grouped together under a single sign. This turned out to be on 7 and 8 September 2006, when the three stars will be situated under the constellation of Virgo.

Therefore, if this interpretation is correct, the quatrain should have the following meaning: '*The Arab Prince bearing the name Lion, when Mars, the Sun together with Venus are united under a single sign, will destroy the Kingdom of the Church from the sea'*.

At this point with all the due caution and reservation that the case calls for, the following chronology could be hazarded:

October–March 2002: death of John Paul II at Lyons, probably through a terrorist attack.

31 December 2001 (or 13 January 2002 or 20 March 2002): election to the pontificate of the *'De Gloria Ulivi'*.

December 2005–March 2006: death of the *'De Gloria Ulivi.'*

January–February 2006 – March 2006: election of *'Petrus Romanus'*, after a tormented Conclave.

7–8 September 2006 – October 2006: capture and death of *'Petrus Romanus'* and transfer of the Holy See to the United States.

According to a strict and logical interpretation of the quatrains, it is not possible to suggest a different chronology. Hence, if these events don't happen, there are only two possibilities: either Nostradamus was wrong, or the magnitude of the current pontiff's work and that of his Church renders him deserving of a different and better fate.

11. Future events up to the end of 2005

In view of the complexity of my argument, I digressed by giving an account of the last years of the Catholic church in one chapter. Now the moment has come to resume the road marked by the passage of the years.

While I have been busy attending to this edition, the dark clouds of war have thickened over the Middle East, especially over Palestine and Israel. In September 2000 a new *Intifada* exploded, and up to now it has caused hundreds of victims, both as a result of terrorist action on the part of the Palestinians and of reactions by the Israeli army under the form of bombardments. There seems to be no easy way out: on the one hand the Palestinians are claiming territory of their own, on the other hand, the Israelis want to hold on to their colonies which sprang up like a rash after their victorious Six-Day War in 1967. The crux is Jerusalem, claimed by the Israelis as their capital, but just as strongly contested on the part of the Arabs.

The Arab world is in an uproar: Saudi Arabia, Iraq, Libya, Egypt, Jordan and particularly Syria have always championed the cause of the Palestinians and so they give their support to Arafat. In the West, however, there is a cautious equidistance on the part of the USA (although many see them as pro-Israeli) as well as on Europe's part. Both have enormous economic interests in Arab oil, which prevents them from taking a more definite stance.

At the moment, it may well be said that the Palestinians are looked upon by the majority as victims of Israeli aggression, forced into defending themselves with what weapons they own from an enemy who can count on formidable military means:

Le regne et loy soubz Venus esleué,
Saturne aura sur Iupiter empire:
La loy et regne par le Soleil leué,
Par Saturnins endurera le pire.

Government and law promoted under Venus (Islam),
Saturn will have its reign over Jupiter,
The law and government drawn up by the Sun,
Through the followers of Saturn will suffer worst.
                    (*Centuries V, quatrain 24*)

This quatrain, in my judgement, has the following meaning: When Saturn is in the same sign as Jupiter, the state created for the Muslims (*soubz Venus*) and its reasons (*loy*) will be promoted, while the state which, thanks to the Western nations and to the Christians (*par le Soleil*), was founded by the Jews will suffer the worst. As is known, the State of Israel was founded in 1948, thanks to international support on the part of the United States and Britain. The Palestinian State, on the other hand, came into being in 1994.

In 2000, Jupiter and Saturn were to start with in Taurus from 15 February until 30 June, then in Gemini from 11 August until 15 October and once again in 2001 from 21 April until 13 July, and on the astrological plane this is a quite extraordinary fact; considering the enormously different times of revolution of the two planets around the Sun (Jupiter, 12 years and Saturn 29 years and six months).

To be more precise, Saturn was *over* Jupiter during the last days of May 2000, when the two planets were situated in Taurus, almost superimposed, with Saturn at 22° and 30' on the 27th, at 22° and 38' on the 28th, at 22° and 45' on the 29th, at 22° and 53' on the 30th and at 23° on 31 May; Jupiter in these days was respectively at 22° and 20', 22° and 34', 22° and 48', 23° 02' and 23° and 16'.

At the end of May 2000, the Israeli's army hurriedly withdrew from Lebanon. Between September and October a bloody *Intifada* broke out with hundreds of victims, terrorist attacks and violent military reprisals. The political situation appears tragic and without any solution. The Israeli premier Sharon, as well as his counterpart Arafat, are obliged to give heed to public opinion in their own states, and these urge for a violent solution to the crisis. Some of his own party in Palestine, where the most extreme and violent elements prevail, contest Arafat and he appears to be even weaker politically than Sharon.

Sharon, however, who came to power promising a rapid solution to the conflict, has found himself having to face a very complex situation, quickly realising that military force is not the key to resolving the problem. In view of this, Sharon has been forced to fall back on a more conciliatory line of conduct, only to find himself being quickly contested by the right wing of his party and by the more extreme Israeli groups, as for example the settlers who had voted for him because of his promise that the colonies, rather than being dismantled, would be extended.

The political weakness of the two heads of state, consequently, makes it impossible to produce solid peace negotiations, as both Arafat and Sharon fear rejection in their own homeland.

There is the risk, therefore, that the conflict will escalate into a real war, which, according to the quatrain, would end with the destruction of the Jewish State. The Seer's prophecies, however, foresee the end of the Israeli State and do not lend themselves to a different interpretation:

La Synagogue sterile sans nul fruit,
Sera receu entre les infideles,
De Babylon la fille du poursuit,
Misere & triste luy trenchera les aisles.

The barren Synagogue, without any fruit,
Will be received among the infidels,
The Daughter of Babylon, miserable and sad,
Will sever the wings of the persecuted.
                    (Centuries VIII, quatrain 96)

Israel, represented by the Synagogue, will be occupied by the followers of Islam (*the infidels*). The inheritors of Babylon, that is, Syria and Iraq, which occupy a great part of the territory of the ancient state, will destroy the Israeli State, which is indicated through the use of the expression '*persecuted*', a description of the fate of the Jews over the centuries.

This is, moreover, confirmed by the letter to Henry, where in paragraph LXXIV the Seer writes: '*And their assaults will not be in vain, and the place which was once the dwelling place of Abraham will be assailed by men who will venerate the "Jovialists"*' (that is, the followers of the Antichrist, whose religion, as will be seen, will sanctify Thursday)' and this is repeated in paragraph LXXVIII '*And the holy sepulchre, of such great veneration, for a long time will remain exposed to the Heavens, under the universal vision of the heavenly gaze of the Sun and Moon.*'

Sestet 34 treats of this sudden conflict and of its consequences:

> Princes & Seigneurs tous se feront la guerre,
> Cousin germain le frere auec le frere,
> Finy l'Arby de l'heureux du Bourbon,
> De Hierusalem les Princes tant aymables,
> Du fait commis enorme & execrable,
> Se ressentiront sur la bourse sans fond.

> *Princes and Lords will go to battle,*
> *Cousins, brother against brother*
> *The happy refuge of the Bourbon has ceased,*
> *From Jerusalem, the very amiable Princes*
> *For enormous, abominable acts committed,*
> *Will resound on the bottomless stock exchange.*
> *(Sestet 34)*

The events surrounding Israel will involve many states, and in each of these there will be two factions, those in favour of and those against the aggression. Prior to these acts of war, there will also follow, however, the reawakening of the ancient blood of the Bourbons, after a long period of oblivion.

In the third line the sestet uses the word '*Arby*', which has no meaning. The fact that it is written with a capital letter, leads me to the conclusion that it is an anagram, and that the correct word is '*abry*', which means *shelter*, *refuge* and which leads to the following of the verse: the Bourbons, after remaining for long under cover and in anonymity, must now make their entrance on to the stage of history.

The war against Israel will have as its consequence a collapse in the stock market, with disastrous effects on the world economy, as we have already seen in *Sestet 24*, dedicated to the crisis in the stock market and the global market.

The consequences of aggression against the State of Israel and its occupation by the followers of Islam are described in *Centuries V, quatrain 11*:

Mer par solaires seure ne passera,
Ceulx de Venus tienderont toute l'Affrique:
Leur regne plus Sol, Saturne n'occupera,
Et changera la part Asiatique.

The sea will not be safe for the followers of the Sun
    (Christians),
Followers of Venus (Islam) *all of Africa will keep,*
In its Kingdom no longer the followers of Saturn
    (Israelis),
And the Asian part will change.
                                    (Centuries V, quatrain 11)

Islamic power, after the fall of Israel, will increase to the extent where the Mediterranean will be dominated by its ships and by those of its ally, Russia, making it dangerous for maritime traffic itself. The Seer in repeating that the State of Israel will no longer exist speaks also of the prospects of profound changes in the Asiatic zone. We noted in the commentary on the letter to Henry, in fact, that in the political play of the Antichrist, a role of primary importance will be attributed to

China, which will be allied with the Arabs and Russians, a fact that will determine an upheaval in the political balances in Asia.

As for the date when Israel will encounter its tragic destiny, the only reference that can be obtained is from the conjunction of Saturn and Jupiter, which will end on 13 July 2001. This, however, does not mean that Israel will succumb on that date (indeed it did not). What is certain, however, as we now see events unfold, is that in establishing dates from the repeated conjunctions of Saturn and Jupiter throughout 2000 and 2001, a continuously tormented period is beginning for Israel, at the end of which her collapse should occur.

If *Centuries VIII, quatrain 96* is anything to go by, it could turn out that the first act of war will have Israeli air power as its first target, with a rapid strike by the Arabs, similar to the Israelis' attack at the beginning of the Six-Day War, when aeroplanes bearing the Star of David (the famous Mirages) destroyed the entire Syrian, Egyptian and Jordanian air forces while they were still on the ground, so obtaining right from the start that mastery of the skies, on which their swift victory depended.

The second basic element that will characterise the near future will be the increasingly close alliance between Russia and the Islamic world, first an economic and then a military one.

The Russia of Vladimir Putin has been trying desperately to regain the role of superpower that the USSR once occupied, but the new leader has found himself in an international political situation which is not a very favourable one: Russia, in fact, very much needs financial intervention; its economy is on the brink of collapse, the greater part of its population is faced with hunger, since galloping inflation has eroded fixed incomes along with pensions. Only a few fortunate individuals, on the whole dishonest speculators, corrupt politicians or organised criminals, have the country's wealth in their hands. Russia in the last years has had considerable economic help from the rest of Europe, particularly Germany, as well as from the USA.

The enormous debt that has been contracted impedes Putin from assuming any aggressive policy whatsoever, in view of the fact that he is well aware of his desperate need of Western financial help. But if on the international chequerboard there should suddenly appear a new economic power which is capable of succouring Russia, relieving it of its indebtedness towards the West, then Putin, finding himself free from financial restraints, could, together with his new ally, resume a determining role on the international plane, regenerating the Russian military machine, which, in any case, has maintained a considerable capacity.

Let us consider, then, a future Islamic world united under one single leader, exceedingly powerful economically thanks to the presence of oil and to the wealth accumulated by the oil-producing Arab States. Even for such a future leader, to rescue Russia financially would be an arduous and terribly burdensome sacrifice. However, the economic capacity of oil-producing Arab States could satisfy such a necessity.

It is then what is prophesied in *Sestet 7* would be realised:

La sangsue au loup se joindra,
Lorsqu'en mer le bled defaudra,
Mais le grand Prince sans enuie,
Par ambassade luy donra
De son bled pour luy donner la vie,
Pour un besoin s'en pouruoira.

Leech will attach itself to Wolf,
When from the sea grain will be lacking,
But the Great Prince, though not besought,
Through embassy will give
Of his grain, in order to give him life,
Through this necessity impoverishment will come.

(Sestet 7)

Russia, in order to emerge from its painful economic crisis, has asked and received economic help from the European countries, most of all from Germany, whose banks are heavily involved in this financial project, while help coming from the United States has been frozen (*when from the sea grain will be lacking*). The last line of the sestet is ambiguous: it might also mean '*For this necessity, he will provide*', though I prefer to think the one I have given is correct.

Taking advantage of such a disastrous situation, the Antichrist (*the Great Prince*), with apparent spontaneity, but in reality with subtle calculation, will offer to help that country economically, not being stingy about massive interventions, which in the end will deprive Russia of all its autonomy, and in this fashion draw its mighty army towards the abyss of the Third World War.

In order to tie Russia in with his design then, Hadrie should in the first place acquire the necessary economic potential, and in my judgement, a victorious war against Israel conducted by him would constitute the solid foundation for his rapid ascent.

In the various Arab countries the *Intifada* has forced into the open the existence of a split between government and people. In fact, while the governments of Saudi Arabia, Jordan, Egypt, the Emirates (save for Iraq and Libya) are inspired with a policy of prudence and caution, limiting themselves to proposing bland diplomatic and economic measures against Israel and mere financial help to the Palestinians, the individual publics have instead poured into the public squares to invoke armed intervention alongside the Palestinians.

In all probability, this situation should worsen within the near future, reaching the point where popular dissent is transformed into *bona fide* revolt, awakened and nourished by Hadrie himself who by then will have become the major hero of the Middle East and champion of Islam.

The fall of the Saudi regime can be found in *Centuries III, quatrain 4*:

> Quand seront proches le default des lunaires,
> De l'un à l'autre ne distant grandement:
> Froit, siccité, dangier vers les frontieres,
> Mesmes ou l'oracle a prins commencement.

When in the Moon followers (Islam) *the distances
    have fallen,
Among them there is no great difference,
Danger at the borders, cold, drought,
Even where the oracle has started from.*
(Centuries III, quatrain 4)

In this quatrain the Seer warns that the Arab countries, whose history, origins and race differ little, not to mention the one religion which binds them together, will in the end come closer to one another in an ever-tightening unity, and through the irresistible process of this closeness, will involve even Saudi Arabia itself, where Mohammed first began his preaching. The Saudi regime is not very well loved by the public in view of the enormous disparity in the distribution of the country's wealth. Furthermore, religious fanaticism plays an important role in Saudi Arabia, fanaticism that is further helped by a rigorous interpretation of the laws of the Koran. In the face of the moderate attitude held by the Saudi rulers, who are worried about jeopardising the advantageous economic relationship they share with the United States through the adoption of an extreme, aggressive position, it is probable that the population aroused by the new charismatic personality, will end up by rebelling, thus decreeing the end of that regime and making way for the birth of a new Islamic State, of which Arabia would come to represent an important part. This quatrain, in my judgement, should be linked to what is written in the letter to Henry in paragraph LXXV, where the Seer writes: *'And the city of Mecca itself will be attacked and assailed from all directions with great violence by armed people.'*

The attack on Saudi Arabia, traditional and faithful ally of the United States, will be an indispensable step in the Antichrist's political manoeuvres: as long as the Saudi regime remains there, every hope of revolution and unification in the Islamic world will be practically impossible, as the Gulf war itself has demonstrated, a war in which Saudi Arabia gave logistic support to the Western forces against Saddam Hussein.

And it is highly probable that almost contemporaneously

with Saudi Arabia, similar events will occur in other Arab states, such as Iraq, and even earlier in the state of Palestine itself, where Yasser Arafat could come to a rapid political decline, because of the more extreme factions and because of the pressing closeness of Syria, which is already practically governing Lebanon.

It is possible that *Sestet 13* is referring to Yasser Arafat:

> L'auanturier six cens & six ou neuf,
> Sera surpris par fiel mis dans un oeuf,
> Et peu apres sera hors de puissance
> Par le puissant Empereur generale,
> Qu'au monde n'est un pareil ny esgal,
> Dont un chascun luy rend obeissance.

> *Six hundred and six or nine, the adventurer*
> *Will be surprised by the gall put in an egg,*
> *And shortly afterwards will be removed from power,*
> *By the mighty General Emperor,*
> *Of whom the world has no peer or equal,*
> *For everyone will pay obedience to him.*

> *(Sestet 13)*

The years mentioned are alternatively 1998 or 2001. Since nothing of the sort took place in 1998, this episode could occur in 2001, unless with the number 9 the Seer meant to refer 2009.

The sestet subsequently clarifies that in that year there will be a *General Emperor* who will have no equal in the world and to whom everyone will have to obey.

The words that are used leave the impression that such an emperor must be identifiable with the Antichrist, who will be an absolute sovereign, rather than the president of the United States, since in a democratic regime the concept of obedience does not exist, unless it is obedience to the law.

In the 2001 or 2009, then, an adventurer belonging to the Arab world will be removed from power.

The term adventurer could be referring to Arafat, in view

of the fact that for many years Arafat was active as a terrorist and ended up by becoming the leader of a faction that was violent and unscrupulous, but events were to favour him to the point where he subsequently received the Nobel Peace Prize. If the sestet is speaking of Arafat, this means that in 2001 or in 2009 there should be an underhand attempt against his life in the form of poisoning, an attempt which will not result in the death of the Palestinian leader but will certainly make him seriously ill.

In any case, the new star of Middle-Eastern politics should in a short while set him aside and bring about his disappearance from the scene of contemporary history.

Alternatively the sestet could be referring to Saddam Hussein, whom the epithet could fit equally well. Iraq is desperately seeking diplomatic relationships that would allow it to emerge from the isolation caused by the disastrous Gulf War.

If Hadrie becomes the overall emperor to which the sestets allude, there is no doubt as to how easy it will be for this new political leader to control Saddam Hussein's Iraq to the point where its very power of decision-making is crushed.

After the conquest of Saudi Arabia through an internal revolution and the easy subjugation of Iraq, the new leader will direct his attention to the other Arab states, whose publics will flood the squares in celebration of the new Mohammed, reaching a point of overthrowing their governments.

When we looked at *quatrain VI, 54*, we noted that the present King of Morocco would be overthrown by an internal revolution, and a destiny that is not dissimilar should be in store for Jordan and the Emirates, as well as the other minor states.

Within a brief time, therefore, *Hadrie*, that is the Antichrist, should succeed in acquiring immense power, such as would perhaps make him the most powerful man in the world.

Thoughts rush suddenly to John's Apocalypse in Chapter 13 where the great mystic writes:

And I stood upon the sand of the sea, and saw a beast rise up out of the sea, having seven heads and ten horns, and upon his horns ten crowns, and upon his heads the name of blasphemy.

And the beast which I saw was like unto a leopard, and his feet were as the feet of a bear, and his mouth as the mouth of a lion: and the dragon gave him his power, and his seat, and great authority.

And I saw one of his heads as it were wounded to death; and his deadly wound was healed: and the entire world wondered after the beast.

And they worshipped the dragon which gave power unto the beast. and they worshipped the beast, saying, Who is like unto the beast? who is able to make war with him?

And there was given unto him a mouth speaking great things and blasphemies; and power was given unto him to continue forty and two months.

And he opened his mouth in blasphemy against God, to blaspheme his name, and his tabernacle, and them that dwell in heaven.

And it was given onto him to make war with the Saints, and to overcome them: and power was given him over all kindred, and tongues, and nations.

And all that dwell upon the earth shall worship him, whose names are not written in the book of life of the Lamb slain from the foundation of the world.

If any man have an ear, let him hear.

He that leadeth into captivity shall go into captivity: he that killeth with the sword must be killed with the sword. Here is the patience and the faith of the saints.

And I beheld another beast coming up out of the earth; and he had two horns like a lamb, and he spoke as a dragon.

And he exerciseth all the power of the first beast before him, and causeth the earth and them which dwell therein to worship the first beast, whose deadly wound was healed.

And he doeth great wonders, so that he maketh fire come down from heaven on the earth in the sight of men,

And deceiveth them that dwell on the earth by means of those miracles which he had power to do in the sight of the beast; saying to them that dwell on the earth, that they should make an image to the beast, which had the wound by a sword, and did live.

And he had power to give life unto the image of the beast, that the image of the beast should both speak, and cause that as many as would not worship the image of the beast should be killed.

And he causeth all, both small and great, rich and poor, free and bond, to receive a mark in their right hand, or in their foreheads: and that no man might buy or sell, save he that had the mark, or the name of the beast, or the number of his name.

Here is wisdom. Let him that hath understanding count the number of the beast: for it is the number of a man; and his number is Six hundred threescore and six.

The last part of the passage reproduced here can be related to *Centuries II, Quatrain 20*:

Freres & seurs en diuers lieux captifz,
Se trouueront passer pres du monarque:
Les contempler les rameaux ententifz,
Desplaisant voir menton, front, nez, les marques.

Brothers and sisters in various places captives,
Will find themselves passing near the monarch,
Contemplating his horns bewitched,
Sad to behold, chin, forehead, nose, the marks.
                                    (*Centuries II, quatrain 20*)

According to John, a beast from the sea will appear on the earth. This beast will represent Evil, that is, the Demon. Another beast will join this one. The beast from the earth, which will be the element destined to intervene among men, entrancing them with words and inducing them into abandoning their faith in order to adore Evil. This beast from the earth is the Antichrist, who will have the task of bringing destruction to a great part of humanity, with the aim of bringing about its regeneration on a radically different basis, one founded on reciprocal respect, with an awareness of the spiritual part of human nature, inclined towards God, the creator of the Cosmos.

Certainly, in the present political situation, such an upheaval in the balance of international power appears somewhat unreal. However, it is not always true that things are resolved even on the basis of well studied and well thought-up plans. Such a thing may take place when an extraordinary personality appears in the limelight of history, a personality capable of overturning even the most well reasoned programme.

History, in fact, teaches us that a man who is gifted, for better or for worse, with a strong personality, with charisma, with the capacity to play the right strings of sentiments and passions, is capable, by himself, of overturning balances and situations which may once have seemed immovable. We need only think, for example, of Napoleon, of Hitler or even of Lenin in order to have an idea of what could happen with a personality endowed with powers that are immensely superior to theirs.

We have seen that the Antichrist will complete unification of the Middle East, subjugating all the Islamic countries and annihilating the State of Israel, aided in this by formidable Russian military potential, which he will obtain by literally buying Russia through enormous economic aid, a policy which will result in such a stringent alliance as not to allow Russia any freedom of decision, practically subjecting it to the power of the new Islamic prince, who at this point will also have been able to define the religious aspect of his policy, instituting a religion, which, though basing itself on Islamic principles, will have its day of worship on Thursday, as emerges in *Centuries I, quatrain 50*:

> De l'aquatique triplicité naistra,
> D'un qui fera le Ieudy pour sa feste:
> Son bruit, loz, regne, sa puissance croistra,
> Par terre & mer aux Oriens tempeste.

From the watery triplicity one will be born,
Who will make Thursday his feast day:
Fame, praise, kingdom, power will increase,
By land and sea to the Eastern tempest.

(Centuries I, quatrain 50)

The water-signs of the Zodiac are three: Cancer, Scorpio and Pisces. In using the expression *watery triplicity* the Seer is pointing to the fact that the Antichrist was born or initiated his rise to power with the Sun in a water sign. The Antichrist will change the day of religious celebration from Friday to Thursday; the quatrain then describes his ascent: he will quickly acquire immense fame and resonance and, through the growth of these, he will progressively increase his power. He will exert this power from the east, and precisely from the east the tempest will come, which will create a tremor in the present political order.

The Antichrist will be venerated as though he were a God as emerges from *Centuries X, quatrain 71:*

La terre & l'air gelleront si grand eau,
Lors qu'on viendra pour Ieudy venerer:
Ce qui sera jamais ne feut si beau,
Des quatre pars le viendront honnorer.

Land and air will freeze water in abundance,
When for Thursday they will come to venerate
Him who will be handsome as none has ever been,
From four parts they will come to pay him honour.

(Centuries X, quatrain 71)

The quatrain is clearly speaking of the Antichrist, since in referring to him, Nostradamus use the same expressions which can be found in Revelations, 13:1,8 (see pp. 175–6)

The similarity between the contents of this quatrain and the passage from Revelations is quite obvious.

Note that in the second line the Seer uses the term '*Ieudy*', which gives rise to several interpretations. Most likely it is

'*Jeudi*'; Thursday. However, the Seer uses a capital letter and precede it by '*pour*'. It is, therefore, quite possibly an anagram of '*Iudey*' and the Judaean *par excellence* is Christ.

The contents of this quatrain would then mean that people would come from every part of the earth to adore the Antichrist as the new Messiah, and this is in perfect accord with what is prophesied in the Apocalypse.

In the meantime, Europe should find itself in extreme difficulty, victim of oil blackmail, along with the concrete threat of an interruption of crude oil supplies, a fact that would practically paralyse the economies and the industries in most European countries. For this reason, in all likelihood, Europe could not react against the destruction of Israel and Europe would witness the rapid consolidation of a new and powerful Arab State.

At the same time, the Russian fleet would be present in the Mediterranean with their tanks loaded, and this would be further obstacle to a reaction by sea.

The Western powers will find themselves without a logistical base in the Middle East, in contrast to their situation during the Gulf war, when Saudi Arabia had provided the necessary logistical support, and within a very short time they would find themselves being forced into reducing their reaction, thus allowing the empire of *Hadrie* to be consolidated.

This situation of extreme tension will be protracted throughout the course of 2002, and this is confirmed by *Sestet 26*, which we have already looked at in the context of the future of the Church.

> *Two brothers are of the ecclesiastical order,*
> *One for France will take the pike,*
> *Once more a blow: if the year six hundred six,*
> *Will not be afflicted by a great malady,*
> *Arms in hand until six and ten,*
> *Scarcely longer than this will his life last.*
>
> *(Sestet 26)*

What is of interest at this moment is that this sestet indicates that France will fighting until 610, which should correspond to the year 2002 (1610+392).

This is also true that in the same year of 2002, Italy, for the first time, could be the object of a violent armed aggression, which would be concentrated on Rome and which would force it to deploy its troops on the battlefield and seek help from neighbouring France:

> La grand Cité où est le premier homme,
> bien amplement la ville je vous nomme,
> Tout en alarme & le soldat és champs,
> Par fer & eaue, grandement affligée,
> Et à la fin des François soulagée,
> Mais ce sera des six cens & dix ans.

> *The great city where the first man is,*
> *I name the town for you most generously,*
> *All in alarm and soldiers in the fields,*
> *By sword and water intensely harassed,*
> *And, in the end assisted by the French,*
> *But that will be when it is six and ten.*
>
> *(Sestet 42)*

The city to which the Seer is alluding is Rome. I have deduced here a play of words in the French text. In the first line we read: '*La grand Cité où est le premier homme*'. Now, if we look at the final '*R*' of '*premier*' and join it with the following '*homme*', we get '*rhomme*', pronounced '*Rome*'. This is the reason why in the second line the Seer draws our attention to his having named the city most generously.

The year 610 is obviously 1610 of the Liturgy and therefore 2002 (1610 + 392). The sestet prophesies that in that year Rome should undergo a violent attack, with bullets raining down from the sky. The situation of extreme danger would force the government to concentrate its armed forces in the vicinities of the capital in order to offset the threatened invasion. The Italian government would then ask for help from neighbouring France, which would presumably guarantee its assistance through the employment of air and naval forces and for the moment the invasion would be thwarted.

The sestet, however, could lend itself to a different interpretation: in 2002 the Italian centre-rightist government could find itself in Rome face to face with protests, making it necessary to intervene with the armed forces for fear of the outbreak of a true revolution. If such were to happen, the Seer in using the name *François* would not be alluding to the French people but rather to two personalities bearing the name *Francesco* (as, for example, the ex-president of the Italian Republic Francesco Cossiga) or the leader of the Left Francesco Rutelli, who through their mediation could restore calm to the violent demonstrations.

In any case, beyond the Italian situation, the international balance of power during the years under examination may undergo profound changes. Islam may become a unique entity almost exclusively governed by *Hadrie*, even if behind a façade of apparent pluralism. This Islamic complex would come to represent a new and particularly violent and aggressive superpower. Russia, thanks to an ever-close alliance with Islamic countries should find itself, on the one hand, put back on its feet economically by the Western financial apparatus, while, on the other hand, it should once again be occupying the primary political and international role it once held, thanks substantially to its renewed military potential.

The opposition existing between the two blocks would become increasingly more radicalised and events taking place in Israel would be a determining factor in this. There would be reprisal, particularly on the part of the Americans, acts of terrorism, skirmishes between the Russo-Islamic block and the NATO periphery, especially Turkey.

This situation of drawn-out war would then be intensified by a growing shortage of fuel, the result of a policy put into practice at Hadrie's behest, intent on forcing Europe to its knees.

In such a scenario, things could further precipitate, until near the brink of a universal conflict.

In these years the Western forces could then conjointly reach a drastic decision: either the cessation of all hostilities and the discussion of a peace plan, or the employment of nuclear weapons and of this there are indications in *Sestet 49*:

> Venus & Sol, Jupiter & Mercure
> Augmenteront le genre de nature,
> Grande alliance en France se fera,
> Et du Midy la sangsue de mesme,
> Le feu esteint par ce remede extreme,
> En terre ferme Oliuer plantera.

> *Jupiter and Mercury, with the Sun and Venus*
> *Will increase the kind in nature,*
> *Grand alliance will be made in France,*
> *And the Leech from the south,*
> *The fire put out by this extreme remedy,*
> *On terra firma will plant the olive.*
>
> *(Sestet 49)*

The astral combination to which the first line refers presupposes that Jupiter, Mercury, Venus and the Sun will find themselves united under the same Zodiacal sign and must be sought in a time which is subsequent to 2002, since the sestet informs us that the state of tension growing into armed conflict, involving, above all, the Middle East, will cease, thanks to a resolute alliance among the Western countries which would be achieved in France, with the concrete threat of total war, Russia (*the Leech*) would be induced into withdrawing for the moment from its warlike intentions alongside the Islamic countries and against Western forces.

Subsequent to 2002, the first days in which the said astral combination will occur will be on 30 July 2003, with the Sun in Leo, Mercury in its last day in Leo, Venus first day, and Jupiter, in that sign since long ago.

Then the four stars will find themselves united under Virgo from 17 August until to the 15 September 2003.

Finally all of them will be in Scorpio from 15 October until 17 November 2006. At one of the dates indicated, therefore, the Western countries, realising the gravity of the situation which is nearing a global catastrophe will find the strength, the resoluteness, and the courage necessary to issue a peremptory '*diktat*' (from which stems the meaning of the second line '*will increase the kind in nature*': Courage, in fact, is a natural endowment, and the situation will be such that it will cause the level of desperation to grow to such an extent as to appear to be the last chance), and with such an attitude of resoluteness, they will succeed for the moment in avoiding the point of no return, by inducing Russia into withdrawing from its warlike intentions. At that point, the Antichrist will remain temporarily without a powerful ally and will be forced to desist.

Among the possible dates, I maintain that the Seer is alluding to 2003, since in October–November 2006, if the theory that I formulate in the next chapter is correct, an appreciable amount of time will have passed since the outbreak of the Third World War, hence the moment for alliances and mediations will long since have been consumed.

And in 2003 a temporary pact is achieved through which a global conflict is avoided. This is confirmed in *Centuries X, quatrain 74*. This same quatrain, examined in the first part of this present work, refers to the completion of the seventh millennium, at the time of the Olympic Games in Greece in 2004. It appears therefore, obvious that if the Olympic Games can take place at the regular time, then there will be a period of peace in the world, seeing that the celebration of the Olympics in times of war is altogether unthinkable.

But such a situation will not last. First of all, the Antichrist will continue to gather followers throughout the world: his words and his speeches will be broadcast in the information media and will endear themselves to that section of mankind who will see in him the new Messiah. '*Petrus Romanus*' will in the meantime have issued his '*voluptuous edict*' creating disapproval and confusion within the Catholic world. This encyclical will be the spark the Antichrist hoped for to set off his war of religion. This encyclical will be deemed as immoral and diabolical, and Muslims will turn it into an emblem by which to justify their aggression, claiming that Allah could never tolerate such impiety, and all this, while the careless leaders of the various Western countries will be underestimating this very grave risk.

The terrible damage, therefore, will take place, and it will be irreparable, overtaking the world, the political and religious institutions in a tragedy of apocalyptic proportions.

La grande perte las que feront les lettres,
Auant le cicle de Latona parfaict:
Feu grand deluge plus par ignares sceptres
Que de long siecle ne se verra refaict.

What grave damage will be caused by letters,
Before the cycle of Latona (the Moon) is complete,
A great flood of fire (due) to inert government,
That in centuries will not be repaired.
                                    (*Centuries I, quatrain 62*)

All that has been exposed above is condensed in this quatrain, which ties in with what the Seer writes in his letter to Henry, where he emphasises the disaster that '*letters*' will cause, letters such as those of the Papal Encyclicals, which are always in an epistolary form and which are addressed to the whole of Christianity. The reference to the '*cicle de Latona*' should be interpreted in light of *Centuries I, quatrain 48*, which we have already looked at. With the name Latona, the mother of Apollo, the Seer means the moon, which, as has been observed, will dominate the destiny of men for 7020 years, in order then to make space for the reign of the Sun. Also on the chronological plane, therefore, *Centuries I, quatrain 62* fits itself perfectly into the context described herein: we are by now at the end of the reign of the moon, and exactly in that period the '*letters*' will deliver the '*coup de grace*' to a shaky world peace.

All this, then, has beginning on the inauspicious deeds of the last pontiff, who should be elected between the end of 2005 and the beginning of 2006, and who with his '*voluptuous Edict*' will provide the Antichrist with the justification for starting his war of religion.

12. The outbreak of the Third World War

The situation will be one of progressive degeneration: after the brief truce, towards the end of 2005 and the beginning of 2006, the Antichrist having assured himself of the support of an economically weakened Russia, now back on its feet, thanks to massive economic interventions from the Arab world, will assume that the moment has come to resume his aggression and conquest, drawing inspiration and justification from the '*voluptuous Edict*' promulgated by '*Petrus Romanus*'.

> Dans peu de temps Medecin du grand mal,
> Et la Sangsue d'ordre & rang inegal,
> Mettront le feu à la branche d'Oliue,
> Poste courir, d'un & d'autre costé,
> Et par tel feu leur Empire accosté,
> Se r'alumant du franc finy saliue.

> *In a little time the Doctor of the great malady,*
> *And the Leech, of unequal order and rank,*
> *Will set fire to the Olive branch,*
> *Travelling speedily from one coast to the other,*
> *With such fire drawing their empire closer,*
> *Reviving themselves on the saliva-less free world.*
>
> *(Sestet 30)*

The Seer uses the term '*Medecin*' in this sestet to mean the Antichrist. The literal translation would be '*Doctor of great malady*' . However, the term '*Mede*' in middle French can mean *Mesopotamian, inhabitant of Media*, and I believe this is what it means in this context. Here the Seer is making use of the so-called '*green language*', in which the real meaning of a word is camouflaged by it having a radically different meaning. However, we cannot exclude the possibility that the Antichrist has a degree in medicine.

If we use this as a premise, the sestet acquires a precise meaning: in the space of a few years, the Antichrist, through the military potential of a Russia practically subjugated to him, will compromise world peace, sending people fleeing from coast to coast. This will set off the rise of his terrible future empire, which will draw vital substenance from the profound crisis in which the free world (*the francs*, that is, the free) will find itself without the necessary energy to fight his ascent. With Arab oil under his control and the pipelines shut off, for the Europeans, there will be enormous problems regarding the availability of fuel for aeroplanes, ships and land vehicles. The reserves will finish rapidly, leaving the Western Europe dry (*saliva-less*). England alone, thanks to oil coming from the North Sea, will be able to withstand the situation, save that in the end, as will be seen, the moment will arrive when it will come under attack.

It will therefore be the availability of oil for the Arabs and the Russians, on the one hand, and the lack of it for Western Europe, on the other, which will cause the balance to swing in favour of the Antichrist's armies, with transport paralysed for his adversaries due to the lack of fuel. Here, therefore, is why Nostradamus refers to the Arabs as '*Roy Temporels*' – the anagram which produced '*Roys en petrol*,' *that* is, *oil kings* – oil being the first indispensable raw material for any war whatsoever.

We need only imagine what would happen today if crude oil from the Arab countries were suddenly absent. As early as the 1970s there was a small energy crisis which forced us to go on foot or by bicycle on alternate days. A drastic closure of the oil market on which 90 per cent of energy production is based and 99 per cent of the system of locomotion would within the space of a few days cause a paralysis of the system, with pumps gone dry and cars at a standstill.

The major part of methane, too, comes either from Russia or from the Tunisian gas duct. If these states too were to cut off the flow of gas, the electricity production would no longer be possible, with all the related consequences, especially in Italy, which does not even have atomic energy, as opposed to France, which is altogether self-sufficient, when it comes to the production of electricity.

The Arab invasion, then, is at hand and will take place after an unexpected attack against the United States, as is foreseen in *Sestet 56*:

> Tost l'Elephant de toutes parts verra,
> Quand pouruoyeur au Griffon se joindra,
> Sa ruine proche, & Mars qui tousjours gronde:
> Fera grands faits aupres de terre saincte,
> Grands estendars sur la terre & sur l'onde,
> Si la nef a esté de deux freres enceinte.

> *Soon the elephant from every part will see,*
> *When the purveyor fights against the Gryphon,*
> *Its end is near, and with Mars continually roaring:*
> *Will perform great deeds in the Holy Land,*
> *Great banners on land and on the sea,*
> *If the vessel is pregnant with two brothers.*
>
> *(Sestet 56)*

The Elephant, as we have seen in other sestets, represents the Arabs, since Mohammed was born in the year of the Elephant, according to the tradition of the Koran.

The Gryphon represents the United States, while 'the purveyor' is the Antichrist. In the second line the verb *joindre* is used, a verb, which in modern French means *join, unite*. In middle French, however, *joindre* could also meant *to engage in combat*.

The sestet means that the Antichrist, having treacherously attacked the United States will, within a brief time, set off the Arab invasion. In that moment, however, when the *Medecin's* banners of victory are fluttering in the wind and his ships ploughing the waves, there is the prediction of his end which is near, because, precisely at the moment of his menacing advance, in the bosom of the agonising Catholic Church (*the vessel*), about to enter upon the stage of history there are the two brothers, who will be the prime movers of the victory and of the deliverance of the world from Evil. And that the year 2006 will be the year which will mark the definitive outbreak of the third global conflict is indicated in *Sestet 28*:

L'an mil six cens & neuf ou quatorziesme,
Le vieux Charon fera Pasques en Caresme,
Six cens & six, par escript le mettra
Le Medecin, de tout cecy s'estonne,
A mesme temps assigné en personne,
Mais pour certain l'un d'eux comparoistra.

The year thousand six hundred and nine or fourteenth,
Old Charon will make Easter in Lent,
Six hundred and six, The Doctor will set all this,
In writing, will be enormously surprised about this,
At the same time decorated in person,
But for sure one or the other will appear.

(Sestet 28)

The sestet prophesies that in the year 1609 or 1614 (of the Liturgy), within the first months, before Easter, the war will begin. By adding 392 the year will be 2001, and the year 1614 will be 2006 (1614 + 392). This second date is the correct one, it being confirmed by other quatrains. However, the reference to 2001 is not without significance, since it has been observed that in that year a grave situation of conflict reached a critical point, with continued slaughter among Israelis and Palestinians. Furthermore, in my judgement, in the sestet the Seer is playing upon the name *Charon*, which in French is pronounced the same way as *Sharon*, that is, the name of the present Israeli prime minister. Sharon, in fact, was nominated as Premier in mid Lent, and celebrated his election in this period after years of waiting and political battles.

But Charon is also the ferryman of Hades, and he will celebrate even more in 2006, when the Third World War should bring monstrous and unimaginable destruction and slaughter.

The sestet makes it clear that in 1998 (1606+392) the '*Medecin*' had already conceived of such a project, after learning that he had been predestined by the powers of Evil for the accomplishment of this eschatological task. To this he had committed himself with the certainty that all would be realised and that war (*Charon*) would come to the world.

The dates which the sestet proposes, therefore, are absolutely accurate and are in perfect accord with those which can be assumed from the quatrains where they refer to an astrological combination. As we saw in the chapter on the Catholic Church, in May–August 2006 Spain will be occupied by the Libyans, which means that the war will intervene within the first months of that year, certainly before Easter, that is, as the Sestet affirms, in the middle of Lent, when Charon, the ferryman of Hades, will have a banquet.

Numerous quatrains predict the invasion of Europe by the Arabs:

> De la felice Arabie contrade,
> Naistra puissant de loy mahometique,
> Vexer l'Espaigne, conquester la Grenade,
> Et plus per mer à la gent lygustique.

> *From the very rich Arab region,*
> *Will be born a powerful Muslim law,*
> *It will bully Spain, will take Granada*
> *And, by sea, up to Liguria and the Adriatic.*
> > (*Centuries V, quatrain 55*)

Arab power, which will be able to rely on the immense economic resources coming from oil and will be equipped with formidable armaments, thanks to close ties with Russia, will direct its attention towards Spain, as happened in the course of the first Arab expansion, which succeeded in subjugating great parts of that country for many centuries.

Contemporaneously with the invasion of Spain, a similar

fate will befall Italy, which will be invaded from sea, from the west as well as from the east coast.

The Ligurians, as well as the inhabitants along the Adriatic are referred to by the Seer as *'Ligustiques'*, which has already been noted in the commentary on the letter to Henry. This comes from a fusion of *'Liguriens'* and *'Hadriatiques'*, through the typical expediency of the *'green language'*. Not even France will be spared, as can be evinced through *Centuries II, quatrain 29*:

> L'Oriental sortira de son siege,
> Passer les monts Appennis voir la Gaule,
> Transpercera ciel, les eaux & neige,
> Et chascun frappera de sa gaule.

> *The man from the East will come out from his seat,*
> *He will pass the Apennines, to see France,*
> *Will mount the sky, the waters and the snow,*
> *Each one will he strike with his spear.*
>
> *(Centuries II, quatrain 29)*

After having invaded Spain and Italy, the Easterners will move up along the Italian peninsula until reaching the French border, which they will cross, notwithstanding resistance from the French.

In order to set his military project into action, the Antichrist, after having unified the Arab world and having assured himself of the unconditional support from Russia, by now in his thrall, will destroy the American fleet with a treacherous attack.

This will be the key moment of the first phase of the war. As the Japanese did during the Second World War, with the destruction of the American Sixth Fleet, the only one endowed with energy, many of its ships and submarines having nuclear propulsion, the Antichrist will become the unchallenged master of the Mediterranean, and the Russian ships will not meet great resistance on the part of the fleets belonging to other Western countries, short as they will be of fuel, and certainly not in a condition to be able to compete with the mighty fleet of the Russian colossus.

> La foi punique en Orient rompue,
> Gang. Iud, Rosne, Loire, & Tag, changeront.
> Quand du mulet la faim sera repue,
> Classe espargie, sang & corps nageront.

> *The Punic faith broken in the East,*
> *Jordan, Jud, Rhone, Loire, Tagus will change,*
> *When hunger is sated in the mule,*
> *The fleet lost, blood and bodies will swim.*
> *(Centuries II, quatrain 60)*

The Islamic religion will undergo profound changes in the process of becoming something different. When this transformation has taken place, the political situation in the Middle East (*Jordan*), in France (*Rhône and Loire*) and in Spain (*Tagus*) will overthrown. The moment in which, Russia, thanks to the Arab aid, has rid itself of its deep crisis (*hunger is sated in the mule*) so that it can intervene with all its military potential, the American fleet will be destroyed.

This interpretation finds ample confirmation in *Centuries I, quatrain 73*:

> France à cinq parts par neglect assaillie,
> Tunys, Argel esmeux par Persiens:
> Leon, Seuille, Barcellone faillie,
> N'aura la classe par les Uenitiens.

> *France assailed unexpectedly in five parts,*
> *Tunisia, Algeria pushed by the Persians:*
> *Leon, Seville, Barcelona failed,*
> *There will be no fleet from the Uenitiens (Americans).*
> *(Centuries I, quatrain 73)*

This quatrain predicts that after the invasion of Spain, the Russian-Arab forces will attack France from five different directions, while, thanks to a military thrust from Iran, Tunisians and Algerians will contribute towards the fall of the principal Spanish cities. Note the last line *n'aura la classe par les Uenitiens*, which has been translated as '*There will be no fleet from the Americans*'. As I have shown in the commentary on the letter to Henry, the term '*Uenise*' could be interpreted as an anagram of '*E. Unies*,' that is, of the United States. In middle French in fact, the '*U*' substitutes the '*V*' and the capital '*U*' is written as though it were a '*V*,' as was true of Ancient Roman writing. '*Uenitiens*', therefore, '*Et. Uniens*', that is, the abbreviation of '*Etatsuniens*'. The quatrain might, therefore, be confirmation of what has been revealed above concerning the strategy that will govern the first phases of the global conflict, which will be characterised by the destruction of the American fleet. As to the place where the American fleet will be destroyed the Seer is even more precise:

> Naufraige à classe pres d'onde Hadriatique,
> La terre esmue sus l'aire en terre mis.
> Egypte tremble augment Mahometique,
> L'Heraul soy rendre à crier est commis.

> *Sinking of the fleet in the Adriatic Sea,*
> *The earth trembles of curdled dust,*
> *Mohammed grows, Egypt is routed.*
> *The Herald is sent to shout surrender.*
> *(Centuries II, quatrain 86)*

According to this quatrain, the American fleet should be annihilated in the Mediterranean, probably in the southern sector, while at the same time Hadrie's land forces should be launching an attack against Egypt, forcing it to surrender.

It is highly probable that on the European and Middle-Eastern fronts the first military moves by Hadrie will be the destruction of the American fleet and the consolidation of power in the Middle East with the defeat and subsequent annexation not only of Egypt but also Turkey, a member country of NATO, which will be left practically to itself in facing the unexpected military aggression:

> Le prince Arabe, Mars, Sol, Venus, Lyon,
> Regne d'Eglise par mer succombera:
> Deuers la Perse bien pres d'un million,
> Bisance, Egìpte ver. serp inuadera.

> *The Arab prince, Mars, Sun, Venus, Leo* (Assad),
> *The reign of the Church from the sea will end,*
> *Toward Persia very close to a million*
> *Turkey, Egypt, serpent, will invade.*
> > *(Centuries V, quatrain 25)*

We look at this quatrain in Chapter 10 on the future of the Catholic church, but it is worthwhile examining it again to offer the following interpretation: '*The Arab leader bearing the name Lion, when Mars, the Sun and Venus are together under the same sign (September, 2006) will destroy the Kingdom of the Church from sea: in the meantime, from the Iranian front with almost one million men he will invade Turkey and Egypt in the name of the serpent.*'

That, apart from Egypt, the very first phases of the conflict also include Turkey is confirmed in *Centuries V, quatrain 27*:

> Par feu et armes non loing de marnegro,
> Viendra de Perse occuper Trebisonde:
> Trembler Pharos, Methelin, Sol alegro,
> De sang Arabe d'Adrie couuert unde.

> *Using fire and weapons, not far from the Black Sea*
> *He will come from Persia to occupy Trebizond,*
> *Pharos, Mitilene and Malta will tremble,*
> *The Adriatic sea will be covered in Arab blood.*
> > *(Centuries V, quatrain 27)*

The Seer foresees flames and weapons not far from the Black Sea and that coming from Persia the Antichrist will occupy

Trebizond (Turkish soil) while Pharos, Mitilene and Malta will tremble from being exposed to the threat of an invasion.

The conquest of Turkey will not be painless, however. In fact, this is a country that boasts a well supplied, organised army at its disposal, so it is altogether logical that the conquest of Turkey by Hadrie will come at the cost of grave losses.

But the strategy of this first phase will not be limited simply to a treacherous attack against the American fleet, it will also be directed towards the American territory itself, and ballistic missiles will destroy the White House.

> Un an deuant le conflict Italique,
> Germain, gaulois, espaignolz pour le fort:
> Cherra l'escolle maison de republicque,
> Ou, hors mis peu seront suffoqué mors.

> *One year before the Italian war,*
> *Germany, France and Spain for the strong:*
> *The school house of Republic will come down,*
> *There, save for a few, death by suffocation.*
> *(Centuries II, quatrain 39)*

This quatrain informs us that in 2005, one year, that is, before the outbreak of the war in Italy, Germany, France and Spain will reach an agreement with the United States (*le fort*) on how to face the continuing situation of tension.

The third line refers to the destruction of a house, which stands as the symbol (school) of a republic. Reference to the White House appears to be more than probable, since, in everyday language, only in reference to the United States does the word '*House*' apply, while just the names of the palaces are used when speaking symbolically of other countries, such as '*Quirinale*' for Italy, '*Elysée*' for France and '*Kremlin*' for Russia. It may well be, then, that by '*emblem-house*' the Seer is referring to the White House, which will be destroyed, causing the death of almost all its inhabitants, including the president of the United States of that time, always supposing that my interpretation given here to *Centuries II, quatrain 62* is correct.

Mabus puis tost alors mourra, viendra,
De gens & bestes une horrible defaite:
Puis tout à coup le vengence on verra,
Cent, main, soif, faim, quand courra la comete.

Mabus then soon will die, there will come,
A horrible ruin to people and beasts,
Then, suddenly one will see vengeance,
A hundred, hand, thirst, famine, when the comet shoots
  over the sky.

(*Centuries II, quatrain 62*)

Many commentators have gone to great pains to identify the personality hidden behind the name '*Mabus*'. In my opinion the Seer is indicating a member of the Bush family, who, in all probability, will become president of the United States. '*Ma*' could hint at a first name: the name of one of the sons of the former American President is Marvin, or '*ma*' could be read backwards, producing 'am', to indicate his American nationality, consequently, '*Mabus*' could be translated as '*Bush the American*'.

I first wrote this at the beginning of 1999. At the end of 2000 George Bush was elected President of the USA: to say anything further would be unnecessary.

In any case, it appears altogether probable that the quatrain is referring to the United States and should be linked to the previously examined quatrain, since it deals with the immediate reaction to a sudden and unexpected attack, with the aftermath of slaughter of men and animals. It is worth noting that since the death of Nostradamus, no-one has appeared on the scene who could be identified with '*Mabus*', and only twenty-five years remain to the end of the prophecies. The Seer also mentions that at *Mabus*'s death, a comet will cross the sky.

The date I have proposed for this coincides with the date that the comet Lexell will appear in the sky: 16 December

2005, it will remain visible until 20 December of that same year, after which it will gradually fade until its final disappearance into the depths of the cosmos in April 2006.

So, if the visibility of the comet is taken into consideration, then the death of '*Mabus*' can be fixed in December 2005; on the other hand, if it is the nearness of the comet to the earth that is the important issue, then the slaughter could take place within the first months of the following year.

In any case, if this were to take place in December 2005, it would signal the moment of the outbreak of the Third World War, which would occur a few days before 2006.

If such were the case, *Centuries II, quatrain 39*, examined above, would a definite date in the future. In fact, we shall see shortly, the war in Italy will take place in 2006; as the destruction of the White House will take place '*one year before the Italian conflict*', it would happen in December 2005.

At this point, it is highly probable that *Centuries II, quatrain 43* is referring to the same comet:

> Durant l'estoille cheuleue apparente,
> Le trois grands princes seront fais ennemis:
> Frappés du ciel, paix terre emulente,
> Pau, Timbre undans, serpens sus le bort mis.

> *When the longhaired star appears,*
> *Three great princes will become enemies:*
> *Peace on earth struck from the sky,*
> *Flooded Po, Tiber, snake on the river bank.*
> (*Centuries II, quatrain 43*)

This quatrain prophesies that when a comet appears – and in view of what has been observed above, this will take place in December 2005 – three great princes will become enemies. We can hypothesise that the three might be the United States, Russia and the Antichrist.

The quatrain goes on to say that peace will receive a blow from the sky, and if what has already been examined is taken into consideration, the bombing of the White House with a missile, would fulfil this prophecy. The last line, then, should be linked to the election of '*Petrus Romanus*', since it indicates Italy (*Po*) and Rome (*Tiber*) and prophesies that in Rome the serpent, symbol of Evil and sinfulness, will find unexpected hospitality. It is worth to quoting here what Centini has to say in his *The Return of the Antichrist*, (page 254):

Saint Hildegond, during a pilgrimage to Jerusalem (1186) had a vision of the so-called triumvirate of the Dies Irae, in which the Pope, the Antipope and the Antichrist appeared together in front of her, giving her a glimpse of sad events in the future.

One day, towards evening, while Hildegond was in the midst of reciting psalms, together with a group of pilgrims, along a lonely road, not far outside Jerusalem, she saw three men appear in front of her. Two were wrapped in long, red capes and the third was dressed in sacred vestments. They proceeded slowly ahead, a few steps in front of the pilgrims, and wherever they placed their feet, there remained a burnt footprint. At a certain point, the three *people* turned towards Hildegond, and each one declared his identity: I am Petrus, said the one dressed in the sacred vestments; I am the AntiPetrus, said the man on the right; I am the Antichrist, said the man on the left.

It is symptomatic that in the vision of Hildegond one of the three does not introduce himself as the *Antipope* but as the '*AntiPetrus*'. This would confirm the almost coeval prophecy of Malachia regarding the final Pope, that is, '*Petrus Romanus*'.

Nostradamus's quatrain is similar to this vision. At the moment the comet appears, the '*serpent*' will be in Rome and will reveal itself, in the person of the last pope, who will put himself forward, asserting principles quite alien to Catholic as well as common morals. We have also seen that nomination of '*Petrus Romanus*' will take place between the end of 2005 and the beginning of 2006, that is, at a time that will coincide with the appearance of the Lexell comet.

It is probable that *Centuries II, quatrain 41* is also referring to this comet:

La grand'estoille par sept jours bruslera,
Nuict fera deux soleilz apparoir:
Le gros mastin toute nuict hurlera,
Qu'un grand pontife changera de terroir.

The great star for seven days will burn,
The night will make two suns appear:
The great mastiff will howl all night long,
When a great pope will change his seat.
                    (Centuries II, quatrain 41)

The comet will be visible in the sky for seven days, and at night it will seem as though there were a second sun.

The great mastiff to which the quatrain alludes, might be identified with the United States, for by using this term Nostradamus probably wished to indicate the Anglo-Saxon countries in which this breed of dog was perfected. So the overall meaning of the quatrain, confirms what I have said above: when a comet will be in the sky that is so luminous that it will brighten the night, something so painful will occur that it will cause the United States to howl with suffering and will determine the immediate transfer elsewhere of the Holy See.

The first countries to suffer an invasion after the destruction of the American fleet and the White House will be Spain and Italy.

In the commentary on the letter to Henry I observed that Nostradamus highlights two clearly distinct phases of the Third World War. This is clearly illustrated in paragraph CXIV:

And on the basis of the aforesaid astrological calculation, made in accordance with the sacred scriptures, the persecution of the people of the Church will stem from the power of the Islamic Kings, united with the people of the East. And this persecution will last for eleven years, more or less, when the principal king of the league will fall, and those years having been completed, his ally from the south will survive and for three years he will persecute the people of the Church more cruelly . . .

Since in another part of the letter, the Seer makes it clear that the empire of the Antichrist will last 25 years and a few months, and precisely until 2 June 2025, we can deduce from this that the third global conflict will have a first phase running from 2006 to 2017 and a second phase running from the beginning of 2022 to 2 June 2025. On this basis we can now examine the quatrains and sestets that relate to the two Mediterranean countries.

> Saturne & Mars en Leo, Espagne captifue,
> Par chef libique au conflict attrapé:
> Proche de Malthe, Heredde prinse viue,
> Et Romain sceptre sera par Coq frappé.

> *Saturn, Mars in Leo, Spain occupied,*
> *Drawn into conflict by Libyan chief,*
> *Near Malta, Infante is captured live,*
> *And Roman sceptre will be broken by the cock.*
> *(Centuries V, quatrain 14)*

We examined this quatrain in Chapter 10 on the future of the Church. The information it provides is that, within a short time, in the space of a few months, that is, Spain will experience the disgrace of an invasion by the 'moors', in the meantime, the Infante of Spain will be captured near Malta, while attempting to flee.

In Spain, meanwhile, a violent war will rage, and Pamplona will put up a strong resistance:

> Vaisseux, galleres auec leur estendar
> S'entrebattront prés du mont Gibattar,
> Et lors sera fors faits à Pampelonne,
> Qui pour son bien souffrira mille maux,
> Par plusieurs fois soustiendra les assaux,
> Mais à la fin unie à la Couronne.

> *Vessels and galleys with their standards*
> *Will battle near Gibraltar,*
> *And then there will be strenuous attack at Pamplona,*

A thousand ills for its own good will suffer,
And time and again will sustain the assaults,
But in the end will become part of the Crown.
                                        (Sestet 41)

While a bitter naval battle is taking place in the straits of Gibraltar, Pamplona will find itself in the midst of a siege and in desperate conditions. The Spaniards will put up a courageous and strenuous resistance, but in the end, overwhelmed by preponderant forces, they will find themselves forced to surrender, and Pamplona will be added to the Empire of the Antichrist. The complete conquest of Spain will require some time, as can be culled from *Centuries VIII, quatrain 51.*

Le Bizantin faisant oblation,
Apres auoir Cordube à soi reprinse:
Son chemin long repos pamplation,
Mer passer proy par la Colongna prinse.

The Byzantine, performing oblation,
After taking Cordoba, will resume,
Its course, at Pamplona after an ample pause,
By sea attempt for Gibraltar taken.
                        (Centuries VIII, quatrain 51)

With the use of the word *Byzantine* the quatrain is alluding to the Islamic countries, and not exclusively to the Turks. In the vision of Nostradamus, the Arabs will conquer Cordoba and Gibraltar, then they will consolidate their position, which will cost them dear, in terms of men and material (*performing oblation*), maintaining Pamplona as a stronghold, in order then to move forward in their conquest.

This conquest will meet with complete success, as we saw earlier in *Centuries I, quatrain 73.*

The war in Italy will be carried on as the same time as the one in Spain, in view of their geographical proximity, as well as Italy's military weakness in terms of armaments and her endemic unpreparedness, politically and militarily, in an emergency situation, as has recently been shown, when her ships were fired on by the Libyans without their reacting, or when Libya directed missiles against our islands off the Italian coast, which, fortunately, missed their targets. The first to collapse will be southern Italy:

> Naples, Palerme, & toute la Secile,
> Par main barbare sera inhabitee,
> Corsicque, Salerne et de Sardaigne l'Isle,
> Faim, peste, guerre, fin de maux intemptee.

> *Naples, Palermo and the whole of Sicily,*
> *By barbarous hands will be depopulated,*
> *To Corsica, Salerno and the Isle of Sardinia*
> *Famine, plague, war, a deliberate end to evil.*
> *(Centuries VIII, quatrain 6)*

> Iardin du monde au près de cité neufue,
> Dans le chemin des montaignes cauees:
> Sera saisi & plongé dans la cuue,
> Beuuant par force eaux soulphre enuenimees.

> *The garden of the world near the new city,*
> *On the road hollowed out of the mountains.*
> *[He] Will be taken and thrown down to the bottom,*
> *Forced to drink sulphurous poisoned water.*
> *(Centuries X, quatrain 49)*

I do not think these two quatrains have any other interpretation except that: southern Italy, Sardinia and Corsica will be invaded and will be destroyed by forces from the Coast. The garden of the world, mentioned in *Quatrain 49* of *Centuries X* is Italy, as the country was so referred to at the time of the Holy Roman Empire, for its climate and its luxuriant vegetation. The '*cité neufe*' is Naples, whose name derives from Greek and means '*new city*'. The quatrain refers to an episode which will take place in those times: a man, probably a politician, will be captured by the invaders, who will have a horrible death in store for him: he will be thrown into a sulphur pit, and there he will die of poisoning and drowning.

But, unfortunately, not even Rome will be spared by the hordes of new barbarians: to this city and to its outrageous end the Seer dedicates numerous quatrains, all of them imbued with unequivocal and sinister significance:

> Un qui les Dieux d'Annibal infernaulx,
> Fera renaistre, effrayeur des humains:
> Onc plus d'horreur ne plus pire journaux
> Qu'auint viendra par Babel aux Romains.

> *One to whom the infernal gods of Hannibal,*
> *Will give rebirth, terror of humanity*
> *Nothing worse will the journals say*
> *Than of what Babel will do to the Romans.*
> *(Centuries II, quatrain 30)*

> De l'Orient viendra le coeur Punique
> Fascher Hadrie, et les hoirs Romulides,
> Accompaigné de la classe Libyque,
> Trebler Mellites & proches Isles vuides.

> *From the East will come the Carthaginian heart,*
> *To offend Hadrie and the heirs of Romulus,*
> *Accompanied by the Libyan fleet,*
> *Malta anxious, empty the nearby isles.*
> *(Centuries I, quatrain 9)*

The person to whom the bloodthirsty Carthaginian divinity will give rebirth is, obviously, the Antichrist. When this takes place and massacres and atrocious violence occur in Rome, the newspapers will dedicate ample space to them as events. (It seems incredible that Nostradamus uses the term *Journaux*, when newspapers had not yet been invented and the word came into use only in 1665, over a century after the quatrain had been written.) In this quatrain, as well as in the subsequent one, the name of *Hadrie* appears. It would seem, then, that the two quatrains are alluding to the same persona, who appears to be both offender and offended. However, the sequence of the two quatrains leads me to think that the name *Hadrie* is there to indicate two distinct subjects. In the quatrain under examination, *Hadrie* might be referring to the Adriatic Sea and to the Italian township (*Adria*) which gave it that name, and which in antiquity was the most important port of that sea.

But *Hadrie* might also be referring to the present Austrian leader Haider, for *Hadrie* is an anagram Haider. In this hypothetical case, the quatrain could mean that the action of the Antichrist will almost simultaneously be directed not only against Rome and the rest of Italy, but also against neighbouring Austria, whose Prime Minister Haider could within the near future become.

In any case, the Romans (*the heirs of Romulus*) will be subject to grave outrages, while the inhabitants of Malta will experience terror and the islands near Italy will become depopulated.

> Combien de fois prinse cité solaire
> Seras changeant les loix barbares & vaines:
> Ton mal s'aproche. Plus seras tributaire
> La grand Hadrie reourira tes veines.

> *How many times taken, solar city,*
> *You will change barbarous and vain laws,*
> *Your malady is near. You must give more,*
> *Great Hadrie will reopen your veins.*
>   (*Centuries I, quatrain 8*)

The *solar city* is Rome, since it represents the seat of the Catholic church, which Nostradamus defines as '*solar*', because it sanctifies *Sun*day. Rome, after the years of the Republic and of the Empire, was repeatedly taken and sacked throughout its history. The immense juridical civilisation of Roman law in the course of the centuries has undergone numerous changes, having been contaminated by barbarian customs.

This will happen once again and is happening now, since the current-day legislator is certainly no paragon of juridical logic and prudence. With the advent of the invaders, also, the legislation will be transformed into arbitrariness and violence. Rome will be subjugated and will become a tributary of the new masters, who will invade and sack it under the leadership of the Antichrist, thus fulfilling of Mohammed's prophecy, which decreed that the power of Islam will not affirm itself until Rome is taken and destroyed.

In this quatrain the term '*Hadrie*' is used, and it has been translated by the majority as *Adria*. In reality, as has been observed in the commentary on the letter to Henry, the name '*Hadrie*' conceals that of the Antichrist.

> La grand cité sera bien desolee,
> Des habitans un seul n'y demourra:
> Mur, sexe, temple & vierge violee,
> Par fer, feu, peste, canon peuple mourra.

> *The great city will be quite desolate,*
> *Of the inhabitants there will not be one,*
> *Wall, sex, temple and violated virgin,*
> *By sword, fire, plague, cannon, will people die.*
> (Centuries III, quatrain 84)

The scenario as it appeared to the eyes of the Seer must have been horrible. As in the times of the fall of the Roman Empire, when Visigoths, Vandals or Huns devastated the Italian peninsula, bringing with them unspeakable suffering and death, so will it occur in these modern times, at the hands of invaders, who will spare neither church nor women. This is confirmed by paragraph CXIX of the letter to Henry, where the Seer writes: '*there will be the most horrible wars and battles and buildings burnt, and destroyed with great bloodshed of virgins, brides and widows raped, suckling children shall be dashed against the city walls and so many evils shall be committed through Satan, Prince of Hell, that almost the entire world shall find itself destroyed and desolate.*'

Ruyné aux Volsques de peur si fort terribles,
Leur grand cité saincte, faict pestilent:
Pillier Sol, Lune, & violer leurs temples,
Et les deux fleuues, rougir de sang coulant.

Ruinations to the Romans, and such a terrible fear,
Their great holy city filled with the plague,
Sun (Gold) and Moon (silver) plundered, temples
*   violated,*
And the two rivers will run red with blood.
(Centuries VI, quatrain 98)

So then, for Rome it will be a barbarous occupation: the
churches will be stripped bare, the works of art plundered,
similar to what took place during the last years of the Empire,
when the barbarians repeatedly pillaged the city.

Owing to the massacres and the presence of unburied
corpses, the plague will reap numerous victims, and the Tiber
along with the Aniene will run red with the blood of the
slaughtered victims.

Vent Aquilon fera partir le siege,
Par murs geter cendres, chauls, & pousiere:
Par pluye apres, qui leur fera bien piege,
Dernier secours encontre leur frontiere.

The north wind will cause the seat to depart,
From walls will be thrown ashes, lime and dust,
Through rains afterwards, which will ensnare them,
Help in extremity near their frontier.
(Centuries IX, quatrain 99)

Bien pres du Tymbre pressé la libitine,
Un peu deuant grand inondation:
Le chef du nef prins, mis à la sentine,
Chasteau palaix en conflagration.

Very near the Tiber in haste Libitina,
A little before the great flood:
The leader of the boat taken prisoner in the sink,
Castle and palace in flames.

(Centuries II, quatrain 93)

Because of the war and the invasion carried out by the forces of the Islamic alliance, the Pope will be forced to escape, while Rome is suffering under a bombardment, which will cause the destruction of historical buildings and monuments, incessant and extraordinary rain will then create difficulties for rescuers, and this is an aspect of the situation which will bring about the capture of the Pope at sea, and thus the prophecy contained in *Centuries V, quatrain 25*, where the Seer writes: '*The reign of the Church will succumb at sea*' will be fulfilled.

The tragic events culminating in the capture of the Pope will cause the transfer elsewhere of the Catholic church: what will remain of the 2,000-year-old institution will abandon Rome, to seek refuge on the American continent. This will make it possible for a regeneration of the Church and of the Catholic religion, based on principles which will hark back to those of the first Christians, before the Church became hierarchical. This much is prophesied in *Centuries VIII, quatrain 99* :

Par la puissance des trois Roys temporelz,
En autre lieu sera mis le saint siege:
Où la substance de l'esprit corporel,
Sera remys & receu pour vray siege.

By the power of the three temporal Kings (the oil kings),
The Holy See will be put elsewhere,
Where the substance of the material spirit,
Shall be recognised and accepted as the true see.

(Centuries VIII, quatrain 99)

As we have said several times, the three '*temporal Kings,*' are the three *oil kings*: Iraq, Iran, and Libya, who with the invasion of Italy and the capture of the pontiff will bring about the transfer of the Holy See. This will be the occasion for survivors to regenerate their religious principles on the basis of the link between man's spiritual and god.

But the Arabs' activities will not be limited to Rome, once the capital has fallen, it will be Florence's turn, as is prophesied by *Centuries VII, quatrain 8*:

> Flora fuis, fuis le plus proche Romain,
> Au Fesulan sera conflict donné:
> Sang espandu, les plus grans prins à main,
> Temple ne sexe ne sera pardonné.

> *Flee, Florence, flee the nearest Roman,*
> *Near Fiesole battle will be engaged,*
> *Bloodshed, the greatest captured,*
> *Neither temple nor sex will be spared.*
>
> *(Centuries VII, quatrain 8)*

Fiesole having been taken, on the threshold of Florence a fierce battle will rage and in consequence of this, the more important political and military figures will be taken prisoner. The hoards of neo-barbarians will then launch into massacres, pillaging and acts of violence against women. Of Fiesole *Centuries VIII, quatrain 16* also speaks:

> Au lieu que HIERON feit sa nef fabriquer,
> Si grand deluge sera & si subite,
> Qu'on n'aura lieu ne terres s'ataquer,
> L'onde monter Fesulan Olympique.

> *Where Henry will have his ship built,*
> *So great a flood will be, and so sudden,*
> *That there will be neither place nor land to assail,*
> *The Olympic wave will mount to Fiesole.*
>
> *(Centuries VIII, quatrain 16)*

The name *Hieron*, in this quatrain, has been translated as Henry. I felt this word was an anagram, since it is written in capital letters, and this is Nostradamus's sign that the name is camouflaged. So *Hieron* becomes '*Roi Hen*', that is, *King Henry*, whose name has been abbreviated to fit into the line and to make it more difficult to understand.

If my interpretation is correct, then the quatrain should have the following meaning: at the place where King Henry, at the end of the conflict, will re-found the Christian church, which is, Rome, there will be a flood, which is so sudden and violent that the inhabitants will be unable to escape, and this exceptional event which will be in addition to the Arabs' invasion, will reach all the way to Florence, after passing through Fiesole, theatre of a ferocious battle.

The natural disaster, as we shall see in other passages, will be throughout the whole of Europe and even the United States. This will be one of the reasons why American intervention will not be possible for a long time.

It is altogether probable for such an extraordinary natural phenomenon to be traceable to the massive use of nuclear weapons, which could cause climatic upheavals of unthinkable proportions.

As far as Henry's religious role within the Church is concerned, what the Seer writes in paragraph CXXVI at the close of his letter is unequivocal:

O, King, the most powerful among all kings, within a brief time exceptional events will come to pass, but I cannot indicate them all in this epistle, nor is it my intention: but in order to understand some among the most dreadful ones, it is sufficient to explain a few even though so great is your majesty, your humanity towards everyone, your faith in God, and you alone are worthy of earning the most authoritative and Christian title of king and worthy of the title of supreme religious authority being conferred upon you.

Henry, in the vision of Nostradamus is destined not only to become the greatest expression of political power, he will also assume a religious role.

This clearly emerges in *Sestet 38*:

> Par eaue & par fer & par grande maladie,
> Le pouuoyeur à l'hazer de sa vie,
> Sçaura combien vaut le quintal du bois,
> Six cens & quinze, ou le dixneufiesme,
> On grauera d'un grand Prince cinquiesme,
> L'immortel nom, sur le pied de la Croix.

> *Through water and sword, and a great illness,*
> *Risking his life, the purveyor,*
> *Will know how much a quintal of wood is worth,*
> *Six hundred fifteen or the nineteenth,*
> *One will engrave of a great fifth Prince,*
> *The immortal name at the base of the Cross.*
>
> (*Sestet 38*)

This sestet requires a few clarifications, the *purveyor* is the Antichrist, whom in other sestets the Seer defined as '*purveyor of the Marine Monster*', that is, representative of Evil. During the conflict, there will be a moment in which the Antichrist will find himself in a delicate position, but he will well be able to evaluate its constituents and come to a decision on the basis of them. The Seer uses the expression '*quintal of wood*': this is a figure of speech to show someone who at a glance is able to judge the weight of a pile of wood, in other words, is able to size up a given situation. The years to which the sestet refers are 2007 or 2011, arrived at through the addition of 1615 or 1619 to 392 (the year of the Liturgy). At one of those two dates, a great *fifth* prince will come into the global limelight. Such a Prince can be none other than Henry of France, in view of the fact that the last king of France to bear this name was Henry IV ('*Paris is worth a mass*'). So, the next Henry can only be Henry V, who will make decisive contributions towards the defeat of the forces of Evil and saving the Christian religion from destruction, thus making himself worthy of his name being etched into the cross. Meanwhile, on the Eastern front, Italy will be attacked by Slavs.

Amas s'approche venant d'Esclauonie,
L'Olestant vieulx cité ruynera:
Fort desolee verra la Romanie,
Puis la grand flamme estaindre ne scaura.

A mass approaches from Slavonia,
The ancient eastern city will be ruined,
Italy will see great affliction,
Then will not be able to extinguish the great flame.
(Centuries IV, quatrain 82)

The Russians along with the Arabs will make a pincer movement, first invading the bordering countries, and then together with Serbia and Slovenia, who will become their allies, they will penetrate Italy from the east, where an ancient city, probably Trieste, the first city they will come upon in their march forward, will be completely destroyed.

They will continue their fight southwards and will reach Italy, which will be set on fire.

It is quite possible that during this war nuclear arms will be used – the great flame of which the quatrain speaks.

In *Centuries IV, quatrain 58* there are further traces of the use of these terrible weapons:

Soleil ardant dans le gosier coller,
De sang humain arrouser terre Etrusque:
Chef seille d'eaue mener son filz filer,
Captiue dame conduicte en terre turque.

Sun aflame in the burnt throat,
Etruscan soil sprinkled with human blood,
The bishop brings away his son,
Captured lady, led away to Turkish soil.
(Centuries IV, quatrain 58)

The quatrain describes the figure of an heroic bishop, who, heedless of the deaths and of throat-burning radiation, does everything in his power to save his followers. We know it is a bishop through the expression 'chef selle d'eau' which literally means 'head with the water seal', clear allusion to the ring with a fish which all bishops are given as a sign of their mission as fishers of souls.

In the course of this courageous effort to rescue his own followers (*his son*), a politically important woman, who has been made prisoner, is transferred by the invaders to Turkey.

Similar considerations regarding the use of nuclear weapons can be drawn upon in *Centuries I, quatrain 3*:

> Pour le chaleur solaire sus la mer,
> De Negropont les poissons demis cuits:
> Les habitans les viendront entamer,
> Quand Rod. & Gennes leur faudra le biscuit.

> *By the sun's heat under the sea,*
> *In the Black Sea the fish half-cooked:*
> *The inhabitants will come to eat them,*
> *When Rhodes and Genoa take their biscuits.*
> > (*Centuries II, quatrain 3*)

It would seem difficult, if not impossible for natural heat from the sun to be able to produce a situation in which the fish in the sea are boiled.

It is therefore probable that because of a nuclear bomb, which is capable of developing immense heat, there will be considerable fish mortality in the Black Sea. The inhabitants along the coast, reduced to hunger and deprived of sustenance, since ships bringing food and assistance will be diverted to Genoa and Rhodes, will be reduced to eating the radioactive fish.

The conquest of Italy and Spain being completed, the Russian and Arab armies will then turn their attention upon France:

Si France passe oultre mer Ligustique,
Tu te verras en isles & mers enclos:
Mahommet contraire plus mer Hadriatique
Cheuaulx & d'Asnes tu rongeras les os.

If you France, go beyond the Italian sea,
You will find Islands and seas blocked,
Mohammed nearer by, more so in the Adriatic sea,
You will gnaw the bones of horses and donkeys.
                              (*Centuries III, quatrain 23*)

The Seer's warning is an eloquent one: the French will make the attempt at a counter-offensive by sea, shifting their fleet to the Ligurian as well as the Adriatic sea. They will be met by a catastrophic defeat, and they will find their country under attack from every direction. The war will bring on frightful scarcity, with a lack of staple foods, and France will be forced into eating horse and donkey flesh.

Centuries I, quatrain 73 has already come under examination above. The quatrain prophesies the terrible siege under which France will fall, coming from five directions: from the sea, down the Pyrenees, across the border with Italy, along the Belgian and German frontiers.

The term '*ligustique*' was translated from the French with the expression '*Italian Sea*'. As we have seen, this adjective is a combination of '*Ligurien*' and '*Hadriatique*' and includes both seas, hence the reference made in the third line to the Adriatic, where Arab power will be great compared with the other side's.

Furthermore, responsibilities for the global disaster attributable to France will be substantial, for it will have been unable to adapt a firm, coherent attitude towards expanding Islamic power.

Par la discorde neglicence Gauloise,
Sera passaige à Mahommet ouuert:
De sang trempé la terre & mer Senoise,
Le port Phoce de voiles & nefz couuert.

Because of French disagreement and negligence,
For Mohammed the passage will be opened,
Drenched with blood the Sienese land and sea,
Marseilles covered with sails and ships.

(Centuries I, quatrain 18)

According to this quatrain, in France there will be uncertainties, perplexities and disagreement as to how the new situation should be dealt with. On the other hand, the Islamic forces will be very determined, and, taking advantage of the French's hesitation they will seize rapidly the port of Marseilles (*the Phoce*).

Another quatrain speaks of the seizure of Marseilles:

Piedz & Cheual à la seconde veille,
Feront entree vastient tout par la mer,
Dedans le poil entrera de Marseille,
Pleurs, crys & sang, onc nul temps si amer.

On foot and horse at the second watch,
All will enter erupting from the sea,
They will enter the port of Marseilles
Tears, cries and blood, never was there such a bitter
*   time.*

(Centuries X, quatrain 88)

In the middle of the night, having subjected Marseilles to an intensive bombardment from sea, the Arabs will succeed in entering and capturing the port. This conquest will be of enormous strategic importance: in fact, the invaders, having conquered Spain and Gibraltar, the entire Italian peninsula and Malta, they will have control over the entire Mediterranean with the fall of Marseilles.

The Arab-Russian troops will also turn towards central Europe, directing their attacks against Germany, Austria and Hungary:

Dans le Dannube & du Rin viendra boire,
Le grand Chameau ne s'en repentira:
Trembler du Rosne & pl'fort ceux de Loire:
Et pres des Alpes coq le ruynera.

In the Danube and the Rhine the great Camel,
Will come to drink and will not repent,
Rhône will tremble and even more Loire,
And near the Alps the cock will lay it to waste.
                    (Centuries V, quatrain 68)

The prophecy of this quatrain is that the Arabs, symbolised
by the camel, will succeed in conquering central Europe, subjugating the regions of the Rhine and Danube. The regions of
the Rhône, and still more those of the Loire, will be exposed
to the perils of invasion. However, these conquests will constitute the maximum limit of the expansion of the new Arabs,
who will subsequently be defeated near the Alps at the hands
of Henry (*the Gaul*), as will shall see later. The Russo-Arabs,
in their advance into the heart of Europe, will not spare
Switzerland, which, after centuries of peace will like other
nations be deeply and cruelly involved in the tragedy.

Migrés, migre de Genesue trestous,
Saturne d'or en fer se changera,
Le contre RAYPOZ exterminera tous.
Auant l'aduent le ciel signes fera.

Quite every one escaped from Geneva,
Golden Saturn will turn to iron,
The hostile RAYPOZ will exterminate everyone.
Before this happens, the sky will give signs.
                    (Centuries IX, quatrain 44)

The quatrain leaves no space for doubts as to what will happen
to Geneva: the Russians, under the command of a general
whose name will be an anagram of *Raypoz,* will exterminate
all the inhabitants of that city. Thus, for Switzerland, the long

period of peace and prosperity will come to an end: the gold from their vaults will be turned into the iron of weapons.

Before this tragic event, an astronomical phenomenon will make its appearance in the sky. For the Genevans this will be a warning of the imminent catastrophe.

Raypoz is written in capital letters, and is most probably an anagram: if this is so, it is a quite special name, and bearing in mind the geographical position of Switzerland and Geneva, it appears probable that the massacre will be committed by an official of the Russian army.

> Le saint Empire viendra en Germanie,
> Ismaelites trouueront lieux ouuerts,
> Anes voudront aussi la Carmanie,
> Les soustenens de terre tous couuerts.

> *The Holy Empire will come into Germany,*
> *The Ismaelites will find open places,*
> *The donkeys will also want Carmania*
> *Defenders of the land all covered.*
> *(Centuries X, quatrain 31)*

Arab power will reach a point where it has the same extant as that of the Holy Roman Empire, and the Islamic troops will encounter very little resistance. At that point, many among them will want to proceed with the conquest, as Alexander the Great did in Carmania (a region identifiable with the territory occupied by today's Iran and Afghanistan), in 325 BC, losing almost his entire army in the region watered by the Minab river, and the invaders, as happened to the army of the great Macedonian, will suffer a terrible defeat.

In any case, the consequences of the war will be horrible for Europe and for France, as is evident in *Centuries VI, quatrain 80*:

> De Fez le regne puiendra à ceulx d'Europe,
> Feu leur cité, & l'ame trenchera:

Le grand d'Asie terre & mer à grand trope,
Que bleux, pers, croix, à mort deschassera.

From Fez the reign will reach those of Europe
The city aflame, life taken away:
The great one from Asia on land and sea a great
    metonym,
Will drive to death blues (French), *light blues* (Italian)
    and the crosses (the Clergy).
                              (Centuries VI, quatrain 80)

The majority of European cities will be destroyed, and Russia
(*the Great one from Asia*), with its troops, will carry out horrible massacres against the French *(bleux)*, Italians *(pers)* and
the clergy *(croix)*. The Seer uses the adjective *bleux*, to indicate
the French, who are known for the colour of the Bourbons'
coat of arms (golden lilies on blue). And to indicate the Italians,
the Seer used *pers*, as this light blue is the colour of the Savoy
coat of arms. Even today in the Italian Republic, the jerseys
of all Italian national teams are light blue.

De gens d'Eglise sang sera espanché,
Comme de l'eau en si grande abondance,
Et d'un long temps ne sera restanché,
Vae, vae au clerc ruyne & doleance.

Of the people of the Church blood will be drawn,
Like water, in such enormous abundance,
And shall not be staunched for a long time,
Alas, alas, to the clergy ruin and torment!
                              (Centuries VIII, quatrain 98)

Ouy soubs terre saincte d'ame voix feinte
Humaine flamme pour diuine voir luire:
Fera des seulz de leur sang terre tainte,
Et les s. temples pour les impurs destruire.

Where under holy ground the false voice of the soul,
Human flame is seem to glitter as divine:
The earth will be tinged with their blood,
And the sacred temples destroyed by an impious throng.
                              (Centuries IV, quatrain 24)

The first of these quatrains presently under examination is saying substantially the same as paragraph CXIV of Nostradamus's letter to Henry:

The blood of the true clergy will flow everywhere, and one
of the terrible temporal (oil) *kings will be greatly praised*
by his followers for having shed more blood of innocent
clergy than how much wine he could have poured, and that
king will commit incredible misdeeds against the Church,
human blood will flow in the public streets and in temples,
like heavy rain and nearby rivers will run red with blood . . .

The second quatrain describes what the Antichrist will accomplish through his power of suggestion that is so immense that many will believe that his words are of divine inspiration. His followers will not hesitate in carrying out massacres among the religious in the name of the new creed.

Persecutee sera de Dieu l'eglise,
Et les sainctz temples seront expoliez:
L'enfant la mere mettra nud en chemise,
Seront Arabes aux Polons raliez.

The Church of God will be persecuted,
And the holy temples stripped bare,
The mother will put her child naked into her blouse,
It will be the Arabs allied with the Poles.
                              (Centuries V, quatrain 73)

This quatrain repeats the fact that the Church will be persecuted. The churches will be deprived of all their wealth. In the meantime, hunger and misery will be of such proportions, that mothers will have nothing with which to cover their children. In the last line the Seer proceeds to make the prophecy of an alliance between the Arabs and the Poles. Note that Nostradamus, when speaking of the Poles, means to refer to the Slavs of Eastern Europe and in particular to Russia, which, as we have seen in the letter to Henry, will in fact be allied to the Arabs in the name of the Antichrist and will involve in its tragic choice of fields its ex-satellite states, which were tied to it through the Warsaw Pact, Warsaw being the capital of Poland.

The fall of the European continent under Arab and Russian aggression, with France almost totally under occupation, and by now at the point of collapse, will throw England – until then territorially intact, because it has been able to maintain an efficient army, air and sea power, with its own oil production – into a deep crisis.

England, however, will also fall victim to the same natural phenomenon as the other European countries, and the United States: torrential rains will cause rivers to swell, and the seas will rise to frightful levels, and continuous floods will bring destruction to crops. The impossibility of maintaining commercial exchanges because of the war, will cause tremendous scarcities.

Un peut davant ou apres l'Angleterre
Par mort de loup, mise aussi bas que terre,
Verra le feu resiter contre l'eau,
Le r'alumant auecques telles force
Du sang humain, dessus l'humaine escorce,
Faite de pain, bondance de cousteau.

A little before or after England,
Through the death of the wolf, also razed lower than the
*   ground,*
Will see fire resist water,
Relighting it with its great force,
With human blood, over human skin,
Absence of bread, abundance of blades.

(Sestet 50)

The moment in which continental Europe discovers that it has become part of the empire of the Antichrist, England will face the extreme gravity of the situation and will find the courage to resist, even against the floods, which will be accompanied by cold and hunger. At that point its economic situation will be a critical one: the necessity of having to direct its economic resources towards armaments, as always happens in such cases, will cause a lowering in life style, and, in contrast to an increasing quantity of weapons, there will a scarcity of foodstuff, a situation already rendered serious by the climatic conditions.

In any case, England will also experience aggression from the Russians and the Arabs, as is prophesied in *Centuries II, quatrain 100*:

> Dedans les isles si horrible tumulte,
> Rien on n'orra qu'une bellique brigue:
> Tant grant sera des prediteurs l'insulte,
> Qu'on se viendra ranger à la grand ligue.

> *Inside the islands so horrible a tumult,*
> *Only a war-like quarrel will be heard,*
> *So great will be the predators' insult,*
> *That there will be alliance with the grand league.*
> > (*Centuries II, quatrain 100*)

England and Ireland, who had remained apart and had not participated in the conflict, are suddenly attacked, and the war is brought into their territory. The attack will cause such an affront, that the two Anglo-Saxon countries will decide to intervene and to ally themselves with what remains of the European forces (only a part of France), together with the United States.

> Le chef d'Ecosse auec six d'Alemaigne,
> Par gens de mer Orientaulx captif:
> Trauerseront la Calpre & Hespaigne,
> Present en Perse au nouueau roy craintif.

The head of Scotland and six of Germany,
Captured by sailors from the East:
Will pass Gibraltar and Spain,
Given in Persia to the horrible new king.
                                        (Centuries III, quatrain 78)

The prophecy of this quatrain is that a noble Scot will be captured at sea together with six Germans. They will be brought through Spain and Gibraltar to Persia, where they will be offered as a gift, almost as sacrificial victims, to the Antichrist.

England, therefore will also be invaded by the Russo-Arab forces, which in the midst of battle will force the queen into a situation from which there will be no escape:

La grande royne se verra vaincu,
Fera exces de masculin couraige:
Sus cheual, fleuue passera toute nue,
Suite par fer: à soy fera oultrage.

The great queen in the face of defeat,
Will make a show of masculine courage,
On horseback will cross the river quite naked,
Pursued by the sword, she will commit outrage on
    herself.

                                        (Centuries I, quatrain 86)

This quatrain could possibly concern Queen Elizabeth II. However, it could also treat of the consort of Prince Charles: Camilla, if he were to marry her. This interpretation is strengthened, in view of the fact that Camilla Parker Bowles is very fond of riding. Whoever is meant by the queen will have no means of escape and in order to flee from the invaders, she will mount a horse naked and commit suicide.

This very same account is repeated in *Sestet 54*:

Six cens & quinze, vingt, grand Dame mourra,
Et peu apres un fort long temps plouura,
Plusieurs pays, Flandres & l'Angleterre,

Seront par feu & par fer affligez,
De leurs voisins longuement assiegez,
Contraints seront de leurs faire la guerre.

Six hundred and fifteen, twenty, a great lady will die,
And shortly afterwards it will rain for a long time,
Many countries, Flanders and England,
Will be vexed by fire and sword,
Long besieged by their neighbours,
Some of them will be against making war.

(Sestet 54)

In the year 2007 or 2012, the queen will die, and after her death, fire and sword will rain down from the sky, striking not only England but Flanders as well. The Russo-Arab invaders will tighten their siege around these two countries, but in spite of this, there will be some who will be against continuing the war. This contrariness, which could appear astonishing, in fact, it will be the result of the politics and religion propagated by the Antichrist himself, who will have created proselytes among these people. It will also be the result of the weariness produced by the long period of war, which will have exhausted a considerable portion of the public.

In the meantime, the Antichrist will proceed with his march through France:

Dans Foix entrez Roy cerulee Turban:
Et regnera moins reuolu Saturne
Roy Turban blanc Bizance coeur ban,
Sol, Mars, Mercure ensemble pres la hurne.

In Foix enter the King in sky-blue Turban,
He will reign for less than a cycle of Saturn,
The King white turban Turk heart exile,
Sun, Mars, Mercury together in the Urn (Aquarius).

(Centuries X, quatrain 73)

The quatrain is clearly giving details as to the duration of the war: the King, who will enter Foix, wearing a sky-blue turban, will remain there less than thirty years, since Saturn employs almost that time span to accomplish its revolution around the Sun.

This implies, therefore, that the occupation will last a long time, as much time, that is, as the empire of the Antichrist will last, which, as has been seen, will continue for an abundant twenty-five years, that is, less than one cycle of Saturn, but, anyhow, a considerable amount of time.

The quatrain speaks of a disagreement arising between the Arabs and the Turks during the course of the war, the latter will, at a certain point retire from the conflict. It should be noted that the Sun, Mars and Mercury are quite frequently united under Aquarius. However, bearing in mind that the Third World War should break out in 2006, and that in this quatrain reference is made to a quite considerable permanence, it seems reasonable to conclude that the event should take place in February 2009, the first astrological combination with the Sun, Mars and Mercury in Aquarius to occur after 2006.

The Turkish turn-about is confirmed by *Centuries V, quatrain 47*:

> Le grand Arabe marchera bien auant,
> Trahy sera par les Bisantinois:
> L'antique Rodes luy viendra au deuant,
> Et plus grand mal par austre Pannonois.

> *The great Arab will march well ahead,*
> *Betrayed he will be by the Byzantines:*
> *Ancient Rhodes will loom before him,*
> *And the greatest evil for Austria and Hungary.*
> *(Centuries V, quatrain 47)*

In their advance through Europe, the Arabs will find themselves being betrayed by the Turks, who will be in obvious disagreement with them as to the plan of invasion.

We have already been able to observe above, in our examination of the expansion of the Antichrist in the Middle East, that Egypt and Turkey will undergo aggression from Iran. It is therefore probable that with the extension of the theatre of war, Turkey will take advantage of the situation by detaching itself from the Arab league. In any case, the quatrain prophesies that the invasion will have a bearing with Austria and Hungary, a fact which is repeated in other parts of the Seer's work.

In 2011 it will then be Paris's turn, after five years of heroic resistance:

> La Ville sans dessus dessous,
> Renuersée de mille coups
> De canons: & forts dessous terre:
> Cinq ans tiendra: le tout remis,
> Et lasche à ses ennemis,
> L'eau leur fera apres la guerre.

> *The City will be upside-down,*
> *Thrown into confusion by a thousand shots*
> *From cannons: the valiant under the ground*
> *Five years will it hold: then totally give in,*
> *Abandoning to its enemies,*
> *The water will come after the war.*
>
> *(Sestet 3)*

In this sestet Nostradamus writes '*Ville*' with a capital letter, and this places us in the position of being able to advance the hypothesis that he intends to indicate the city *par excellence*, that is, Paris. The French capital will find itself under bombardment for five years, and the heroic French people will put up a strong resistance. However, what the violence of weapons alone will not succeed in accomplishing will be accomplished by water. Once again the Seer alludes to an extraordinary natural phenomenon whose effects will be felt by a considerable part of the globe and which will cause immense flooding of cities and countryside, weakening the resistance of the West, already exhausted by the terrible war. Thus the Antichrist will have the opportunity to assert that Allah protects him and assists him in destroying Evil and Sin: all this will endow the invaders with an incredible moral force and will act as a psychological counter-blow against those who will have been desperately resisting.

The sestet makes use of a septenarius instead of hendecasyllabic verse, in order to underline the excitement of the moment and the dramatic succession of events.

At that point, with the occupation of Spain, Italy and great parts of France and England and of the entire Middle East being assured, the Antichrist will succeed in administering a boundless territory, when it is considered that Russia will be under submission to him and that he will have secured for himself the alliance of China, until then outside the conflict.

In high spirits after victory, the *Médecin* will be present everywhere, paying visits to his lugubrious empire, made up of destroyed cities and unburied bodies:

> Le pouruoyeur du monstre sans pareil,
> Se fera veoir ainsi que le Soleil,
> Montant le long la ligne Meridienne,
> En poursuiuant l'Elephant & le loup,
> Nul Empereur ne fit jamais tel coup,
> Et rien plus pis à ce Prince n'aduienne.

> *The purveyor of the peerless monster,*
> *Will make himself seen like the Sun,*
> *Rising along the meridian line,*
> *In pursuing the Elephant and the Wolf,*
> *No Emperor has ever made such a coup,*
> *And nothing worse will happen to this Prince.*
>
> *(Sestet 39)*

This sestet leaves no doubt at all regarding this point: the Antichrist, after having established dominion over the Arab world and over continental Europe, like a peacock, will go from place to place, by now certain of having achieved his goals, goals which numerous people through history have tried in vain to achieve prior to him, people such as Napoleon and Hitler.

The Seer warns, however, that that moment of glory will soon pass and that complete disgrace will follow on its heels.

Sestet 46 has similar contents but is chronologically more precise:

> Le pouruoyeur mettra tout en desroute,
> Sangsue & loup, en mon dire n'escoute
> Quand Mars sera au signe du Mouton
> Ioint à Saturne, & Saturne à la Lune,
> Alors sera ta plus grande infortune,
> Le soleil lors en exaltation.

> *The purveyor will put everything to rout,*
> *Leech and Wolf do not listen to me.*
> *When Mars will be in the sign of the Ram,*
> *With Saturn, and Saturn with the Moon,*
> *Then will be your greatest misfortune,*
> *The Sun at that point in exaltation.*
>
> *(Sestet 46)*

As we have seen, in the sestets, the Antichrist is given the title of '*purveyor of the Marine Monster*', a clear allusion to the '*Beast of the Sea*' in the Apocalypse where the demon has come from the pit to corrupt and destroy humanity. Then, through the intervention of the Beast of the Sea, the '*Beast of the Earth*' is created, which represents the beast of the sea and propagates his worship among men: the purveyor (or provider), therefore, is the Antichrist, the same as the one present in John's Book of Revelations.

In this sestet as well as in the one preceding it, the Seer warns that the Antichrist will destroy everyone, Russia and Europe, but, unfortunately, he will not be heeded.

However, the sestet is important for another reason: it mentions an astral conjunction of Saturn, Mars and the Moon in the sign of Aries, with the Sun in exaltation. A celestial body goes into exaltation when it enters under a sign which lends

force to it. The house in which the Sun is in exaltation is
Aries, therefore the sestet is indicating an astral conjunction
in Aries of the Sun, the Moon, Mars and Saturn, and this will
occur exclusively on 16 and 17 April 2026: at that moment,
the fatal hour of death will have arrived ('*your greatest misfortune*') for the Antichrist. At that point, about a year will have
passed since the end of the war, and if it is true that the
Antichrist succeeds in surviving for some months more, it
means that he will be taken prisoner and will die of an illness
in prison.

His death will be the final act of a tragedy and will give
rise to jubilation and a great sense of relief for all mankind.
The Sun itself, which, after more than 7,000 years will shine
once more on human destinies, will do so with a more vivid
and exalting light.

But prior to this important event, the Calvary which mankind
will be forced to undergo will be quite difficult, and there will
be occasion to witness the temporary triumph of the forces of
Evil.

> Le grand Empire chacun an deuoir estre,
> Un sur les autres le viendra obtenir,
> Mais peu de temps sera son regne & estre,
> Deux ans aux naues se pourra soustenir.

> *Each one was to have the great empire,*
> *One above all others will succeed in obtaining it,*
> *But his reign and life will last only a short time,*
> *For two years will the ships hold forth.*
>
> (Centuries X, quatrain 32)

The Antichrist, with his forces at their maximum extent, will
succeed, therefore, in obtaining that empire which, throughout
history, after Rome, no one has been able to achieve. But his
dominion will last only a short time, as will his own life too.
The initial strategy will be that of destroying the American
fleet, as the Japanese did during the Second World War; then
the powerful Russian fleet will emerge as master of the seas.

This fleet will be able to guarantee dominion to the Antichrist for only two years, then, slowly, but inexorably, the resurgence of Western forces will progressively succeed in eroding his empire, bringing it to its complete destruction.

13. The second phase of the war: 2011–17 and four years of truce: 2017–21)

The second phase of the war will be characterised by the West's reaction: it will gradually liberate a great part of Europe from the invaders. This phase will mark Henry's prominence, who, in the space of six years, with a great expenditure of effort and at the cost of millions of human lives, will succeed in achieving his goal, as is prophesied in paragraph LXXXI of the letter to Henry: *'the major part of the troops of the principal Eastern leader will be annihilated by the northerners and the people of the West, defeated and exterminated and the rest in flight and their children, born of different wives, will be imprisoned and the prophecy of the Royal Prophet will then come true: 'Ut audiret gemitus compenditorum, ut solveret filios interemptorum'.*

Nostradamus uses two distinct terms to indicate Henry, one already identified by numerous interpreters, which boils down to the name of *'Chiren'* and which is an anagram of *'Henric'*. The other is not correctly defined and consists of the name of *'Selin'*, by itself or accompanied *'Chiren'* (an anagram). That the name *'Selin'* refers to Henry gains substance from the letter dedicated to Henry himself, whose own name is preceded by the hyperbole *'l'invictissime'* and is followed by the adjective *'second'*. So the Seer is using the *green language*, fusing the first part of the adjective with that of the hyperbole, thus *'Selin'* is *SE*(cond) *L'IN*(victissime), and that is *Henry the Second, the Invincible*.

> Comme un Gryphon viendra le Roy d'Europe,
> Accompaigné de ceux d'Aquilon,
> De rouges & blancz conduira grande troppe,
> Et iront contre le Roy de Babylon.

> *Like a Gryphon the King of Europe will come,*
> *Allied with those of Aquilon* (the North),
> *Of reds and whites will he lead a great troop,*
> *And then will go against the King of Babylon.*
>
> *(Centuries X, quatrain 86)*

The Seer compares Henry to a Gryphon, the mythical bird of the regions of Scythia, which preyed upon navigators who sailed the Black and the Ionian seas. Henry will be the military leader of the troops of the north who will have set aside their political and ideological differences, with the aim of facing their common enemy (*reds and whites*). He will launch the power of his army against the leader of the Arab League.

In the meantime, another military leader (the second of the three brothers), of Italian origin, will move against the Libyans, driving them out of European territory.

> Par grand fureur le roy Romain belgique,
> Vexer vouldra par phalange barbare:
> Fureur grinsant chassera gent libique,
> Depuis Pannons jusques Hercules la hare.

> *With great fury, the Roman king of Belgium,*
> *Will want to attack with foreign troops,*
> *Will chase the Libyans with great fury,*
> *From Hungary all the way to the altar of Hercules*
>   (Gibraltar).
>
> *(Centuries V, quatrain 13)*

Belgium under Libyan occupation is attacked by this military leader, who, with the help of a multinational army (foreign) succeeds in his attempt and liberates central Europe, forcing the Arabs back beyond the straits of Gibraltar indicated as '*Altar of Hercules*', which refers to the mythical *Pillars of Hercules*, which lent their name to the straits of Gibraltar in ancient times. The Roman king to whom the quatrain refers is probably the same as described in *Centuries V, quatrain 74*:

De sang Troyen naistra coeur Germanique,
Qu'il deuiendra en si haulte puissance:
Hors chassera gent estrange Arabique,
Tournant l'eglise en pristine preeminence.

Of Trojan blood will be born a German heart,
That he will become so high powered:
He will drive away the Arab stranger,
Putting the Church back to its pre-eminence.
(Centuries V, quatrain 74)

The reference to Troy should not direct our thoughts to Turkey, but rather, to Virgil and to his *Aeneid:* Aeneas is the mythical progenitor of the ancient Romans, and so the Seer is referring to Italy here. This future personality will be of Italian origin, therefore, but will have a German mother (*German heart*).

In the meantime, after so much suffering, what will remain of the Western nations will organise and predispose the counter-attack. Here, the alliance between France and Spain will be of fundamental importance, and with their remaining forces they will organise a common army:

Croix, paix, soubs un accomply diuin verbe,
Espaigne & Gaule seront unis ensemble:
Grand classe proche, & combat tres acerbe,
Coeur si hardy ne sera qui ne tremble.

Cross, peace, under an accompanying divine verb,
Spain and France will be united together:
A great fleet approach, and very sharp conflict,
The heart, courageous though it is, can do nought but
*   tremble.*
(Centuries IV, quatrain 5)

Between Spain and France, partially liberated from the invasion, a close alliance will be forged in preparation for the hard battles that are going to have to be faced. The two countries will also be united in the name of Christianity and God.

Numerous verses are dedicated to the great Henry:

> Nay subs les umbres & journee nocturne,
> Sera en regne & bonté souueraine:
> Fera renaistre son sang de l'antique urne,
> Renouuelant siecle d'or pour l'aerain.

> *Born in the shadow, at a nightly hour,*
> *With his sovereign goodness he will reign,*
> *His blood will be reborn from the antique urn,*
> *Renewing the golden century with bronze.*
> *(Centuries V, quatrain 41)*

Henry will be born at night-time and will reign with magnanimity. His ancient blood (that of the Bourbons) will be resurrected from the antique urn containing the ashes of his ancestors, as a valiant military leader of the armed forces that will defeat the invaders. The last line is ambivalent: it could mean "Renewing the century with gold in place of bronze", or it could mean: "With weapons (*bronze*) he will renew the golden century". A similar concept to this is given in *Sestet 40*:

> Ce qu'en viuant le pere n'auoit sceu,
> Il acquerra ou par guerre ou par feu,
> Et combatre la sangsue irritée,
> Ou jouyra de son bien paternel,
> Et fauory du grand Dieu Eternel,
> Aura bien tost sa Prouince heritée.

> *What, while the living father did not know,*
> *He will acquire either by war or by fire,*
> *And fight the wrathful Leech,*
> *Or will rejoice in his paternal goods,*
> *And, favoured by the great Eternal God,*
> *Will very soon inherit his Province.*
> *(Sestet 40)*

While his father was still alive, Henry still did not have awareness of himself and of his immense inner resources. This self-
awareness will be acquired in the course of bitter combat
against the Arabs. Only at that moment will his ancient lineage
assure him of that heroic glow by which he will be surrounded.
God will assist him in his efforts and will give him the possibility of reacquiring in a brief time dominion over the territory
that had belonged to his ancestors, that is, France.

Sestet 4 has similar contents but gives a precise indication
of a date.

> D'un rond, d'un lis, naistra un si gran Prince,
> Bien tost, & tard venu dans sa Prouince,
> Saturne en Libra en exaltation:
> Maison de Venus en decroissante force,
> Dame en apres masculin soubs l'escorse,
> Pour mantenir l'heureux sang de Bourbon.

> *From a ring, from a lily, such a great Prince will be*
>   *born,*
> *Quite soon and later he will come to his Province,*
> *Saturn in Libra in exaltation:*
> *The house of Venus in decline,*
> *Masculine woman under the skin,*
> *To conserve the felicitous Bourbon blood.*
>   *(Sestet 4)*

The sestet informs us that Henry, when Saturn is situated in
Libra and Venus is in Virgo, will reach his province. The
astrological references are in need of a few comments. Each
planet acquires force when it finds itself in a particular house.
The house in which Saturn is exalted is Libra. The opposite
house with respect to the sign in which each planet is exalted
is that in which the planet becomes weak. Venus acquires
force and becomes exalted in Pisces, and becomes weak in
the opposite sign, which is Virgo.

Consequently, the year in which Saturn is in Libra and
Venus is in Virgo must be identified. Saturn will be found in

Libra in October 2009 and will remain in that sign until 8 April 2010, when in its retrograde phase, it will return to Virgo. It will then re-enter Libra on 22 July 2010 to remain there until the 5 October 2012. Venus will be situated in Virgo from the 22 August 2011 until 15 September of the same year. Then it will re-enter Virgo on 4 October 2012; but Saturn on the 6 October will enter Scorpio, so its period of exaltation on 4 October will have reached a minimum.

This means that the event being narrated must be referred to August–September 2011, with Venus in Virgo and Saturn in Libra.

And the fact that the year 2011 is correct is confirmed by *Sestet 38*, which we have already studied, where the Seer indicates that in 615 or 619 the name of Henry V will be engraved on the base of the cross. The year 615 corresponds to 2007, while 619 correspond to 2011, and so, the two sestets point to exactly the same year as being that of the advent of Henry.

Henry, in order to escape from the Antichrist and to save the blood of the Bourbons, will use the stratagem of masquerading as a woman ('*masculine woman under the skin*').

> Soubz le colleur du traicté mariage,
> Fait magnanime par grand Chyren selin,
> Quentin, Arras recouurez au voyage,
> D'Espaignolz fait second banc macelin.

> *Of marriage alliance made under the flag,*
> *Magnanimous deed by the great Henry,*
> *Quentin, Arras retaken in the excursion,*
> *Of Spaniards a second slaughter.*
> *(Centuries VIII, quatrain 54)*

The alliance between France and Spain will allow Henry to rely on an adequate army, which will put him in the position of being able to regain San Quentin and Arras with a well executed incursion. In the encounter, however, numerous Spaniards will meet their death.

Dans les Espaignes viendra Roy tres-puissant,
Par mer & terre subjugant le Midy:
Ce mal fera, rebaissant le croissant,
Baisser les aisles à ceux du Vendredy.

An all-powerful king will come to Spain,
Subjugating the south by land and by sea,
He will do evil, lowering the crescent,
Lowering the wings of those of Friday (Mohammed).
(Centuries X, quatrain 95)

Subsequently there will be the beginning of the Spanish campaign, through which Henry will succeed in liberating the entire southern region of that nation, bringing about a collapse of Arab forces, which, in their defeat, will lose a great part of the Iberian territory.

Dedans les isles de cinq fleuues à un,
par le croissant du grand Chyren Selin:
Par les bruynes de l'aer fureur en l'un,
Six eschapés cachés fardeaux de lyn.

In the isles of five rivers to one
By the crescent of the great Henry Selino
Through the misty airs, the wrath of one
Six escaped, hidden in bundles of linen.
(Centuries VI, quatrain 27)

Henry's action will also be directed at England and Ireland, defined by the Seer as the islands of five rivers to one. With this, Nostradamus intends to refer to Great Britain, which at the highest point of its glory and expansion, held dominion over territories furrowed by five rivers: the Thames, the Nile, the Ganges, the Niger and the Euphrates. With the fading of its power, the British Empire was reduced to only one river, the Thames.

In the course of his action aimed at liberating England, Henry whose name is accompanied by the adjective *Selin* (an abbreviation of *Second l'Invictissime*), will exert all his military might and his wrath, routing Russians and Arabs, six of whose leaders will escape by hiding in bundles of linen.

> Passer Guienne, Languedoc & le Rosne,
> D'Agen tenens de Marmande & la Roole,
> D'ouurir par foy parroy, Phocen tiendra son trosne,
> Conflit aupres Saint Pol de Manseole.

> *Through Guienne, Languedoc and Rhône,*
> *The lands of Agen, Marmande and the Roole,*
> *His objective to open resolutely the Phocen wall*
>   (Marseilles),
> *Conflict near Saint Paul de Mansol.*
>> *(Centuries IX, quatrain 85)*

Once again, line 3 is open to other interpretations: it could also mean *'By opening with pillage, Marseilles shall seize her objective'*, though I prefer the interpretation given above.

Henry will then proceed towards the liberation of France, and this action on this part will lead to the re-acquisition of Marseilles, after a violent battle near Saint Paul de Mansol in Provence.

> Proche à descendre l'armee Crucigere,
> Sera guettee par les Ismaelites,
> De tous cottez batus par nef Rauiere,
> Prompt assaillis de dix galeres eslites.

> *Near to descending, the crusading army,*
> *Will be lain in wait for by the Israelites,*
> *Harassed on every side by the ship* Raviere
> *Soon attacked by ten elite galleys.*
>> *(Centuries IX, quatrain 43)*

The allied forces, as during the times of the Crusades, will proceed with the liberation of France by land and by sea.

The warship *Raviere*, a name which, possibly is an anagram

of something else, probably of Russian origin, harasses them from all sides with continual cannonades, and from sea, then it will be attacked by ten ships from the Western fleet and will thus be sunk.

Dominion of the seas will be a decisive element during the third global conflict. For a certain period of time, the powerful Russian fleet, having destroyed the American fleet, will guarantee powerful support to the forces of the Antichrist, impeding the Western ships from bringing help to the countries under attack. Subsequently, as happened during the second global conflict, the West will succeed in creating a powerful fleet, with which they will force a reversal in the fortunes of the conflict.

> Gaulois par saults, monts viendra penetrer:
> Occupera le grand lieu de l'Insubre:
> Au plus profond son ost fera entrer,
> Gennes, Monech poulseront classe rubre.

> *Through passes and across mountains the French will*
>   *penetrate,*
> *And will occupy the greater part of Italy,*
> *His army will penetrate far within,*
> *They will push out the Russian fleet from Genoa and*
>   *Monaco.*
>
> *(Centuries IV, quatrain 37)*

According to this quatrain, the Western forces, under the command of Henry, will begin the campaign from Italy, part of which will come under occupation, in particular the northwestern sector, where the Russian fleet will be forced to abandon Genoa and the principality of Monaco.

I have concluded that the expression '*Classe rubre*' refers to Russia: it is a fact that the Romans used to refer to Russia as '*Rubria*', that is, *red*, and on the basis of this adjective and of its ambivalence Nostradamus created a splendid quatrain, which though it regards the past, and merits being cited for the fact that until now it has not been understood:

A soubstenir la grand cappe troublee,
Pour l'esclaircir les rouges marcheront:
De mort famille sera presque accablee,
Ler rouges rouges le rouge assomeront.

To uphold the great muddied cloak,
To make it clean the reds (Russians) *will march:*
The family will be almost annihilated,
The red reds (the Bolsheviks) *will kill the red* (Russians).
(Centuries VIII, quatrain 19)

In this quatrain the Seer plays on the double meaning of the adjective '*rouge*', which has the meaning of red, but which in its Latin derivation also means '*Russian*'.

To me the quatrain is obviously about the death of Tsar Nicolas II and the extermination of his family at the hands of Lenin's Bolsheviks, after the white Russians had made the vain attempt at a counteroffensive in defence of the Tsar. It must be added that, surprisingly, the same quatrain informs us that one member survives the extermination ('*the family almost annihilated*'), and that is the infant Anastasia, about whose mysterious fate rivers of ink have flowed.

At this point the Western world will have been entirely liberated. The Arabs will be forced to retreat to their territories; in the meantime the Russians will suffer a military collapse and will be completely destroyed, as is prophesied in *Sestet 58*:

Sangsue en peu de temps mourra,
Sa mort bon signe nous donra,
Pour l'accroissement de la France,
Alliance se trouueront,
deux grands Royaumes se joindront,
François aura sur eux puissance.

In a little while the Leech will die,
Its death for us will be a good sign,
For the growth of France,

An alliance will be sealed,
Two great kingdoms will unite,
The French will have power over them.
(Sestet 58)

This is the end, therefore, of Russia, a fact which will signal the expansion of French military and political power. The war will furthermore force the nations to come to an understanding as to the necessity for closer and more precise military and political alliances capable of guaranteeing an improved and a more timely defence.

There will be the fusion of two states, over which France will exert a great influence.

With the precipitous retreat by the invading forces thousands of prisoners will regain their freedom.

En barbe crespe & noire par engin,
Subiuguera la gent cruelle & fiere:
Un grand Chyren ostera du longin,
Tous les captifz par Seline baniere

With a curly black beard, with engine of war,
He will subjugate the cruel, proud people,
The great Henry will remove the leash,
Of the prisoners under the Moon's (Arab) *flag.*
(Centuries II, quatrain 79)

Line 1 is open to another interpretation: '*Par engin*' might mean '*with cleverness*', but I prefer the interpretation above.

The description of the great future military leader brings back memories of the Second World War, particularly, in France, where after the landing in Normandy, the allied forces progressively liberated the country from Nazi occupation. In many films of the period the faces of generals and troops can be seen protruding from the turrets of tanks, blackened by dust and smoke, weary from fatigue and tension, faces, however, which shine with the brightness of proud smiles.

As happened in France in the Second World War, also in

the Third World War, after victory and liberation, there will be scenes of jubilation and celebration:

> Crier victoire du grand Selin croissant,
> Par les Romains sera l'Aigle clamé:
> Turin, Milan & Gennes n'y consent,
> Puis par eulx mesmes Basil grand reclamé.

> *Through the growing victory of Henry,*
> *The Romans eagle will acclaim,*
> *Turin, Milan and Genoa not assenting,*
> *But by themselves, Basel will be reclaimed.*
> *(Centuries VI, quatrain 78)*

As often happens in such cases, after the victory celebrations, protests will arise. While the Romans will without reserve acclaim the French eagle and will consequently push for the unification of Italy, France and other European states under Henry, in the north there will be those who will want to maintain the autonomy and the sovereignty of Italy. However, on the wave of the enthusiasm of the entire Italian population, the voices of dissent will be silenced, and Henry will by then be destined to become that '*Monarch of the Universe*', whose advent is prophesied by the entire work of Nostradamus.

The unification of Italy with the great new European State at the hands of Henry is furthermore confirmed by *Centuries IV, quatrain 77*:

> Selin monarque l'Italie pacifique,
> Regnes unis Roy chrestien du monde:
> Mourant vouldra coucher en terre blesique,
> Apres pyrate auoir chassé de l'onde.

Henry the monarch pacifies Italy,
Kingdoms united, Christian king of the world,
When he dies, he will want to rest in the ground at Blois,
After pirates are driven from the sea.
(Centuries IV, quatrain 77)

Apart from the pacification of Italy by Henry and its subsequent union with the powerful new state, the quatrain tell
us that Henry, after having earned the title of Christian King
of the World, will want to be buried when he dies at Blois
and that his death will come after the enemy ships have been
finally destroyed.

The war, lasting a good eleven years, will have brought
with it such frightful consequences, as will throw doubt upon
the very survival of the human race itself.

In this war, in fact, nuclear weapons will have been put to
use, a fact which will have made it so that in great parts of
the globe, it will have become impossible to cultivate the soil
and to raise animals. To this will be added the scarcity of
manpower, since the death toll will reach into the millions,
while many infants will be born with monstrous deformities,
because of the radiation by which their mothers will have been
contaminated during pregnancy.

This has already been made clear in the commentary of the
letter to Henry, where in paragraph LXX it is written that '*in
these circumstances there will arise a pestilence so great that
more than half the world will perish*,' the Seer then adds
in paragraph LXXX: '*what calamitous affliction will strike
pregnant women then!*'

A frightful prophecy about famine and scarcity that will
afflict the world is contained in *Sestet 33*:

Bien peu apres sera tres grande misere,
Du peu de bled, qui sera sur la terre,
Du Dauphiné, Prouence & Viuarois,
Au Viuarois est un pauure presage,
Pere du fils, sera entropophage,
Et mangeront racine & gland du bois.

Very soon afterwards, there will be very great misery,
For lack of grain, everywhere in the land,
From Dauphiné, Provence and Vivarois,
For Vivarois there is a terrible presage,

The father will be cannibal of his son,
And will eat the roots of tree and acorns.

(Sestet 33)

The immediate post-war period is well represented in *Centuries I, quatrain 63*:

Les fleaux pasés, diminue le monde,
Long temps la paix terres inhabitées,
Seur marchera par ciel, terre, mer & onde,
Puis de nouueau les guerres suscitees.

When the scourge has passed, the world will diminish,
A long-lasting peace in uninhabited lands,
Certainty will walk through heaven, earth, sea and wave,
Then once again the wars will begin.

(Centuries I, quatrain 63)

Radiation from the nuclear war will cause flowers to wither. Many zones of the earth will be uninhabitable. The peace which flows through the world is no longer the joyous dove of peace, but almost a sad and black crow which soars above deserted and arid expanses, without woods, fields, houses: only heaps of debris and desolation.

Notwithstanding this disaster, human sufferings will not yet be over: the quatrain prophesies, in fact, that war will return to what will have remained of mankind.

14. Resumption of the war by China: 2022–25

Du pont Euxine, & la grand Tartarie,
Un roy sera qui viendra voir la Gaule:
Transpercera Alane & l'Armenie,
Et dans Bisance lairra sanglante Gaule.

From the Euxine bridge and the great Tartary,
There will be a king who will come to see France,
He will cross Sarmatia and Armenia,
And in Byzantium he will wound the Gaul bloodily.
(Centuries V, quatrain 54)

Euxine Sea was an ancient name for the Black Sea. The quatrain prophesies that a king coming from what was once the land of the Tartars, across the territories adjacent to the Black Sea – Armenia and Russia (*Sarmatia*, land of the ancient people of the Alans) – will go all the way to France. In his advance, he will encounter the forces of Henry in Turkey and will succeed in prevailing.

In any case, the new offensive, at the outset, will meet with success, as can be seen in paragraph CXVII of the letter to Henry: '*the third king of the Arab alliance, hearing the laments of the people of his principal territory, will put together a great army and will pass through the districts of his forebears and his ancestors and he will succeed for the greater part in restoring the situation to its previous state.*'

In this passage also the reference is to China, since the Huns, the Mongols and the Tartars devastated great parts of Europe with their invasions, and, they can rightly be defined as antecedents (*the Huns*) and as forebears (*the Mongols and the Tartars*) with respect to the future invaders. Across the

territories adjacent to the Black Sea and Turkey, therefore, the
new invaders will extend their reach into the Middle East as
well as into southern and insular Italy, flanked in this under-
taking by the remaining Arab forces, which have returned to
their original territories.

Sicily and Sardinia will come face to face with a new
Calvary:

> Paterne orra de la Sicile crie,
> Tous les aprests du goulphre de Trieste,
> Qui s'entendra jusque à la Trinacrie,
> De tant de voiles fuy, fuy l'horrible peste.

> *From Paternò will be heard Sicilian cries,*
> *Haste is made in the gulf of Trieste,*
> *When can be heard as far away as Trinacria,*
> *With so many ships fleeing, fleeing the horrible plague.*
>
> (*Centuries VIII, quatrain 84*)

While near the Gulf of Trieste the Western forces will seek
to organise themselves for a counter-offensive, Sicily will be
devastated by the Arabs and the Chinese, who will attack from
the sea, spreading death and destruction. The fate of Sardinia
will be similar:

> Par feu du ciel la cité presque aduste,
> Urna menasse encor Deucalion.
> Vexé Sardaigne par la punique fuste,
> Apres que Libra lairra son Phaeton.

> *By fire from the sky, the city almost burnt,*
> *Again the urn Deucalion threatens,*
> *Sardinia harassed by Punic ships,*
> *After Libra leaves its Phaeton.*
>
> (*Centuries II, quatrain 81*)

Through a terrible air attack, a city will be almost completely
burnt to the ground. The moment of Aquarius (*the urn*) con-

tinues to undermine justice and civilisation. Deucalion, in fact, was the son of Prometheus, considered as the most just among men. The Libyan fleet will harass Sardinia after the Sun leaves Libra (23 September).

Phaeton, according to Greek mythology, was the son of the sun. When he learnt who his father was, Phaeton went to him and succeeded in persuading him to let him drive his flaming chariot for one day. Phaeton foolishly brought the sun too close to the earth, running the risk of setting it aflame. Jupiter, at that point, struck him with a thunderbolt. This intervention for certain peoples came too late, hence their skins were burnt and they became black.

It seems obvious that in the quatrain the Seer is using Phaeton to indicate the Sun, but obviously, it is not possible to determine the year in which the prophecy will come true, even if it appears to be altogether probable that the event being described refers to the resumption of war, seeing that in the second line the Seer writes that '*Again the urn threatens Deucalion*' and the use of *again* presupposes a fact which has been repeated and should have the meaning of '*once more*'.

The renewed aggression will also be against France, as can see from *Centuries II, quatrain 96*.

Flambeau ardant au ciel soir sera veu,
Pres de la fin & principe du Rosne:
Famine glaiue: tard le secours pourueu,
La Perse tourne enuaihir Macedoine.

A burning flame will be seen in the evening sky,
At the mouth of the Rhône and at the source,
Famine and sword, late will assistance be brought,
Persia turns to invade Macedonia once more.
(Centuries II, quatrain 96)

War, then, will once again be brought to the Western world, and French soil will submit to yet another aggression, while the allied forces will be slow in organising a counter-offensive.

Iran, in the meantime, supported by the Chinese war machine, will take courage and will cross into Macedonia.

Seront oyes au ciel les armes battre,
Celuy an mesme les diuins ennemis:
Voudront loiz sainctes injustement debatre,
Par foldre & guerre bien croyans à mort mis.

Weapons will be heard fighting in the sky,
That very year, the enemies of God
Will want impiously to demolish the sacred laws,
Through lightning and war, the faithful will be put to
  death.

(*Centuries IV, quatrain 43*)

The persecution of the clergy will resume, and the religious laws will once again be flouted. Meanwhile, the faithful will be massacred in great numbers, in the name of the Antichrist.

The new and bloody occupation of Western Europe by the Arabs and Chinese will cause a universal cry of suffering from the Rhine all the way to Malta and to the Italian peninsula:

En lieu bien proche esloigné de Venus,
Les deux plus grands de l'Asie & d'Affrique:
Du Rhin & Hister, qu'on dira sont venus,
Crys, pleurs à Malte & coste ligustique.

In a place nearby, far away from Venus (Islam),
The two great ones of Asia and Africa:
They say have come from the Rhine and Danube estuary,
As far Malta and the Mediterranean coast cries and
  weeping.

(*Centuries IV, quatrain 68*)

The quatrain prophesies that at a certain moment during the conflict, when the Chinese and the Arabs have obtained their best results with the new war, the Antichrist (*the great one from Africa*) and the Chinese leader (*the great one from Asia*)

will meet in Provence to review the situation. In that moment
a universal cry of suffering will be raised all over Europe,
from the north to the deepest south. To indicate Islam, the
Seer uses the name Venus to symbolise Islam, which has
Friday *(Vendredi)* as its holy day.

Ligustique, as we have already seen, comprises the Ligurian
and the Adriatic seas, thus meaning the European countries
adjoining the Mediterranean.

But by now the moment has come, and the fall of the Antichrist is at hand. An army under the leadership of '*Ogmion*'
is marching towards Turkey:

> Logmion grande Bisance approuchera,
> Chassee sera la barbarique Ligue:
> Des deux loix l'une l'est inique lechera,
> Barbare & franche en perpetuelle brigue.

> *Ogmion will march on great Byzantium,*
> *The barbarous league will be driven out,*
> *Of two laws, he will expel the iniquitous,*
> *Barbaranism and liberty in eternal disagreement.*
> *(Centuries V, quatrain 80)*

This quatrain tells us that the Gallic hero will take Constanti-
nople and Turkey, and succeed in driving the forces of the
new barbarians out of that region. He will find that country
lacerated by religious divisions, since there will be a clash
between those who will continue to uphold the doctrine of the
Antichrist and those who will want to return, instead, to the
old moral principles. Ogmion will do what is necessary to have
the iniquitous doctrine abandoned, either through diplomacy or
by force, imposing a clear distinction between the concept of
liberty and that of absolute power.

> Par le cinquieme & un grand Hercules,
> Viendront le Temple ouurir de main bellique.
> Un Clement, Iule & Ascans recules,
> L'espe, clef, aigle, n'eurent onc si grand picque.

By way of a fifth and a great Hercules,
Will come to the temple to open a warlike hand.
Clement, Julius, Ascanius, pushed back,
Sword, key, eagle never suffered so much bickering.
                              (Centuries X, quatrain 27)

Henry and Ogmion will be forced to undertake an expedition to an Italy which has been newly devastated. In their war campaign they will in the end reach Rome, where they will set the Christian religion back on its feet at the cost of arduous combat and a noteworthy loss of human lives.

The *'great Hercules'* is almost certainly *'Ogmion'*, the name of a Celtic divinity, very similar in characteristics to the mythical Greek hero. The *'Fifth'* is obviously Henry, who as monarch will be, precisely, *Henry the Fifth. Clement, Julius* and *Ascanius* are all names, which bring Rome to mind: Clement, in fact, is a name frequently given to popes; with Julius, the Seer is referring to Julius Caesar; Ascanius was the son of Aeneas and, according to Virgil, he emigrated together with his father to Lazio and the greatest of his descendants was Emperor Octavian.

With these names the Seer is showing that the war will be so furious and so violent, that in the face of one similar to it, even the most illustrious personalities of Roman and religious history would have backed away.

In the last line *'sword'*, *'key'* and *'eagle'* refer respectively to the army, the Church and France.

Aux lieux sacrez animaux veu à trixe,
Auec celuy qui n'osera le jour:
A Carcassonne pour disgrace propice,
Sera posé pour plus ample sejour.

In holy places hairy animals shelter,
With him who will not dare (to appear by) day,
At Carcassonne through propitious ill-fortune,
Will be buried for a longer sojourn.
                              (Centuries IX, quatrain 71)

The last moments of the Antichrist, by now, have come. On realising this, he will reduce the Church to a shelter for animals. Nostradamus defines him as '*he who will not dare (to appear by) day*', that is, he who loves only the night, as the symbol of evil and iniquity.

Destiny will not save him, however, from the humiliation of being captured and imprisoned.

The last act will take place in Milan, where the invaders will be annihilated, and the Antichrist will be captured and led, bound in golden chains, to the presence of Henry, who will thus celebrate his victory before the enemy of humanity.

> Le grand mené captif d'estrange terre,
> D'or enchainé au roy Chyren offert:
> Qui dans Ausone, Milan perdra la guerre
> Et tout son ost mis à feu & à fer.

> *The great one led captive from foreign land,*
> *In golden chains offered to King Henry,*
> *He who in Milan will lose the war,*
> *And all his army put to fire and sword.*
> *(Centuries IV, quatrain 34)*

The quatrain leaves no room for doubt. The '*great one*' can be none other than the Antichrist, who will be captured, probably in his own country of origin (*foreign land*) after having lost the decisive battle in the vicinity of Milan, where the Western forces will annihilate his army, on 2 June 2025.

At that point for the '*Médecin*' there is in the making a brief humiliating imprisonment, which will last until his death, which will come when the Sun, Mars, Saturn and the Moon are in Aries, and that is 16–17 April 2026, as prophesied by *Sestet 46*, at which point he will be buried in the '*deep pit*' at Carcassonne.

The destruction and the end of the Antichrist will be down to the '*three brothers*', Henry, Ogmion and the Roman King, who together will have saved what will have remained of mankind, and will have prepared for the return of the Reign of Saturn, the golden century:

> L'Antechrist trois bien tost annichilez,
> Vingt & sept ans sang durera sa guerre,
> Les heretiques mortz, captifs exilez.
> Sang corps humain eau rogie gresler terre.

> *The Antichrist soon annihilated by the three,*
> *Twenty-seven years of blood his war will last,*
> *Dead heretics, prisoners exiled,*
> *Blood, human bodies, reddened water hails down upon*
>   *the earth.*

(Centuries VIII, quatrain 77)

Here then is the epilogue to the human drama, after twenty-seven years of malevolent activity and of horrible destruction. From 2000, the year of his rise to power, until his death on 16 or 17 April 2026, are exactly twenty-seven years, which confirms exactly the chronology that has been proposed.

In 2026 the Antichrist will then disappear. His followers will be killed, imprisoned or forced to flee. But the epic eschatological battle between Good and Evil will have cost an immeasurable price in term of human life: from this sacrifice a new beginning for mankind will emerge, that is based on morality and on much improved and more diverse relationships between men and with God. We shall return to the reign of the Sun and of Saturn and the Seer's long prophecy will be understood.

> Au chef du monde le grand Chyren sera,
> Plus oultre apres aymé, craint, redoubté:
> Son bruit & loz cieulx surpassera,
> Et du seul tiltre victeur fort contenté.

> *Great Henry will be leader of the world,*
> *More loved, more feared, formidable than any other*
>   *after,*

His fame and glory will pass into Heaven,
And his unique title of victor will make him very happy.
                              (Centuries VI, quatrain 70)

After his final victory, Henry will be truly world leader. No one will be more loved and at the same time feared for his immense power, which he will exercise in an enlightened way. His fame and glory will be greater than that of anyone else in history, as much on earth as in Heaven, from the moment he ascends there, as the ancient kings of Rome, whether it be a question of temporal or religious power. His titles will be numerous, but he will only favour that of '*victor*' in eternal memory of the role which God in his inscrutable wisdom had wished to reserve for him. Upon his death, as in his own wish, the French hero Ogmion will succeed him, as we learn in *Centuries VI, quatrain 42*:

> A Logmion sera laissé le regne,
> Du grand Selin qui plus fera de faict:
> Par les Italies estendra son enseigne,
> Regi sera par prudent contrefaict.

> *To Ogmion will the kingdom pass,*
> *Of the great Henry who will do no more deeds,*
> *He will extend his standard into Italy,*
> *A king who for prudence will be appreciated.*
>   *(Centuries VI, quatrain 42)*

Ogmion, according to this quatrain, will succeed in completing the work of Henry: Italy will receive him with great favour, and in substance he will completely integrate himself.

Ogmion, not withstanding his value and his audacity demonstrated in the long war, will be a prudent and conscientious leader, and for this he will be appreciated in a time of peace.

In that moment the predominance of the Christian religion accepted by everyone as the true faith will become certain:

Religion du nom des mers vaincra,
Contre la secte fils Adaluncatif,
Secte obstinee deploree craindra,
Des deux blessez par Aleph et Aleph.

Religion in the name of the seas will triumph,
Against the sectarian sons of the malignant,
The stubborn and deplored sect will fear,
Two wounded by Aleph and Aleph.
                    (Centuries X, quatrain 96)

Nostradamus, in this quatrain, defines Christianity as the
'*Religion in the name of the seas,*' this, because in Latin the
plural of sea (*mare*) is '*mari*' thus alluding to the name of
Mary (*Maria*). The quatrain sheds light on the fact that the
false religion of the Antichrist, a religion of his own making
and of his master, Satan (*the two*) will be completely annihilated by '*Aleph*' and '*Aleph*': Aleph is the first letter of the
Hebrew alphabet, and the repetition of it has a mystical meaning: in *Aleph* the principle of the beginning and the end of
mankind is epitomised ('*In Principio era il Logos*'). With
Aleph the world came to be created, with *Aleph* the world will
renewed, returning to its pure origins.

La loy du Sol & Venus contendens,
Appropriant l'esprit de prophetie.
Ne l'un ne l'autre ne seront entendens,
Par Sol tiendra la loy du grand Messie.

The law of the Sun (Catholicism) and Venus (Islam)
    competing,
To appropriate the spirit of prophecy,
Neither one nor the other will be understood,
With the Sun will be the law of the great Messiah.
                    (Centuries V, quatrain 53)

As to the differences between Islamic (*Venus*) and Catholicism
(*Sun*), neither one or the other will be prioritised in the true

faith: when the war is over and the Kingdom of the Sun is achieved, the only point of reference for the soul will be the teachings of Christ. The simplicity of his teaching, without lists or dogma and conforming to the moral laws felt by everyone, will be the only law for mankind: man will feel within himself how to discriminate between God and Evil, without the need for sermons.

Temples sacrés prime façon Romaine,
Reietteront les goffres fondements:
Prenant leur loix premieres & humaines,
Chassant, non tout, des saincts les cultements.

Sacred temples as for the early Romans,
Will reject the deep divides,
Will take up their early, human laws,
Driving out, though not completely, the worship of Saints.
                              (Centuries II, quatrain 8)

The new creed will be founded on the simplicity of the early Christians and the places of worship will be simple and plain, no longer sumptuous and gigantic churches. Faith and praying will be directed almost exclusively towards God, and the cult of numerous saints who are part of the Catholic church of today will be abandoned almost entirely.

Le corps sans ame plus n'estre en sacrifice,
Jour de la mort mys en natiuité:
L'esprit diuin fera l'ame felice,
Voyant le verbe en son eternité.

The body without soul is no longer to be sacrificed,
The day of death changes into one of birth,
The divine spirit will make the soul happy,
Seeing the word in its eternity.
                              (Centuries II, quatrain 13)

The contents of the quatrain reflect the Rosicrucian doctrine: the first line points out that in the future creed there will no longer be the sacrament of the Eucharist, that is, the sacrifice of the holy Host. The second line makes it clear that the day of death will be like that of birth. According to the Rosicrucians death is nothing, if it is not a step forward along the road to cosmic perfection, according to the law of the Karma: each time a man is born, he has a goal to accomplish, which is that of improving himself and remedying the errors he committed in a previous life. Through this coming and going the soul travels along the path of improvement leading towards perfection, and when this is reached, new births will no longer be necessary. Death is, therefore, looked up on by the Rosicrucians as a new stage along an extensive journey, not to be feared but to be greeted with the serene awareness that another stretch has been covered. The divine spirit, which through the new teachings will enlighten man, will make it possible for him to contemplate the word with the eyes of the soul, bringing him happiness and an awareness of his mission in the limitless context of cosmic harmony. The contents in *Centuries III, quatrain 2* are similar:

> Le diuin verbe pourra à la substance,
> Comprins ciel terre, or occult au fait mystique,
> Corps, ame, esprit ayant toute puissance,
> Tant soubz ses piedz, comme au siege celique.

> *The divine word will be made flesh,*
> *To include Heaven and earth, hidden gold in the mystic act,*
> *Body, soul and spirit having every power,*
> *Under its feet as in the celestial seat.*
>
> *(Centuries III, quatrain 2)*

This quatrain says that in those times the word of God will be manifested to man, and it will permeate heaven and earth. The truth, which was concealed under mysticism and faith, will become obvious and will be understood. Thus the Kantian

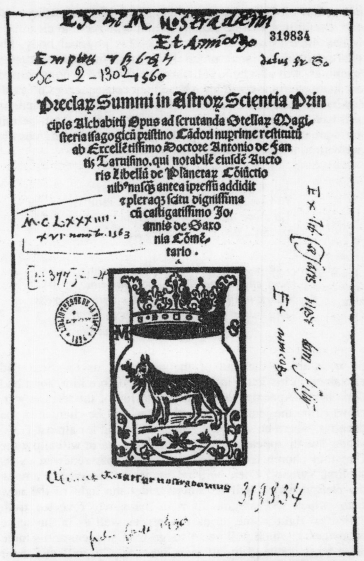

Frontispiece of a manual on astronomy which belonged to Nostradamus

noumenon of the existence of God and of immortality will end: everything will be explained and will become clear.

The three aspects of man, that is, his physical body, his vital spirit and his soul, precisely the tripartite of Rosicrucian teachings, will also be in full harmony, and the actions carried out in this harmony will have beneficial consequences on earth (*under the feet*) as well as in Heaven, seeing that those actions will have the effect of improving earthly life and will permit the soul to earn merits in its long journey towards cosmic perfection, according to the law of Karma.

> Le seducteur sera mis en la fosse,
> Et estaché jusques à quelque temps,
> Le clerc uny le chef auec sa crosse:
> pycante droit attraira les contents.

> *The seducer will be put in the pit,*
> *And enchained there for some time,*
> *Clerk united with the leader with his cross,*
> *The bitter truth shall attract the happy.*
> *(Centuries VIII, quatrain 95)*

So now are at the end of the prophecy: as the Seer had explained in his letter to Henry and as, before him, John had done in the Apocalypse, at the conclusion of the terrible war, crowned by the victory of Good, Satan will be chained in the deep pit, where he will be destined to remain for almost 1,000 years. The disappearance of Evil from the earth will allow the Christian church to be rebuilt and the cross renewed as its sublime symbol. There will no longer be dissension among the clergy, which will be united under the light of the new faith, which will assume form in the newly revealed truth ('*droit*' = right in the juridical sense as well as in the sense of justness), which will be so suggestive, so clear and simple as to be understood by all men, who, finally, will no longer be anguished by the doubts which have always afflicted humanity and tormented generations of philosophers and theologians, problems such as the existence of God, the immortality of the Soul, the eschatological aim of existence.

With this quatrain the prophecy of Nostradamus comes to an end, and in it the aim of his work is accomplished: that of offering to the world the concrete hope of a better future.

15. A summary of events 2000–25

After the eclipse of the sun on 11 August 1999, a malevolent personality will come to power in that zone which is historically known as Mesopotamia. He will present himself as the new Messiah or as a second Mohammed and will succeed in unifying the Arab world. He will at the same time turn to a Russia afflicted by enormous economic problems. Thanks to considerable financial interventions, the Antichrist will succeed in nailing that country to his politics, thus gaining the possibility of counting on its enormous military potential. The Antichrist will set off a war initially against the State of Israel, which will be cancelled from the map of the world. This will cause a series of repercussions at an international level. War, however, will be avoided for the moment, thanks to the firm position that will be assumed by the West; consequently a precarious peace will be achieved in 2003.

In the meantime, gloomy times are in prospect for the Catholic church. After the death of John Paul II, at Lyon, the two popes to succeed him will be immoral and malevolent men, a fact that will cause an irreversible crisis within the Church, a crisis that within a brief span of time will lead to its ruin.

In December 2005, or within the first months of 2006, through a treacherous and sudden attack by the Russian fleet, the West's naval forces in the Mediterranean will be annihilated, and, at the same time, a missile, bearing a nuclear warhead, will strike the White House, killing the president of the United States. Thus the Third World War will begin. The Russians and the Islamic States will rapidly conquer Spain and Italy, a considerable part of France, Germany, Austria, Hungary and Switzerland. The invading forces will spare no one. Men, women and children will be massacred in masses.

Cities will be completely destroyed and religious dignitaries will be the object of a bloody persecution, as in the time of Nero.

Britain also will undergo an attack as well as an invasion. The war will continue until 2011, a year during which the Russian and Islamic states will achieve their maximum expansion.

Their victory will, for the most part, be due to the lack of oil and of alternative energy on the part of the Europeans: ships and tanks will not be able to go into action, aeroplanes will be unable to take off. European military forces will find themselves at the mercy of their aggressors, once their reserves of fuel have been exhausted.

The forces of the West, however, brought to crisis, will succeed in reorganising themselves and in launching a counter-offensive. Three leaders will distinguish themselves particularly in this context of war: Henry, Ogmion, both of them French, and an Italian, born of a German mother. In the space of six years the Western forces will progressively succeed in regaining possession of the territories and in expelling the invaders. The epilogue of this phase of the war will be in Italy, where the invading forces will be defeated, and the forces of Islam and Russia will be completely annihilated. This will force the Arabs to withdraw to their own territories, while Russia will succumb completely, following an attack from the Western forces.

The Antichrist, however, will not yet have come to an end: having returned to his country, he will be under the protection of China, whose armed forces will have remained intact, and the West at that moment will not have sufficient military strength to be able to carry out a second war against the Asian colossus.

There will therefore be a truce of four years, and in that period it will be possible to evaluate the enormous disaster caused by the war, which will have left behind radioactive soil, lack of foodstuff and a depopulated world.

In 2022 war will resume at the hands of China. The resumption of hostilities will lead to a successful new invasion, which

Michel Nostradamus

in turn will lead to an almost total re-occupation of the liberated territories.

The reaction after an initial dispersal will not be long in coming: the zones of occupation will be liberated anew; the invaders will be destroyed in a decisive battle in the vicinity of Milan, and the Antichrist will be taken prisoner and, in gold chains, will be brought into the presence of Henry, who in this way will celebrate his great victory (2 June 2025).

The Antichrist will then be imprisoned, and his death will come in the following year, when the Sun, Saturn, Mars and the Moon will be in Aries (16–17 April 2026).

The world population surviving the catastrophe will be only a third of that which existed prior to the war, and the problem of sustenance will be a grave one, with the economy reduced to zero and with a considerable part of the land having been rendered absolutely sterile and unproductive. In any case, at the end of the war, the survivors will become aware of the necessity to re-establish human relationships on a different basis. This necessity will be fulfilled, with the revival of Christianity, which, having abandoned ornamentation, hierarchy and pomp, will return to its simple origins, and every mystery regarding birth and death will be revealed, a fact which will favour the spiritual growth of humanity and its freedom from Evil.

With these last vicissitudes and the comforting hope for the return of the Reign of the Sun and for a radically different future and peace for 1,000 years, the prophecy of Nostradamus comes to an end.

Conclusion: the future of mankind

The scenario which awaits us in the coming years will be a terrifying one. It will witness the overthrow of every existing political balance of power and every economic principle.

Industry will be reduced almost to zero. Money will lose its value. The same will be true of emergency resources common in times of economic crisis. The principal problem will be that of survival, since very few regions of the earth will be capable of offering sustenance. The coming war will make it impossible to cultivate lands or raise animals in many parts of the globe, because of radiation, and very little will remain of Europe: the main cities will be destroyed, the immense historical and artistic heritage dispersed; the few people who will have survived the catastrophe will be severely contaminated by radiation. The situation will not be very different in the United States, since in that country, too, the war will have left terrible, deep scars.

And yet, notwithstanding the monstrous catastrophe, a period of peace, fraternity and prosperity will return for the survivors. The second Revelations ('*the divine word will be made flesh*') will, in fact, come about, and with it a new way of looking at human relationships: the times will be such that it will no longer be courts or judges who administer the law in their imperfect fashion; every individual, in fact, will give of himself and lend a hand in the common emergency, while an awareness of what is to come after death will make the rat race and the accumulation of wealth seem useless, since everyone will understand that earthly life is only a means given to man by God to allow him to better himself as a spiritual entity, until the achievement of cosmic perfection, free from all his animal and material instincts.

This state of things will last for almost 1,000 years, a period in which Evil will remain chained in the pit, as John prophesied in the Apocalypse. At the end of this period, Evil will return to strike the earth, and thus, the last epic conflict of the human drama will take place, with God's final victory, the end of this material world and the advent of cosmic harmony, without any more anxiety, violence and ugliness. It is this that will be the definitive final Judgement of the Christian tradition.

To modern man all this could appear as absurd and inconceivable, because man of today is drenched with materialism and plagued by anxiety through the quest for his own economic well being and often through his thirst for power over other men, at whatever cost.

But all this is written in the great book of the future of Humanity, that same book which the Angel made John swallow in his mystic vision, making it possible for him to prophesy and to see what would come to pass in the future.

John, within the moment of a heartbeat, in a state of mystical ecstasy saw the future of the world, and wrote down what he saw with a symbolism of rare power, transferring to this work all the prophetic spirit he had received as a gift.

The work of Nostradamus does not stray from of the writings of John. However, while the purpose of the Apocalypse was to encourage men towards the observance of moral principles, warning them of the consequences otherwise, stimulating them, therefore, to exercise their free will in order to avoid such an outcome, Nostradamus knew by his time, that time had run out and that there was no longer any time to remedy the irreparable: the four horsemen of the Apocalypse were already venting their fury against the world with continuous wars, famine, civil and religious conflicts; after which would come the pollution that we are personally experiencing today; then the beast of the earth will appear, that is, the Antichrist, to carry out his mission, the mission willed by God in order to purify mankind.

What the Seer transmits to us through the *Centuries* is, in reality, a message of hope and comfort, notwithstanding the dark and ominous future depicted:

Resist and overcome the trials to which God has submitted you in order to re-create the world on different bases, in harmony with the cosmos, you will then be rewarded with the return of the Reign of light.

The coming of the eighth Millennium is at hand, and it will dawn in the year 2004. It will be a gloomy dawn, as when, in winter, cold black clouds threaten to obscure the rising sun. But the strong wind blowing, shaking the trees and sending into flight the dry leaves which have remained desperately clinging to the branches, will drive the clouds away, allowing light to spread. That tremendous and impetuous wind will be the Antichrist, who will rage against the vice-ridden and corrupt humanity of our times, disoriented in its moral values, and distracted in the soul by its search for its own physical satisfaction, no longer in harmony with the law of the cosmos.

But when the wind ceases its fury, in the end, it offers the earth a clear and serene sky, making it possible for the sun to free its rays, with their life-giving light and heat.

Appendix I: Nostradamus's non-coded work

At the end of such a long gallop through the future, it is time to look at one last mystery: when will Nostradamus's *'non-coded'* work be rediscovered?

In *quatrain 94* of *Centuries III*, Nostradamus writes:

De cinq cens ans plus compte on tiendra,
Celuy qu'estoit l'ornement de son temps:
Puis à un coup grande clarté dourra,
Que par ce siecle les rendra tres contenzs.

Commentators all agree in the meaning of this quatrain: Nostradamus, who was the pride and the glory of his times, will be taken seriously for more than 500 years. Then, unexpectedly, he will shed light on the contents of his work. This is because his prophecies, written in prose, and giving precise dates, facts and personalities will be rediscovered. Such a rediscovery will bring happiness to those whose fortune it will be to be living in that moment.

That the *'non-coded'* work exists, there can be no doubt, in view of the fact that Nostradamus, in the letter to his son, César, writes:

Then, more than once, during the sinister storms, 'I shall ground them to powder', the Lord will say, 'I shall destroy them and I shall have no pity' and a thousand other happenings will come with the waters of the earth and continual rains, as I have set down in writing more extensively in my other prophecies, which are composed in free speech 'in soluta oratione' and which define the places, the times and the pre-determined limit in which future mankind will

unerringly recognise the events when they happen, as others
have noticed doing with greater clarity.

What emerges from reading the quatrain is that the rediscovery of the work in prose, stripped of camouflage and ambiguity, should come about after a passage of more than 500 years from the publication of the *Centuries*, and therefore, after 2055.

This quatrain has caused me some perplexity, for, if the chronology I have proposed is accurate, with the end of the prophecies fixed at a date of 2 June 2025, that those living in 2055 or beyond can be *'tres contents'* about finding the *non-coded* work would make no sense if the events prophesied have already taken place by then. The discovery of the *non-coded* work will make sense only if it is a source of comfort and happiness for those living in that moment, and provides them with the necessary strength to resist, and give them faith in the time that is yet to come.

I am convinced that the rediscovery of the *non-coded* work will fulfil such a purpose and that it will not just be a pure and simple discovery of a historical document, as exceptional and as interesting it may be. The work of Nostradamus is not the work of a common reader of cards, but a text inspired by God, as Nostradamus himself writes in his letter to his son César. It was God who gave him the power to tear away the veils of time; it was God who delegated to him the power to reveal the future to mankind.

John was a sublime prophet: God empowered him to put mankind on its guard against the terrible risks it was facing. If mankind had purged itself and had taken the road towards cosmic harmony, giving heed to conscience and moral laws, the inauspicious events prophesied would not have taken place. As Nostradamus points out, the prophet has the capacity to define future occurrences with his prophecy, since time within itself contains all possibilities and is absolutely indifferent as to whether a defined event does or does not take place. The prophet, at the moment in which he makes his prophecy, isolates what will take place from amongst an infinity of future options.

In the Apocalypse the prophetic message is conditional; it is not an anathema. Its purpose is constructive, it points out the way to avoid the irreparable events it indicates, the warnings are repeated frequently: *'repent, change direction. Otherwise, what is predicted will come true.'*

Nostradamus, as he himself points out, is a Seer: he does not have the power to be effective in future time, but, notwithstanding, his work has a very precise purpose of its own. It contains a message of hope, a spur for the better part of mankind not to be resigned, to resist the events.

If this is its aim, seeing that it is inspired by God, then it cannot be that the mystery of the *Centuries* is to be revealed when everything has finished.

During the Second World War the work of Nostradamus heartened the spirits of the French people, since it came to be understood that many quatrains gave unequivocal indication of the way in which the war would end, so much so that the Nazis bribed translators to produce a version which coincided with their expectation of victory. In our case, in view of the much graver situation presenting itself on the horizon, it is vital to have not just a *possible* interpretation of his hermetic text, but one that is absolutely accurate, and this can only happen through founding the work *in soluta oratione,* that is, *non-coded*, and if this makes mankind 'very happy', so much the better.

If this to happen, then, it seems obvious that the *'non-coded'* work will be revealed when the Third World War is raging and when a desperate, seemingly hopeless situation has presented itself. Only then would the revelations of the work be able to fulfil its precise purpose, which will be that of giving those persecuted by the Antichrist the certainty of a final victory over Evil, as prophesied by John.

Were the secrets of the *Centuries* to be revealed now, however, mankind would draw little happiness from what is written therein, seeing that the future, for the next twenty years or so, is shown to be terrible and overwhelming.

This much, as we have seen, emerges as unequivocal in *Centuries IV, quatrain 30.*

Plus onze fois Luna Sol ne vouldra,
Tous augmentés & baissés de degré:
Et si bas mis que peu or on couldra,
Qu'apres faim peste descouuert le secret.

More than eleven times Moon and Sun will not come,
Everything increased and lowered by degree,
And so badly reduced that little gold will flow,
Then famine, pestilence and the secret revealed.
                    (Centuries IV, quatrain 30)

Nostradamus is telling us that the *'non-coded work'* will be revealed at the apex of a grave crisis, in the midst of famine and plague (radioactive contamination), therefore, at a moment when such a revelation can prove itself to be of comfort to mankind.

Even more unequivocal is *Centuries II, quatrain 27*:

Le diuin verbe sera du ciel frappé,
Qui ne pourra proceder plus auant:
Du reserant le secret estoupé,
Qu'on marchera par dessus & dauant.

The divine word shall be struck from the sky,
And will not be able to proceed further:
They will conceal the mute secret,
It will be walled over and in front.
                    (Centuries II, quatrain 27)

This quatrain predicts that faith in God, together with his Churches, will receive a violent blow, such that the profession of its own religious creed will no longer be possible.

Precisely at that moment the secret of the *Centuries* will be revealed, but the Antichrist, as the Nazis did previously, will attempt to conceal such a revelation, by mystifying its contents or by impeding its divulgence with violence.

If this is the purpose of the *Centuries,* and if the interpretation of these two quatrains under discussion is accurate, then it seems that *Centuries III, quatrain 94* ought to have a quite different meaning.

After a lengthy study, I came to the conclusion that, in this quatrain, the Seer has provided proof yet again of a unique capacity to confer a double meaning to the lines and of a striking, almost diabolical sense of humour.

The key to the interpretation of the quatrain is all contained in the first line and particularly in the word *'compte'*. The Seer, in fact, does not write *'en compte'*, but simply *'compte'*, the object of the verb *'tenir'*. *'Tenir compte'* in middle French as well as in modern French means to *make a calculation, to count*. The next step in resolving the enigma is to understand that the *'celuy'* , in the second line, is not object of the first line but subject of the third line. In fact, once it is understood that *tenir compte* means to make a calculation, the *'Celuy'* of the second line cannot depend on it. So, the line assumes a radically different meaning, of *'a sum will be made of more than five hundred years'*. And the entire quatrain can be translated as follows:

> *Five hundred years and more will be counted,*
> *Then, he who was the honour of his times,*
> *Will suddenly grant great clarity,*
> *That in that century will make men happy.*

The quatrain is saying that it will be *erroneously* concluded that the prophecies cover a certain time span, which is greater than 500 years, and that only after that period of time will the *non-coded* work be discovered. The quatrain adds that all of a sudden and beyond all expectations, the work will be discovered much before then, a fact that will create great happiness.

What is diabolical here is that only because of the quatrain and because of the ambiguity of the first line, people have thought erroneously that the time span exceeded 500 years: if the quatrain had not been written, no one would have been able to commit such an error, since there are no other chronological indications as to the moment of discovery of the work 'in soluta oratione'.

So, not only is this quatrain not an obstacle to my thesis concerning the end of the prophecies, it also implicitly confirms that their ending and the discovery of the *non-coded* work will take place before the conclusion of 500 years.

The rediscovery of the '*non-coded*' work is prophesied in two distinct quatrains:

> Dessoubz de chaine Guien du ciel frappé,
> Non loing la est caché le tresor:
> Qui pour longs siecles auoit esté grappé,
> Trouué mourra, l'oeil creué de ressort.
> *(Centuries I, quatrain 27)*

> Quand l'escripture D.M. trouuee,
> Et caue antique à lampe descouuerte,
> Loy, Roy & Prince Ulpian esprouuee,
> Pauillon Royne et Duc sous la couuerte.
> *(Centuries VIII, quatrain 66)*

The translation of these two quatrains will not be forthcoming: my preference is to leave every possible interpretation open to the reader, since these verses enclose within them the secret of the place in which the *non-coded* work is hidden.

Numerous people have attempted to interpret them, and it can be said that every version that has been offered has seemed very distant from their true meaning.

But this is not the moment in which to come face to face with the interpretation: that moment has not yet arrived, and when it comes, the work '*in soluta oratione*' will see light after a darkness lasting 450 years.

Appendix II: The original French text of the letter to César

Ad Caesarem Nostradamum filium, Vie & felicité.

Ton tard aduenement César Nostradame mon filz, m'a faict mettre mon long temps par continuelles vigilations nocturnes referer par escript, toy delaisser memoire apres la corporelle extinction de ton progeniteur, au commun profit des humains, de ce que la diuine essence par Astronomiques reuolutions m'ont donné congnoissance. Et depuis qu'il à pleu au Dieu immortel que tu ne fois venu en naturelle lumiere dans ceste terrene plaige, & ne veulx dire tes ans qui ne sont encores acompaignez, mais tes moys Martiaulx incapables à receuoir dans ton debile entendement, ce que je seray contrainct apres mes jours de finer: veu qu'il n'est possible te laisser par escript ce que seroit par l'injure du temps obliteré: car la parolle hereditaire de l'occulte prediction sera dans mon estomach intercluse: considerant aussi les aduentures de l'humain definement estre incertaines, & que le tout est regi & gouuerné par la puissance de Dieu inestimable, nous inspirant par baccante fureur, ne par limphatique monument, mais par astronomiques assertions soli numine diuino afflati praesagiunt e spiritu prophetico particularia. Combien que de long temps par plusieurs fois j'aye predict long temps au parauant, ce que despuis est aduenu, & en particulieres regions, attribuant le tout estre faict par la vertu & inspiration diuine, & autres felices & sinistres aduentures de accelerée promptitude prononcées, que despuis sont aduenues par les climatz du monde: ayant volu taire & delaissé par cause de l'injure, & non tant seulement du temps present, mai aussi de la plus part du futur de mettre pae escript pource que les regnes, sectes, & religions feront changes si opposites, voire au respect du present diametralement, que si je venois à referer ce que à l'aduenir sera, ceulx de regne, secte, religion, & foy trouueroient si mal accordant à leur fantasie auriculaire, qu'ilz viendroient à damner, ce que par les siecles aduenir on congnoistra estre veu & apperceu. Considerant aussi la sentence du vray Sauueur: Nolite sanctum dare canibus nec mittatis margaritas ante porcos ne conculcent pedibus & conuersi dirumpant vos. Qui à esté la cause de faire retirer ma langue au populaire, & la plume au papier, puis me suis volu estendre declarant pour le commun aduenement, par obstruses & perplexes sentences les causes futures, mesmes les plus urgentes, & celles que j'ay apperceu quelque humaine mutation que aduienne ne scandalizer l'auriculaire fragilité, & le tout escript soubz figure nubileuse, plus que du tout prophetique, combien que Abscondisti haec a sapientibus, et prudentibus, id est potentibus et regibus, et enucleasti ea exiguis et tenuibus, & aux Prophetes: par le moyen de Dieu immortel & des bons anges ont receu l'esprit de vaticination, par lequel ilz voyent les causes loingtaines, & viennent à preuoir les futures aduenements: car rien ne se peult parachever sans luy, ausquelz si grande est la puissance & la bonté aux subiectz, que pendant qu'ilz demeurent en eulx, toutesfois aux autres effectz subiectz, pour la similitude de la cause du bon genius, celle chaleur & puissance vaticinatrice s'approche de nous: comme il nous aduient des rayons du Soleil, qui se viennent gettans leur influence aux corps elementaires. Quant à nous qui sommes humains, ne pouuons rien de nostre naturelle congnoissance & inclination d'engin, congnoistre des secretz obstruses de Dieu le Createur. Quia non est nostrum noscere tempora, nec momenta etc. Combien que aussi de present peuuent aduenir & estre personnaiges, que Dieu le Createur aye voulu reueler par imaginatiues impressions, quelques secretz de l'aduenir, accordés à l'astrologie iudicielle, comme du passé, que certaine puissance & volontaire faculté venoit par eulx, comme flambe de feu apparoit, que luy inspirant, on venoit à iuger les diuines & humaines inspirations. Car les oeuures diuines, que totallement sont absolues, Dieu les vient parachever: la moyenne qui est au millieu les Anges: la troisiesme, les mau-

uais. Mais mon filz, je te parle icy un peu trop obstrusement: mais quant aux occultes vaticinations que ont vient à receuoir par le subtil esperit du feu qui quelque fois par l'entendement agité, contemplant le plus hault des Astres comme estant vigil-ant, mesme que aux prononciations estant surprins escriptz, prononcant sans crainte moins attaint d'inuerecunde loquac-ité: mais quoy? Tout procedoit de la puissance diuine du grand Dieu eternel, de qui toute bonté procede. Encores, mon filz, que j'aye inferé le nom de prophete je ne me yeux attribuer tiltre de si haulte sublimité, pour le temps present: car qui propheta dicitur hodie, olim vocabatur videns: car prophete proprement, mon filz, est celuy qui voit choses loingtaines de la congnoissance naturelle de toute creature. Et cas aduenant que le prophete, moyennant la parfaicte lumiere de la prophetie, luy appaire manifestement des choses diuines, comme humaines que ce ne peult faire, veu les effectz de la future prediction s'estendent loing. Car les secretz de Dieu sont incomprehensibles, & la vertu effectrice contingent de longue estendue de la congnoissance naturelle, prendent leur plus prochain original du liberal arbitre, faict apparoir les causes qui d'elles mesmes ne peuuent acquerir celle notice pour estre cognues, ne par les humains augures, ne par autre congnoissance ou vertu occulte, comprinse soubz la concauité du ciel, mesme du faict present de la totale eternité, que vient en foy embrasser tout le temps. Mais moyennant quelque indi-uisibile eternité par comitiale agitation Hiraclienne les causes par le celeste mouuement sont congneues. Je ne dis pas mon filz afin que bien l'entendes que la congnoissance de ceste matiere ne se peut encores imprimer dans ton debile cerueau que les causes futures bein loingtaines, ne soient à la con-gnoissance de la creature raisonable: si sont nonobstant bon-nement la creature de l'ame intellectuelle des causes presentes loingtaines, ne luy sont du tout ne trop occultes, ne trop reserées: mais la parfaicte des causes notices ne se peult acquerir sans celle diuine inspiration: veu que toute inspi-ration prophetique recoit prenant son principal principe mou-ant de Dieu le createur, puis de l'heur & de nature. Parquoy estant les causes indifferantes indifferentement produictes &

*non produictes, le presaige partie aduient ou à esté predit.
Car l'entendement crée intellectuellement ne peult voir occultement, sinon par la voix faicte au lymbe, moyennant la exigue flamme, en laquelle partie les causes futures se viendront à incliner. Et aussi mon filz, je te supplie que jamais tu ne vueilles emploier ton entendement a quelles resueries & vanités, qui feichent le corps, & mettent à perdition l'ame, donnant trouble au foible sens: mesmes la vanité de la plus que execrable magie, reprouuée iadis par les secrées escriptures & par les diuins canons, au chef duquel est excepté le iugement de l'astrologie iudicielle: par laquelle & moyennant l'inspiration & reuelation diuine par continuelles supputations auons noz propheties redigé par escript. Et combien que, celle occulte Philosophie ne fusse reprouuée, n'ay onques volu presenter leurs effrenées persuations: combien que plusieurs volumes qui ont esté cachés par long siecles ne sont estés manifestés. Mais doutant ce qui aduiendroit en ay faict apres la lecture, present à Vulcan, que ce pendant qu'illes venoit à deuorer la flamme leschant l'air rendoit une clarté insolite, plus claire que naturelle flamme, comme lumiere de feu de clistre fulgurant illuminant subit la maison, come si elle fust esté en subite conflagration. Parquoy afin que à l'aduenir ne fusses abusé, perscrutant la parfaicte transformation, tant seline solaire, & soubz terre metualx incorruptibles & aux undes occultes, les ay en cendres conuertis. Mais quant au iugement qui se vient paracheuer moyennant le iugement celeste, cela te veulx je manifester: parquoy auoir congnoissance des causes futures, reiectant loing les fantastiques imaginations qui aduiendront, limitant la particularité des lieux, par diuine inspiration supernaturelle: acordant aux celestes figures, les lieux & une partie du temps de proprieté occulte par vertu, puissance, & faculté diuine: en presence de laquelle les trois temps sont comprins par eternité, reuolution tenant à la cause passée presente & future: quia omnia sunt nuda et aperta etc. Parquoy mon filz tu peulx facilement comprendre, que les chose qui doiuent aduenir, se peuuent prophetiser par les nocturnes & celestes lumieres, que sont naturelles, & par l'esprit de prophetie non que je me vueille attribuer nomination ny effect prophetique,*

mais par reuelée inspiration, comme homme mortel esloigné non moins de sens au ciel, que des piedz en terre. Possum non errare falli decipi: fuis pecheur plus grand que nul de ce monde, subiect à toutes humaines afflictions. Mais estant surprins par fois la sepmaine limphatiquant, & par longue calculation, rendant les estudes de souefue odeur: je ay composé liures de propheties, contenant chascun cent quat-rains astronomiques de propheties, lesquelles j'ay un peu voulu rabouter obscurement & sont perpetuelles vaticinations, pour d'icy à l'année 3797. Que possible fera retirer le front à quelque uns, en voyant si longue extension, & par soubz toute la concauité de la Lune aura lieu & intelligence: & ce entendant uniuersellement par toute la terre, mon filz. Que si tu nis l'aage naturel & humain, tu verras deuers ton climat au propre ciel de tà natiuité, les futures aduentures preuoir. Combien que le seul Dieu eternel, soit celuy qui congnoit l'eternité de sa lumiere, procedant de luy mesmes: & je dis franchement que à ceulx à qui sa magnitude immense, ha volu par longue inspiration melancolique reueler, que moyennant icelle cause occulte manifestée diuinement: principallement de deux causes, qui sont comprinses à l'entendement de celuy inspiré, qui prophetise, l'une est que vient à infuser esclarciss-ant la lumiere supernaturelle, au personaige qui predit par la doctrine des Astres, & prophetise par inspireé reuelation laquelle est une certaine participation de la diuine eternité, moyennant le prophete vient à iuger de cela que son diuin esperit luy à donné, par le moyen de Dieu le createur, & par une naturelle instigation: c'est assauoir ce qu'il predit estre vray, & à prins son origine etheréement: & telle lumiere & flambe exigue est de toute efficace & de telle altitude, non moins que la nature, la clarté, & naturelle lumiere ren les philosophes si asseurés, que moyennant les principes de la premiere cause ont attainct à plus profondes abysmes des plus haultes doctrines. Mais à celle fin mon filz que je ne vague trop profondement pour la capacité future de ton sens, & aussi que je trouue que les lettres feront si grande & incomparable jacture que je trouue le monde auant l'uniuerselle confla-gration aduenir tant de deluges & si hautes inondations, qu'il

*ne sera guieres terroir qui ne soit couert d'eau & sera par si
long temps que hors mis enographies & topographies, que le
tout ne soit peri: aussi auant telles & apres inundations, en
plusieurs contrées les pluyes seront si exigues, & tombera du
ciel si grande abondance de feu & de pierres candentes qui
ny demourera rien qu'il ne soit consummé: & ceci aduenir,
en brief, & auant la derniere conflagration. Car encores que
la planette de Mars paracheue son siecle, & à la fin de son
dernier periode, si le reprendra il mais assemblés, les uns en
Aquarius par plusieurs années, les autres en Cancer par plus
longues & continues. Et maintenant que sommes conduictz par
la lune, moyennant la totale puissance de Dieu eternel que
auant qu'elle aye paracheué son total circuit, le soleil viendra
& puis Saturne. Car selon les signes celestes le regne de
Saturne sera de retour, que le tout calculé le monde, s'aproche,
d'une anaragonique reuolution: & que de present que cecy
j'escripz auant cent septante sept ans trois moys unze jours
par pestilence, longue famine, & guerres, & plus par les inundations le monde entre cy & ce terme prefix, auant & apres
par plusieurs foys, sera si diminué & si peu de monde sera,
que lon ne trouuera qui vueil le prendre les champs qui deuien-
dront liberes aussi longuement qu''lz sont estés en seruitude:
& ce quant au visible iugement celeste, que encores que nous
soions au septiesme nombre de mille qui paracheue le tout,
nous approchant du huictiesme ou est le firmament de la huictiesme sphere, qui est en dimension latitudinaire: ou le grand
Dieu eternel viendra paracheuer la reuolution: ou les images
celestes retourneront à se mouuoir & le monument superieur
qui nous rend la terre stable & ferme, non inclinabitur in
saeculum saeculi: hors mis que son vouloir sera accomply, ce
sera, mais non point autrement: combien que par ambigues
opinions excedants toutes raisons naturelles par songes Mach-
ometiques, aussi aucune fois, Dieu le createur par les ministres
de ses messagiers de fleu en flamme missiue vient à proposer
aux sens exterieurs, mesmement à noz yeulx les causes de
future prediction significatrices du cas futur qui se doit a celuy
qui presaige manifester. Car le presaige qui se faict de la
lumiere exterieure vient infalliblement à iuger partie auecques*

& moyennant le lume exterieur: combien vrayement que la partie qui semble auoir par l'oeil de l'entendement, ce qui n'est par la lesion du sens imaginatif la raison est par trop euidente, le tout estre predict par afflation de diuinité, & par le moyen de l'esprit angelique inspiré à l'homme prophetisant rendant ioinctes de vaticinations le venant à illuminer luy esmouuant le deuant de la phantasie par diuerses nocturnes aparitions que par diurne certitude prophetise par administration astronomique coioincte de la sanctissime future prediction, ne considerant ailleurs que au couraige libre. Vient asture entendre mon filz que je trouue par mes reuolutions que sont accordantes à reuelée inspiration que les mortel glaiue s'aproche de nous maintenant, par peste, guerre plus horrible que à vie de tres hommes n'à esté, & famine lequel tombera en terre, & y retournera souuent, car les Astres s'accordent à la reuolution: & aussi à dict, Visitabo in virga ferrea iniquitates eorum et in verberibus et percutiam eos: car la misericordie du Seigneur ne sera point dispergée un temps, mon filz, que la pluspart de mes propheties seront accomplies, & viendront estre par accomplissement reuolues. Alors per plusieurs fois durant les sinistres tempestes, Conteram ergo, dira le Seigneur, et confringam, & non miserebor: & mille autres aduentures, qui aduiendront par eaux & continuelles pluies comme plus à plain j'ay redigé par escript aux miennes autres propheties, qui sont composées tout au long, in soluta oratione, limitant les lieux, temps, & le terme prefix que les humains apres venuz, verront cognoissants les aduentures aduenues infalliblement comme auons noté par les autres parlant plus clairement: nonobstant que soubs nuee seront comprins les intelligences: sed quando submouenda erit ignorantia, le cas sera plus esclarci. Faisant fin mon fils, prends donc ce don de ton pere Michel Nostradamus, esperant toy declarer une chacune prophetie des quatrains icy mis. Priant au Dieu immortel qu'il te vueille prester vie longue, en bonne & prospere felicité.

De Salon ce premier jour de Mars 1555

Appendix III: The original French text of the letter to Henry

A L'INVICTISSIME TRES-PUISSANT ET TRES-CHRESTIEN HENRY ROY DE FRANCE SECOND

MICHEL NOSTRADAMUS TRES-HUMBLE TRES-OBEYSSANT SERUITEUR ET SUBJECT

VICTOIRE ET FELICITE'

(I) Pour icelle souueraine obseruation que i'ay eu, ô tres-chrestien et tres-victorieux Roy, depuis que ma face estant long temps obnubilee se présente au deuant de la deité de vostre majesté immesuree, depuis en ça j'ay esté perpetuellement esblouy ne desistant de honnorer et dignement venerer iceluy jour que premierement deuant icelle je me presentay comme à une singuliere majesté tant humaine. (II) Or cherchant quelque occasion par laquelle je peusse manifester le bon coeur et franc courage, que moyennant iceluy mon pouuoir eusse faict ample extension de cognoissance enuers vostre serenissime majesté. (III) Or voyant que par effects le declairer ne m'estoit possible, joint auec mon singulier desir de ma tant longue obtenebration et obscurité, estre subitement esclarcie et transportee au deuant de la face du souuerain oeil, et du premier monarque de l'uniuers, (IV) tellement que j'ay esté en doute longuement à qui je viendrois consacrer ces trois Centuries du restant de mes Propheties, paracheuant la milliade, (V) et apres auoir longuement cogité d'une temeraire audace, ay prins mon addresse enuers vostre majesté, n'estant pour cela estonné, comme raconte le grauissime aucteur Plutarque en la vie de Lycurgue, que voyant les offres et presens qu'on faisoit par sacrifices aux temples des dieux immortels d'iceluy temps et à celle fin que l'on ne s'estonnast par trop

*souuent desdictes fraiz et mises ne s'osoyent presenter aux
temples. (VI) Ce nonobstant voyant vostre splendeur Royalle,
accompagnee d'une incomparable humanité ay prins mon
addresse, non comme aux Rois de Perse, qu'il n'estoit nullement permis d'aller à eux, ny moins s'en approcher. (VII)
Mais à un tres-prudent, à un tressage Prince j'ay consacré
mes nocturnes et prophetiques supputations, composees plustost d'un naturel insitinct, accompagné d'une fureur poëtique,
que par reigle de poësie, (VIII) et la plus part composé et
accordé à la calculation Astronomique, correspondant aux
ans, moys et sepmaines des regions, contrees, et de la pluspart
des villes et citez de toute l'Europe, comprenant de l'Affrique,
et une partie de l'Asie par le changement des regions, qui
s'approchent la plus part de tous ces climats, et composé
d'une naturelle faction: (IX) respondra quelqu'un qui auroit
bien besoin de soy moucher, la rithme estre autant facile,
comme l'intelligence du sens est difficile. Et pource, ô tres-
humanissime Roy, la plus part des quatrains prophetiques sont
tellement scabreux, que l'on n'y scauroit donner voye ny moins
aucuns interpreter, (X) toutesfois esperant de laisser par escrit
les ans, villes, citez, regions ou la pluspart aduiendra, mesmes
de l'annee 1585 et de l'annee 1606, accomençant depuis le
temps present, qui est le 14 de Mars 1557, (XI) et passant
outre bien loing jusques à l'aduenement qui sera apres au
commencement du 7 millenaire profondement supputé, (XII)
tant que mon calcul astronomique et autre sçauoir s'a peu
estendre, où les aduersaires de Iesus-Christ et de son Eglise,
commenceront plus fort de pulluler, (XIII) le tout a esté
composé et calculé en jours et heures d'election et bien dispo-
sees, et le plus justement qu'il m'a esté possible. (XIV) Et le
tout Minerva libera, et non invita, supputant presque autant
des aduentures du temps aduenir, comme des aages passez,
comprenant de present, et de ce que par le cours du temps par
toutes regions l'on cognoistra aduenir, tout ainsi nommement
comme il est escrit, ny meslant rien de superflu, combien que
l'on dit: Quod de futuris non est determinata ommino veritas.
(XV) Il est bien vray, Sire, que pour mon naturel instinct
qui m'a esté donné par mes auites ne cuidant presager, et*

adioustant et accordant iceluy naturel intinct auec ma longue supputation uny, et vuidant l'ame, l'esprit, et le courage de toute cure, solicitude, et fascherie par repos et tranquilité de l'esprit. (XVI) Le tout accordé et presagé l'une partie tripode æneo. (XVII) Combien qu'ils sont plusieurs qui m'attribuent ce qu'est autant à moy, comme de ce que n'en est rien, Dieu seul eternel, qui est perscrutateur des humains courages pie, juste, et miséricordieux, est le vray juge, auquel je prie qu'il me vueille defendre de la calomnie des meschans, (XVIII) qui voudroyent aussi calomnieusement s'enquerir pour quelle cause tous vos antiquissimes progeniteurs Roys de France ont guery des escrouelles, et des autres nations ont guery de la morsure des serpens, les autres ont eu certain instinct de l'art diuinatrice, et d'autres cas qui seroyent loing icy à racompter. (XIX) Ce nonobstant ceux à qui la malignité de l'esprit malin ne sera comprins par le cours du temps apres la terrenne mienne extinction, plus fera mon escrit qu'à mon vivant, (XX) cependant si à ma supputation des aages je faillois on ne pourroit estre selon la volonté d'aucuns. (XXI) Plaira à vostre plus qu'imperialle Majesté me pardonner, protestant deuant Dieu et ses saincts. que je ne pretends de mettre rien quelconque par escrit en la presente epistre, qui soit contre la vraye foy Catholique, conferant les calculations Astronomiques, jouxte mon sçauoir: (XXII) car l'espace du temps de nos premiers, qui nous ont precedez sonts tels, me remettant sous la correction du plus sain jugement, que le premier homme Adam fut deuant Noé enuiron mille deux cens quarante deux ans, (XXIII) ne computant les temps par la supputation des Gentils, comme a mis par escrit Varron: mais tant seulement selon les sacrees Escriptures, et selon la foiblesse de mon esprit, en mes calculations Astronomiques. (XXIV) Apres Noé, de luy et de l'universel deluge, vint Abraham environ mille huictante ans, lequel a esté souuerain Astrologue, selon aucuns, il inuenta premier les lettres Chaldaïques : (XXV) apres vint Moyse enuiron cinq cens quinze ou seize ans, (XXVI) et entre le temps de Dauid et Moyse ont esté cinq cens septante ans là enuiron. (XXVII) Puis apres entre le temps de Dauid, et le temps de nostre sauueur et redempteur Iesus-Christ nay

de l'unique Vierge, ont esté (selon aucuns Cronographes) mille
trois cens cinquante ans : (XXVIII) pourra objecter quelqu'un
ceste supputation n'estre veritable, pource qu'elle differe à
celle d'Eusebe. (XXIX) Et depuis le temps de l'humaine
redemption jusque à la seduction detestable des Sarrazins,
sont esté six cens-vingt et un an, là enuiron, (XXX) depuis en
ça l'on peut facilement colliger quels temps sont passez, si la
mienne supputation n'est bonne et valable par toutes nations,
(XXXI) pource que tout a esté calculé par le cours celeste,
par association d'esmotion infuse à certaines heures delaissees
par l'esmotion de mes antiques progeniteurs. (XXXII) Mais
l'injure du temps, ô serenissime Roy, requiert que tels secrets
evenemens ne soyent manifestez que par enigmatique sentence,
n'ayant qu'un seul sens et unique intelligence, sans y auoir
rien mis d'ambigue n'amphibologique calculation: (XXXIII)
mais plustost sous obnubillee obscurité par une naturelle
infusion approchant à la sentence d'un des mille et deux Prophetes, qui ont esté depuis la creation du monde, jouxte la
supputation et chronique punique de Ioël, Effundam spiritum
meum super omnem carnem et prophetabunt filii vestri, et filiae
vestrae. (XXXIV) Mais telle prophetie procedoit de la bouche
du S. Esprit, qui estoit la souueraine puissance eternelle,
adjoincte auec la celeste à d'aucuns de ce nombre ont predit
de grandes. et esmerueillables aduentures. (XXXV) Moy en
cest endroict je ne m'attribue nullement tel tiltre. ja à Dieu
ne plaise, je confesse bien que le tout vient de Dieu, et luy en
rends graces, honneur, et louange immortelle, sans y avoir
meslé de la diuination que prouient à fato: mais à Deo, à
natura, (XXXVI) et la pluspart accompagnee du mouuement
du cours celeste, tellement que voyant comme dans un miroüer
ardent, comme par vision obnubilee, les grands euenements
tristes, prodigieux, et calamiteuses aduentures qui s'approchent par les principaux culteurs. (XXXVII) Premierement des
temples de Dieu, secondement par ceux qui sont terrestrement
soustenus s'approcher telle decadence, auecques mille autres
calamiteuses aduentures, que par le cours du temps on cognoistra aduenir: (XXXVIII) car Dieu regardera la longue sterilité
de la grand dame, qui puis apres conceura deux enfans

principaux: (XXXIX) mais elle periclitant, celle qui luy sera adjoustee par la temerité de l'aage de mort periclitant dedans le dixhuictiesme, ne pouuant passer le trentesixiesme qu'en delaissera trois masles. et une femelle, et en aura deux, celuy qui n'en eut jamais d'un mesme pere, des trois freres seront telles differences, puis unies et accordees, que le trois et quatre parties de l'Europe trembleront: (XL) par le moindre d'aage sera la monarchie Chrestiène soustenue et augmentee: sectes esleuees, et subitement abaissees, Arabes reculez, Royaumes unis, nouuelles Loix promulguees : (XLI) des autres enfans le premier occupera les Lions furieux couronnez, tenans les pattes dessus les armes intrepidez. (XLII) Le second se profondera si auant par les Latins accompagné, que sera faicte la seconde voye tremblante et furibonde au mont Iouis descendant pour monter aux Pyrennees ne sera translatee à l'antique monarchie, sera faicte la troisiesme innondation de sang humain, ne se trouuera de long temps Mars en Caresme. (XLIII) Et sera donnee la fille par la conseruation de l'Eglise Chrestiène, tombant son dominateur à la paganisine secte des nouueaux infidelles, elle aura deux enfans, l'un de fidelité, et l'autre d'infidelité par la confirmation de l'Eglise Catholique. (XLIV) Et l'autre qui à sa grande confusion et tarde repentance la voudra ruiner, seront trois regions par l'extreme difference des ligues, c'est assauoir la Romaine, la Germanie, l'Espaigne, qui feront diuerses sectes par main militaire, (XLV) delaissant le 50 et 52 degrez de hauteur, et feront tous hommages des religions loingtaines aux regions de l'Europe et de Septentrion de 48 degrez d'hauteur, qui premier par vaine timidité tremblera., puis les plus occidentaux. meridionaux et orientaux trembleront, (XLVI) Telle sera leur puissance, que ce qui se fera par concorde et union insuperable des conquestes belliques; (XLVII) De nature seront esgaux: mais grandement differents de foy. (XLVIII) Apres cecy la Dame sterile de plus grande puissance que la seconde sera receüe par deux peuples, par le premier obstiné par celuy qui a eu puissance-sur tous, par le deuxiesme et par le tiers qui estendra ses forces vers le circuit de l'Orient de l'Europe aux pannons l'a profligé et succombé et par voile marine fera ses extensions à la Trinacrie

Adriatique par Mirmidon, et Germaniques du tout succombé,
et sera la secte Barbarique du tout des Latins grandement
affligee et deschassee. (XLIX) Puis le grand Empire de
l'Antechrist commencera dans la Atila et Zerfes descendre en
nombre grand et innumerable, tellement que la venue du sainct
Esprit procedant du 48 degré, fera transmigration, dechassant
à l'abomination de l'Antechrist, faisant guerre contre le royal
qui sera le grand Vicaire de Iesus-Christ, et contre son Eglise,
et son regne per tempus et in occasione temporis. (L) Et prece-
dra deuant une eclypse solaire le plus obscur, et le plus tenebre-
reux, qui soit esté depuis la creation du monde jusques à la
mort et passion de Iesus-Christ, et de la jusques icy, (LI) et
sera au moys d'octobre que quelque grande translation sera
faicte, et telle que l'on cuidera la pesanteur de la terre auoir
perdu son naturel mouuement et estre abismee en perpetuelles
tenebres, seront precedens au temps vernal, et s'en ensuyuant
apres d'extremes changemens, permutations de regnes, par
grand tremblement de terre, auec pullulation de la neuue
Babylonne, fille miserable augmentee par l'abomination du
premier holocauste, (LII) et ne tiendra tant seulement que
septante trois ans, sept moys, (LIII) puis apres en sortira du
tige celle qui auoit demeuré tant long temps sterile, procedant
du cinquantiesme degré, qui renouuellera. toute l'Eglise Chre-
stienne. (LIV) Et sera faicte grande paix, union et concorde
entre uns des enfans des fronts esgarez, et separez par diuers
regnes (LV) sera faicte telle paix que demeurera attaché au
plus profond baratre le suscitateur et promoteur de la martiale
faction par la diuersité des relígieux, et sera uny le Royaume
du Rabieux: qui contrefera le sage. (LVI) Et les contrees,
villes, citez, regnes, et prouinces qui auront laissé les premiers
voyes pour se deliurer, se captiuant plus pronfondement seront
secrettement faschez de leur liberté, et parfaicte religion per-
due, commenceront de frapper dans la partie gauche, pour
retourner à la dextre, (LVII) et remettant la. saincteté profligee
de long temps, avec leur pristin escrit, qu'apres le grand chien
sortira le plus gros mastin, qui fera destruction de tout, mesmes
de ce qu'au parauant sera esté perpetré, seront redressez les
temples comme au premier temps, et sera restitué le clerc à

*son pristin estat (LVIII) et commencera à meretricquer et lux-
urier, faire et commettre mille forfaits. (LIX) Et estant proche
d'une autre desolation, par lors qu'elle sera à sa plus haute
et sublime dignité, se dresseront de potentats et mains milit-
aires, (LX) et luy seront ostez les deux glaiues, et ne luy
demeurera que les enseignes, (LXI) desquelles par moyen de
la curuature qui les attire, le peuple le faisant aller droict, et
ne voulant se condescendre à eux par le bout opposite de la
main aigue, touchant terre, voudront stimuler jusques à ce que
naistra d'un rameau de la sterile de long temps, qui deliurera
le peuple uniuers de celle seruitude benigne et volontaire, soy
remettant à la protection de Mars, spoliant Iupiter de tous ses
honneurs et dignitez, pour la cité libre, constituee et assise
dans un autre exigue Mezopotamie. (LXII) Et sera le chef et
gouuerneur jetté du milieu, et mis au lieu de l'air, ignorant
la conspiration des conjurateurs, auec le second Trasibulus,
qui de long temps aura manié tout cecy. (LXIII) Alors les
immundicitez des abominations seront par grande honte objec-
tees et manifestees aux tenebres de la lumiere obtenebre, ces-
sera deuers la fin du changement de son regne, (LXIV) et les
clefs de l'Eglise seront en arriere de l'amour de Dieu, (LXV)
et plusieurs d'entre eux apostatizeront de la vraye foy, (LXVI)
et des trois sectes, celle du milieu, par les culteurs d'icelle,
sera un peu mis en decadence. (LXVII) La prime totallement
par l'Europe, la plus part de l'Affrique exterminee de la tierce,
moyennant les pauures d'esprit, que par ensensez esleuez par
la luxure libidineuse adultereront. (LXVIII) La plebe se leuera
soustenant, dechassera les adherans des legislateurs, et sem-
blera que les regnes affoiblis par les Orientaux que Dieu le
Createur aye deslé Satan des prisons infernalles, pour faire
naistre le grand Dog et Dohan, lesquels feront si grande frac-
tion abominable aux Eglises, que les rouges ne les blancs sans
yeux ne sans mains plus n'en jugeront et leur sera ostee leur
puissance. (LXIX) Alors sera faicte plus de persecution aux
Eglises, que ne fut jamais. (LXX) Et sur ces entrefaictfes naistra la pestilence si grande que trois pars du monde plus que
les deux defaudront, (LXXI) Tellement qu'on ne se sçaura
cognoistre ne les appartenans des champs et maisons, et nais-*

tra l'herbe par les ruës des cités plus haute que les genous: (LXXII) Et au clergé sera faicte toute desolation. et usurperont les martiaux ce que sera retourné de la cité du Soleil de Melite, et des isles Stechades, et sera ouuerte la grand chaisne du port qui prend sa denomination au boeuf marin. (LXXIII) Et sera faicte nouuelle incursion par les maritimes plages, volant le saut Castulum deliurer de la premiere reprinse Mahumetane. (LXXIV) Et ne seront de leurs assaillemens vains, et au lieu que jadis fut l'habitation d'Abraham, sera assaillie par personnes qui auront en veneration les Ioujalistes. (LXXV) Et icelle cité d'Achem sera enuironnee et assaillie de toutes parts en tresgrande puissance de gens d'armes. (LXXVI) Seront affoiblies leurs forces maritimes par les Occidentaux. (LXXVII) Et à ce regne sera faicte grande desolation, et les plus grandes citez seront depeuplees, et ceux qui entreront dedans, seront comprins à la vengeance de l'ire de Dieu. (LXXVIII) Et demeurera le sepulchre de tant grande veneration par l'espace de long temps soubs le serain à l'uniuerselle vision des yeux du Ciel, du Soleil, et de la Lune. (LXXIX) Et sera conuerty le lieu sacré en ebergement de troupeau menu et grand, et adapté en substances prophanes. (LXXX) O quelle calamiteuse affliction sera par lors aux femmes enceintes: (LXXXI) Et sera par lors du principal chef Oriental, la plus part esmeu par les Septentrionaux et Occidentaux vaincu, et mis à mort, profligez. et le reste en fuite. et ses enfans de plusieurs femmes emprisonnez. et par lors sera accomplie la prophetie du Royal Prophete : Ul audiret gemitus compeditorum, ul solueret filios interemptorum. (LXXXII) Quelle grande oppression que par lors sera faicte sur les Princes et gouuerneurs des Royaumes, mesmes de ceux qui seront maritimes et orientaux, et leurs langues entremeslees à grande societé: (LXXXIII) la langue des Latins et des Arabes, par la communication Punique, et seront tous ces Roys Orientaux chassez, profligez, exterminez, (LXXXIV) non du tout par le moyen des forces des Roys d'Aquilon. et par la proximité de nostre siecle par moyen des trois unys secrettement cerchant la mort, et insidies par embusches l'un de l'autre, (LXXXV) et durera le renouuellement de Triumuirat sept ans, que la renommee de telle secte sera son *estenduë par l'uniuers, et sera soustenu le sacrifice de la saincte et immaculee hostie (LXXXVI) et seront lors des Seigneurs deux en nombre d'Aquilon, victorieux sur les Orientaux, et sera en iceux faict si grand bruit et tumulte bellique, que tout iceluy Orient tremblera de la frayeur d'iceux freres, non freres Aquilonaires. (LXXXVII) Et pource, Sire, que par ce discours je mets presque confusement les predictions, (LXXXVIII) et quand ce pourra estre et l'advenement d'iceux, pour le denombrement du temps que s'enfuit, qu'il nest nullement ou bien peu conforme au superieur: (LXXXIX) lequel tant par voye Astronomique, que par autres mesmes des sacrees ecritures, qui ne peuvent faillir nullement, que si je voulois à un chacun quatrain mettre le denombrement du temps, le pourroit faire: (XC) mais à tous ne seroit agreable, ne moins les interpreter jusques à ce, Sire, que vostre Majesté m'aye octroyé ample puissance pour ce faire, pour ne donner cause aux calomniateurs de me mordre. (XCI) Toutesfois, contans les ans depuis la creation du monde jusques à la naissance de Noë, sont passez mil cinq cens et six ans (XCII) et depuis la naissance de Noë jusques à la parfaicte fabrication de l'Arche, approchant de l'uniuerselle mondation, passerent six cens ans (si les dons estoyent Solitaires ou Lunaires, ou des dix mixtions) je tiens ce que les sacrees escritures tiennent qui estoyent Solaires. (XCIII) Et à la fin d'iceux six ans Noë entra dans l'Arche pour estre sauué du deluge, (XCIV) et fut iceluy deluge, uniuersel sur la terre, et dura un an et deux mois. (XCV) Et depuis la fin du deluge jusques à la natiuité d'Abraham, passa le nombre des ans de deux cens nonante cinq. (XCVI) Et depuis la natiuité d'Abraham jusques à la natiuité d'Isaac, passerent cent ans. (XCVII) Et depuis Isaac jusques à Iacob, soixante ans dès l'heure qu'il entra en Egyptes jusques à l'yssue d'iceluy, passerent cent trente ans. (XCVIII) Et depuis l'entree de Iacob en Egypte jusques à l'yssue d'iceluy, passerent quatre cent trente ans. (XCIX) Et depuis l'yssue d'Egypte jusques à l'edification du Temple faicte par Solomon au quatriesme an de son regne, passerent quatre cens octante ou quatre vingts ans. (C) Et depuis l'edification du Tèmple, jusques à Iesus-Christe selon la supputation des hierographes, passeront quatre cens nonante ans. (CI) Et ainsi par ceste supputation que j'ay faicte, colligee par les sacrees lettres, sont enuiron quattre mille cent septante trois ans et huict mois, peu ou moins. (CII) Or de Iesus-Christ en ça, par la diuersité des sectes, je laisse, (CIII) et ayant supputé et calculé les presentes Propheties, le tout selon l'ordre de la chaisne qui contient sa reuolution, le tout par doctrine Astronomique, et selon mon naturel instinct, (CIV) et apres quelque temps et dans iceluy comprenant depuis le temps que Saturne qui tournera entre à sept du mois d'Auril, jusques au 15 d'Aoust, Iupiter à 14 de Iuin jusques au 7 Octobre, Mars depuis le 17 d'Auril jusques au 22 de Iuin, Venus depuis le 9 d'Auril jusques au 22 de May, Mercure depuis le 3 de Feurier, jusques au 24 dudit. (CV) En apres le premier de Iuin, jusques au 24 dudit, et du 25 de Septembre, jusques au 16 de Octobre, Saturne en Capricorne, Iupiter en Aquarius, Mars en Scorpio, Venus en Pisces, Mercure dans un moys en Capricorne, Aquarius et Pisces, la Lune en Aquarius, la teste du Dragon en Libra: (CVI) la queuë à son signe opposite suyuant une conjonction de Iupiter à Mercure, avec un quatrin espect de Mars à Mercure, et la teste du Dragon sera auec une conjonction du Soleil à Iupiter, l'année sera pacifique sans eclipse, et non du tout, et sera le commencement comprenant ce de ce que durera (CVII) et commençant icelle annee sera faicte plus grande persecution à l'Eglise Chrestienne, que n'a esté faicte en Afrique, et durera ceste icy yusques à l'an mil sept cens nonante deux que l'on cuydera estre une renouation de siecle: (CVIII) apres commencera le peuple Romain de se redresser, et de chasser quelques obscures tenebres, receuant quelque peu de leur pristine clarté. non sans grande diuision et continuel changement. (CIX) Uenise en apres en grande force et puissance levera ses aisles si tres-haut ne disant gueres aux forces de l'antique Rome. (CX) Et en iceluy temps grandes voyles Bisantines associees aux Ligustiques par l'appuy et puissance Aquilonaire, donnera quelque empeschement que des deux Cretenses ne leur sera la Foy tenuë. (CXI) Les arcs edifiez par les antiques Martiaux s'accompagneront aux ondes de Neptune. (CXII) En l'Adriatique sera faicte discorde grande, ce que sera uny sera* separé, approchera de maison ce que parauent estoit et est grande cité, comprenant le Pempotam la Mesopotamie de l'Europe à quarante cinq et autres de quarante un, quarante deux et trente sept. (CXIII) Et dans iceluy temps, et en icelles contrees la puissance infernale mettra à l'encontre de l'Eglise de Iesus-Christ la puissance des aduersaires de sa loy, qui sera le second Antechrist, lequel persécutera icelle Eglise et son vray Vicaire, par moyen de la puissance des Roys temporels, qui seront par leur ignorance seduict par langues, qui trencheront plus que nul glaiue entre les mains de l'insensé. Le susdict regne de l'Antechrist ne durera que jusques au definement de ce nay pres de l'aage et de l'autre à la cité de Plancus, accompagnez de l'esleu de Modone Fulcy, par Ferrare, maintenu par Liguriens Adriaticques, et de la proximité de la grande Trinacrie: Puis passera le mont Iouis. Le Gallique ogmium, accompagné de si grand nombre que de bien loing l'Empire de sa grande loy sera presenté, et par lors et quelque temps apres sera espanché profuseement le sang des Innocents par les nocens un peu esleuez : alors par grands deluges la memoire des choses contenues de tels instrumens receura innumerable perte, mesmes les lettres : qui sera deuers les Aquilonaires par la volonté diuine, et entre une fois lié Satan. Et sera faicte paix universelle entre les humains, et sera deliuree l'Eglise de Iesus-Christ de toute tribulation, combien que par les Azos-tains voudront mesler dedans le miel du fiel, et leur pestifere seduction : et cela sera proche du septiesme millenaire, que plus le sanctuaire de Iesus-Christ ne sera conculqué par les infideles qui viendront de l'Aquillon, le monde approchant de quelque grande conflagration combien que par mes supputations en mes propheties le cours du temps aille beaucoup plus loing. Dedans l'Epistre que ces ans passez ay dedié à mon fils César Nostradamus j'ay assez appertement declaré aucuns poincts sans presage. Mais icy, ô Sire, sont comprins plusieurs grands et merueillieux aduenemens, que ceux qui viendront après le verront. (CXIV) Et durant icelle supputation Astrologique, conferee aux sacrees lettres, la persecution des gens Ecclesiastiques prendra son origine par la puissance des Roys Aquilonaires, unis auec les Orientaux. Et *ceste persecution durera onze ans, quelque peu moins, que par lors defaillira le principal Roy Aquilonaire, lesquels ans accomplis suruiendra son uny Meridional, qui persecutera encore plus fort par l'espace de trois ans les gens d'Eglise, par la seduction apostastique, d'un qui tiendra toute puissance absoluë à l'Eglise militaire, et le sainct peuple de Dieu obseruateur de sa loy, et tout ordre de religion sera grandement persecuté et affligé tellement que le sang des vrais Ecclesiastiques, nagera par tout, et un des horribles Roys temporels par ses adherans luy seront donnes telles loüanges, qui il aura plus respandu de sang humain des innocens Ecclesiastiques, que nul ne sçauroit auoir du vin: et iceluy Roy commertra de forfaicts enuers l'Eglise incroyables, coulera le sang humain par les rues publiques, et temples, comme l'eau par pluye impetueuse, et rougiront de sang les plus prochains fleuues, et par autre guerre nauale rougira la mer, que le rapport d'un Roy à l'autre luy sera dit: Bellis rubuit navalibus aequor. (CXV) Puis dans la mesme annee et les suivantes s'en ensuiura la plus horrible pestilence, et la plus merueilleuse par la famine precedente, et si grandes tribulations que jamais soit aduenue telle depuis la premiere fondation de l'eglise chrestienne, et par toutes les regions Latines, (CXVI) demeurant par les vestiges en aucunes contrees des Espaignes, (CXVII) Par lors le tiers Roy Aquilonaire entendant la plaincte du peuple de son principal tiltre, dressera si grande armee, et passera par les destroits de ses derniers auites et bisayeuls, qui remettra la plus part en son estat, (CXVIII) et le grand Vicaire de la cappe sera remis en son pristin esta: mais desolé et puis du tout abandonné, et tournera estre Sancta sanctorum destruicte par Paganisme et le vieux et nouueau Testament seront dechassez, bruslez, (CXIX) en apres l'Antéchrist sera le prince infernal, encores par la derniere foy trembleront tous les Royaumes de la Chrestienté, et aussi des infideles, par l'espace de vingt cinq ans, et seront plus grieues guerres et batailles, et seront villes, citez, chasteaux, et tous autres edifices bruslez, desolez, destruicts, auec grande effusíon de sang vestal, mariees, et vefues violees, enfans de laict contre les murs des villes allidez et brisez, et tant de maux se commettront par le*

moyen de Satan. prince infernal que presque le monde uniuer-
sel se trouuera defaict et desolé: (CXX) et auant iceux aduene-
mens, aucuns oyseaux insolites crieront par l'aire Huyhuy, et
seront apres quelque temps esuanouys. (CXXI) Et apres que
tel temps aura duré longuement sera presque renouuellé un
autre regne de Saturne, et siecle d'or, (CXXII) Dieu le createur
dira entendant l'affiction de son peuple, Satan sera mis, et lié
dans l'abysme du barathre dans la profonde fosse: (CXXIII)
et adonc commencera entre Dieu et les hommes une paix
uniuerselle, et demeurera lié enuiron l'espace de mille ans, et
tournera en sa plus grande force, la puissance Ecclesiastique,
et puis tourne deslié. (CXXIV) Que toutes ces figures sont
justement adaptees par les diuines lettres aux choses celestes
visibles, c'est à sçauoir, par Saturne, Iupiter, et Mars, et les
autres conjoincts, comme plus à plain par aucuns quadrains
l'on pourra voir. (CXXV) Je eusse calculé plus profondement,
et adapté les uns auecques les autres. (CXXVI) Mais voyant,
ô Serenissime Roy, que quelqu'uns de la censure trouueront
difficulté, qui sera cause de retirer ma plume à mon repos
nocturne, Multa etiam, ô rex omnium potentissime praeclara
et sane in brevi ventura, sed omnia in hac tua epistola innec-
tere non possumus, nec volumus : sed ad intelligenda quaedam
facta horrida fata, pauca libanda sunt, quamvis tanta sit in
omnes tua amplitudo et humanitas homines, deosque pietas,
ut solus amplissimo et Christianìssimo Regis nomine, et ad
quem summa totius religionis auctoritas deferatur dignus esse
videare. (CXXVII) Mais tant seulement je vous requiers, ô Roy
tres-clement; par icelle vostre singuliere et prudente humanité,
d'entendre plustost le desir de mon courage, et le souuerain
estude que j'ay d'obeyr à vostre Serenissime Majesté, depuis
que mes yeux furent si proches de vostre splendeur Solaire,
que la grandeur de mon labeur n'attainct ne requiert.

De Salon, ce 27 de Iuin, mille cinq cens cinquanta huict.